The
ELEMENTS
of
POWER

ALSO BY TERRY R. BACON

Selling to Major Accounts:
Tools, Techniques, and Practical Solutions for the Sales Manager (1999)

Winning Behavior:
What the Smartest, Most Successful Companies Do Differently
(2003, with David G. Pugh)

The Behavioral Advantage:
What the Smartest, Most Successful Companies Do Differently
to Win in the B2B Arena
(2004, with David G. Pugh)

Powerful Proposals:
How to Give Your Business the Winning Edge
(2005, with David G. Pugh)

Readers can find more information on these books, as well as *The Elements of Power* and other current topics in talent management and human performance, at www.terryrbacon.com. Additional information on the research behind *The Elements of Power,* including power-and-influence profiles of forty-five countries, is also available at www.kornferryinstitute.com or www.theelementsofpower.com.

The

ELEMENTS

of

POWER

TERRY R. BACON

AMACOM

AMERICAN MANAGEMENT ASSOCIATION
New York • Atlanta • Brussels • Chicago • Mexico City • San Francisco
Shanghai • Tokyo • Toronto • Washington, D.C.

Bulk discounts available. For details visit:
www.amacombooks.org/go/specialsales
Or contact special sales:
Phone: 800-250-5308
E-mail: specialsls@amanet.org
View all the AMACOM titles at: www.amacombooks.org

This publication is designed to provide accurate and authoritative information in regard to the subject matter covered. It is sold with the understanding that the publisher is not engaged in rendering legal, accounting, or other professional service. If legal advice or other expert assistance is required, the services of a competent professional person should be sought.

Disclaimer: The opinions expressed here are the views of the writer and do not necessarily reflect the views and opinions of Korn/Ferry International.

Library of Congress Cataloging-in-Publication Data

Bacon, Terry R.
    The elements of power : lessons on leadership and influence / Terry R. Bacon.
        p.   cm.
    Includes index.
    ISBN-13: 978-0-8144-1511-5 (hardcover)
    ISBN-10: 0-8144-1511-3 (hardcover)
    1. Leadership.   2. Control (Psychology)   3. Interpersonal
communication.   I. Title.
    HD57.7.B323   2011
    658.4'092—dc22

                                                                    2010027654

About AMA

American Management Association (www.amanet.org) is a world leader in talent development, advancing the skills of individuals to drive business success. Our mission is to support the goals of individuals and organizations through a complete range of products and services, including classroom and virtual seminars, webcasts, webinars, podcasts, conferences, corporate and government solutions, business books, and research. AMA's approach to improving performance combines experiential learning—learning through doing—with opportunities for ongoing professional growth at every step of one's career journey.

Printing number

10   9   8   7   6   5   4   3   2   1

PERMISSIONS AND CREDITS

Introduction: Katharine Graham (Photo by Arnold Newman/Getty Images); Jim and Tammy Faye Bakker (Photo by Scott Miliman/AFP/Getty Images).

Part I: Cover photo © iStockphoto.com/Cimmerian.

Chapter 1: Bill Gates (Photo by Chuck Nacke/Getty Images); Maya Angelou (Photo by Frederick M. Brown/Getty Images); Martin Fleischmann and B. Stanley Pons (Photo by Diana Walker/Time Life Pictures/Getty Images).

Chapter 2: Dr. Martin Luther King (Photo by Rolls Press/Popperfoto/Getty Images); President George W. Bush (Photo by Brendan Hoffman/Getty Images).

Chapter 3: Arsenal fans at Waterloo Station (Photo by S. R. Gaiger/Topical Press/Getty Images); Robert Young as Dr. Marcus Welby (Photo by ABC Television/Courtesy of Getty Images); Xu Jinglei (Photo by Carlos Alvarez/Getty Images); Quotation from the film *Taxi Driver* courtesy of Columbia Pictures. Used with permission.

Chapter 4: Brad Pitt and Angelina Jolie (Photo by Robyn Beck/AFP/Getty Images); Ann Coulter (Photo by Rob Hill/FilmMagic).

Chapter 5: Eleanor Roosevelt (Photo by Joseph Scherschel/Time Life Pictures/Getty Images); Eliot Spitzer (Photo by Timothy A. Clary/AFP/Getty Images).

Part II: Cover photo © iStockphoto.com/fstop123.

Chapter 6: Quotations from the film *Network* courtesy of MGM Studios. Used with permission. Indra Nooyi (Photo by Brian Ach/WireImage); Ali al-Naimi (Photo by Hassan Ammar/AFP/Getty Images).

Chapter 7: Quotations from the film *Serenity* courtesy of Universal Pictures. Used with permission. Dr. Peter Pronovost (Johns Hopkins University School of Medicine. Used with permission); Fareed Zakaria (Photo by Joe Kohen/WireImage).

Chapter 8: Rahm Emanuel (Photo by Justin Sullivan/Getty Images); Vice President Dick Cheney with President George W. Bush (Photo by Alex Wong/Getty Images); Cartoon of Dick Cheney (Mike Peters EDTCTN (New) © King Features Syndicate).

Chapter 9: Aung San Suu Kyi (Photo by Pornchai Kittiwongsakul/AFP/Getty Images); Warren Buffett (Photo by Nicholas Roberts/AFP/Getty Images).

Chapter 10: Mark Zuckerberg (Photo by Suzanne Plunkett/Bloomberg via Getty Images); Jeff Bezos (Photo by Toru Yamanaka/AFP by Getty Images).

Part III: Cover photo © iStockphoto.com/Viorika.

Chapter 11: Sister Mary Scullion (Photo by Jeff Fusco/Getty Images); Jeremy Gilley (Photo by Astrid Stawiarz/Getty Images).

CONTENTS

PREFACE

TWENTY-FIVE YEARS AGO, BRITISH POP DUO TEARS FOR FEARS RELEASED their hit song "Everybody Wants to Rule the World." I remembered that song five years later when a senior human resources manager at a division of General Electric asked me to develop an educational program on influence effectiveness. She felt that many of the employees she was responsible for were not skilled at influencing upward or laterally within their matrix organization and were not nearly as persuasive as they needed to be with customers. "Many of them don't have strong enough presence," she said, "and they aren't good at getting their ideas across. They can't read audiences and don't know how to adapt to them. All they do is tell customers about the features of our products and services. Too many of our recent hires are going to fail if we don't teach them how to use power and influence."

To meet her need, I spent several months in university libraries searching for and reading everything I could on the topic of power and influence in organizations. Although the research was often enlightening, none of it offered what I felt was a comprehensive picture of how people develop the power necessary to influence others effectively. I sought a model of power and influence that could describe every instance of influence—from street beggars to dictators, from friends doing favors for one another to colleagues working together on teams, from athletic coaches to executive coaches, and from mail room clerks to CEOs. As a business consultant, I was primarily interested in how power and influence were used in the world of work, but I quickly realized that there were numerous parallels with how power works in politics and government, the military, the church, the media, social organizations, and families. In fact, the exercise of power in politics and nonbusiness organizations is essentially indistinguishable from the exercise of power in companies, so businesspeople can learn much about power from how it is used in other domains.

In the literature on power and influence, I couldn't find the comprehensive model that I sought, so I stitched together a new model based on insights from the existing research as well as my own experiences in business and my observations of people at work. That model became the basis for the Survey of Influence Effectiveness (SIE), which was published in 1990 by my company, Lore International Institute (the company was acquired in 2008 and is now part of Korn/Ferry International, and the SIE is now available at www.kornferry.com). Subsequent psychometric studies of the framework and survey showed that the item structure was valid and the survey accurately measured power and influence. During the past twenty years, we've been using the SIE to assess the power bases and influence effectiveness of tens of thousands of businesspeople around the world. The data we have collected have given us some unique insights into how people develop power and how they use that power to lead and influence others. Some of that research appears in this book, some of it will appear in a companion book on influence, and some will be available on my websites: www.terryrbacon.com and www.theelementsofpower.com. With these books and websites, my aim is to help people in business (and other walks of life) learn how to become more powerful and, consequently, how to have more impact.

I don't agree with Tears for Fears that everybody wants to rule the world. Surely, not *everybody*. We are not all megalomaniacs. But I haven't met anyone in the business world who doesn't want to make a difference. No one wants to be powerless. People want their ideas to be heard and acted upon. They want their proposals to be accepted. They want to be persuasive and to change people's minds. They want customers to adopt their products or solutions and know that they improved their customers' lives or businesses. In short, people want to be influential. And as this book shows, you cannot be as influential as you want unless you understand the elements of power and build a strong enough power base to be effective wherever you are working. Without power, there is no influence or leadership.

ACKNOWLEDGMENTS

Many people helped me during the creation of this book, and I deeply appreciate their contributions. First, I would like to thank my colleagues at Korn/Ferry International for their assistance. Bruce Spining helped with my research at various points during the project. Joey Maceyak managed the SIE database and built the programs that helped me extract and analyze the data. Sheri Ligtenberg proofread the manuscript and prevented me from making some egregious errors. Susan Kuhnert kept me organized and assisted me with research and management of the project, and David Gould created the figures that appear in this book. Many thanks to these fine people.

Nancy Atwood, Maryann Billington, Martin Moller, Carolyn Archuleta, and Laurie Voss read parts of the manuscript and offered invaluable feedback and suggestions on the ideas and their expression. Ken DeMeuse and Guangrong Dai helped me with the Power Sources Self-Assessment that appears in chapter 12. Their expertise in the creation of assessments made this one a far better product. Finally, I would like to thank Kevin Cashman for his insights and suggestions, particularly in chapter 5. Kevin's stature as one of the top thinkers on leadership in the world was amply demonstrated with his generosity and the quality of his suggestions.

I am also indebted to Donna Stewart for her cross-cultural research and insights. Her work was invaluable in interpreting how the findings of the SIE apply to different cultures. Among Donna's many gifts are curiosity and tenacity, which make her a fine researcher. Many thanks as well to Dr. Marilee White, a friend and professor of art history whose expertise was helpful in my exploration of the different ways of knowing. Few people were as helpful as Dr. Joel Jones, who read the entire manuscript and offered thoughtful comments and suggestions throughout. My discussions with him about power, influence, and leadership were very fruitful. Now and then, you encounter someone whose help is truly instrumental in shaping your thinking, and that's what Joel has been to me.

I would also like to thank Ellen Kadin, my longtime editor at the American Management Association, as well as everyone else at AMACOM who helped with this book. Book publishing is a collaboration between the author and the publisher, and I appreciate everything Ellen and her colleagues did on behalf of *The Elements of Power*. Their guidance made it a better book.

Finally, I would like to thank my wife, Debra, for her unending patience and support throughout a lengthy writing process. She knows, as much as anyone, that a writer's brain never stops working and that it's perfectly natural for someone to get out of bed at three in the morning to go write. She is my soul mate and my inspiration, and I am grateful to have her as my companion on my life's journey.

A WORD ABOUT PRONOUNS

As much as possible, I have avoided the awkward use of dual pronouns: he or she, his or her, him or her, and himself or herself. Although these constructions are meant to be inclusive, they are a clumsy use of English. Instead, when I am speaking hypothetically or illustratively, I have either used the plural forms of these pronouns, which do not signify gender, or varied my pronoun usage, sometimes referring to someone as *he* and sometimes as *she*. My pronoun choices are random and are meant to illustrate that the gender of my hypothetical subjects is irrelevant.

COMPANY NAMES

Throughout the book, readers will see references to Lore, Lore International Institute, Korn/Ferry International, and Lominger. Korn/Ferry International is the parent company. Korn/Ferry began as an executive search firm but has been expanding into leadership and talent consulting through internal growth and acquisition. It acquired Lore International Institute in November 2008 and Lominger several years earlier. We are all now part of Korn/Ferry, but if earlier work had been done under an original company name, I use that name for the sake of accuracy.

MY GLOBAL RESEARCH STUDY ON POWER AND INFLUENCE

Readers will see references throughout this book to a research study I led at Lore on global power and influence. This research began in 1990 and continues today. It is based on Lore's proprietary 360-degree assessment, the Survey of Influence Effectiveness. During the past twenty years, our database has grown to more than 64,000 subjects and over 300,000 respondents, and it has given me and my colleagues insight into the strength of people's power sources, how frequently they use different influence techniques, how effectively they use them, how appropriate those techniques are for their culture, and how skilled they are in twenty-eight areas related to leadership and influence effectiveness. Because this is a global study, it has allowed us to identify differences in the uses of power and influence in forty-five countries around the world. Throughout the book, when I refer to our global research, I am referring to this extensive study.

The
ELEMENTS
of
POWER

INTRODUCTION

WHAT MAKES PEOPLE POWERFUL? WHERE DOES THEIR POWER COME FROM?
Whether you are an individual contributor, a professional, a supervisor, a midlevel manager, a senior executive, or the CEO, you must develop enough power to be persuasive, to gain the agreement or cooperation of others, and to stimulate action. Otherwise, you could not do your job. One of the undeniable facts of life is that people who lack power exert very little influence on others. Those who are powerful and use their power effectively are the people who have impact. They get things done. They make a difference. In the world at large, some people or groups amass the power necessary to influence social trends, change minds, shape history, and create or destroy great things, including social movements and nations. In the business world, the most powerful people use their power to lead and motivate others, build high-performing teams, manage projects, drive new initiatives, develop new business and new enterprises, harness the creative energies of groups, and guide organizations toward the successful accomplishment of their mission. If you want to make a difference, you must develop some strong sources of power.

It would be tempting to assume that all leaders need is the power vested in them by virtue of their position, that the formal authority inherent in their management role is sufficient. However, a quick look around any organization will show that some leaders and managers are much more influential than their peers—just as Bill Gates had more impact as CEO of Microsoft than most CEOs have in their industries. Some leaders are more credible, more visible, and more highly respected. Some, like Gates, Warren Buffett, and Richard Branson, have influence far outside their organizations. On a more modest scale, some midlevel managers have the CEO's ear and are considered rising stars. Others are less influential, despite their positions and the formal authority they have by virtue of their roles. Moreover, leading principally through the power and authority of a position is passé today. As *One-Minute Manager* author Ken Blanchard has noted, "In the past a leader was a boss. Today's leaders must be partners with their people. They no longer can lead solely based on positional power."

Some leaders are inspirational and motivating, capable of leading large groups of people in new directions. Others struggle to build a following and are never able to lead as capably in real life as they do in their dreams. We could attribute the difference between more effective and less effective leaders to differences in their skills, or situational differences, or just plain luck. But this misses an important point. Today, effective leadership and management is a function of influence, not command and control, and influence is a function of power. It's as simple as this: The more powerful you are, the more influence you can have on others, and the more influential you are, the more impact you are likely to have in your organization and beyond. The formal authority vested in a management role is one source of power, but it is not the only source. Moreover, it's not the most powerful source.

What makes a manager, leader, or executive powerful? For that matter, what makes *anyone* powerful? How do leaders build their power bases? How do they use them? And what can cause their power bases to be diminished? These are important questions not only in business but in everyday life. Since the dawn of humanity, people have been obsessed with power, which is understandable, given the enormous impact power has had in our collective history, our organizations, and our daily lives. Great works of literature have explored power, among them *The Iliad, Lord of the Flies, Animal Farm, The Autumn of the Patriarch,* and *All the King's Men.* The corrupting effect of power was one of Shakespeare's principal themes (e.g., *Antony and Cleopatra, King Lear, Hamlet, Othello, Richard III,* and especially *Macbeth*). And power has been an abiding concern of many psychologists (Sigmund Freud, Carl Jung, Alfred Adler, and David McClelland), philosophers (Niccolò Machiavelli, Michel Foucault, Friedrich Nietzsche, Karl Marx, Steven Lukes, and Alvin Toffler), and business authors (Mary Parker Follett, Lillian Gilbreth, Robert Greenleaf, Douglas McGregor, John Kotter, Gary Yukl, Warren Bennis, Robert P. Vecchio, and Peter Drucker).

The aim of this book is not to recount all that has been written about power, but I would be remiss not to acknowledge the extraordinary amount of thought many insightful people have given to the topic. It has been the subject of endless fascination, debate, and discussion through the ages. Perhaps only love, death, and God have captivated the human imagination as much as power.

In the modern era, and on a much more practical level, a number of researchers have explored the role of power in organizations, particularly in business. In a now-classic exploration of personal and organizational power, social psychologists John R. P. French Jr. and Bertram Raven published an essay in 1959 called "The Bases of Social Power."[1] They identified five sources of power (reward, coercive, legitimate, referent, and expert) and later added a sixth (information). Since then, numerous other researchers have explored these sources of power, as well as power's effects, and identified additional sources of power that French and Raven did not. The model of power and influence presented in this book is derived from an extensive review of contemporary research on personal power and organizational power and on the twenty years of original research I conducted at Lore International Institute. My aims were to formulate a comprehensive model of power and influence that could describe any act of leadership or influence in any domain, and to describe that model in terms that people in business and other walks of life could use to improve their ethical use of power and understand and defend themselves against unethical uses of power. This book focuses on power—what it is, where it comes from, how it's built, and how it is used to lead and influence others. In a companion book, I will be discussing ethical and unethical forms of leadership through influence.

In my model of power and influence, there are five sources of power that stem from your position and participation in an organization: *role* power; *resource* power; *information* power; *network* power; and *reputation* power. Additionally, there are five sources of power that stem from your personal assets: *knowledge* power; *expressiveness* power; *attraction* power; *character* power; and *history* power, which derives from your history or familiarity with the people you are trying to lead or influence. Finally, there is one meta-source of power, *will,* which is related to the popular concept of willpower. I refer to "will" as a meta-source of power because it can have a substantial magnifying effect on all the other power sources.

This book explores these power sources in depth. Chapter 1 discusses knowledge power, although I relate it not only to what you know, but also to what skills and talents you have. Knowledge power catapulted Bill Gates to the forefront of his industry and made Maya Angelou one of the most admired people in her profession. Gates illustrates the virtues of technical knowledge coupled with business savvy, and Angelou illustrates the virtue of versatility. But there is a cautionary tale in this chapter, too, about two scientists whose careers were derailed by a premature announcement of a discovery that was later proven to be untrue, which illustrates the impact on knowledge power when you are wrong.

Chapter 2 discusses the power of expressiveness, which is the power of speech, or the power derived from being eloquent and articulate. Gifted speakers like Winston Churchill and Martin Luther King had a special ability to capture people's imaginations and move them to action. In contrast, George W. Bush's frequent inability to speak eloquently and persuasively diminished his presidential power (while the power of expression helped put his successor into office). What we'll learn from each of these examples explains why expressiveness is one of the strongest sources of power you can have—and why it's never too late to join Toastmasters.

Chapter 3 explores history power, which is the power derived from the length and extent of your relationship with, or familiarity with, the person you are trying to lead or influence. History typically refers to a real relationship (in general, the longer you know someone the more influence you may have with that person), but it also refers to virtual relationships, which is why advertising firms hire movie stars and famous athletes to represent their clients' products. In this chapter, you'll meet a Chinese actor and entrepreneur who has leveraged the Internet to build a remarkable base of personal power—and learn how you can use social networking similarly. Attraction power, the subject of chapter 4, is much more than how physically attractive you might be. Attraction power is mainly the capacity to cause others to like you. It is one of the foundations of charisma. You'll see how Brad Pitt and Angelina Jolie have used this power source to great advantage, and consider why it's a power drain for author and political commentator Ann Coulter. The lesson for business leaders? It is helpful but not essential to be well liked by your followers, but it's crippling to antagonize a large number of potential supporters.

Chapter 5 examines character power, the last of the personal power sources in my model. This is the power derived from other people's perceptions of your honesty, integrity, courage, and other elements of character. Eleanor Roosevelt built a phenomenal career on the strength of her character, while Eliot Spitzer ruined his career through almost comically stupid behavior that revealed a fatal flaw in his character. The lesson for business leaders is that character matters a great deal more than you even imagine it does—and the rules *do* apply to you, no matter who you are or how highly regarded you might be in every other respect.

In chapter 6, I begin exploring organizational power by focusing on sources of power that derive chiefly, but not exclusively, from your role in an organization and your control of organizational resources other people need. Role power can also come from previous roles you've held, and you may have high resource power if you can access resources outside your organization. We'll see how Indra Nooyi uses her role power effectively as

CEO of PepsiCo—and learn from the poisonous regime of Nicolae Ceausescu of Romania why the consent of the governed is so critical. While exploring the power bestowed by the control of resources, I'll also explain what my marble-collecting childhood friend Steven had in common with Saudi Oil Minister Ali al-Naimi.

Chapter 7 discusses information, a source of power that is rapidly transforming business and life in the twenty-first century. In this chapter we'll meet Dr. Peter Pronovost, an award-winning physician who is transforming postoperative care through information, and Fareed Zakaria, a media and publishing star whose command of information has given him a global platform for influencing people and opinion. Chapter 8 examines network power, which is rapidly evolving through social networking technologies. The power of networking derives not only from who you know and how many of the right people you know, but what sources of power they have and how accessible they are to you. We'll look at Rahm Emanuel, current White House Chief of Staff, whose power is magnified by his network, and former U.S. Vice President Dick Cheney, whose network power was diminished not only because he left office but because of his bellicose words and behavior. And in chapter 8 I'll introduce you to a current business leader whose extensive networks are one of the hallmarks of her power in her organization.

Chapter 9 concludes my discussion of organizational power sources by focusing on the power of reputation. How you are known and how widely you are known can be a tremendous source of power—and it can transcend your current organization. In this chapter, I discuss what business leaders can learn from the tawdry tale of John and Elizabeth Edwards, on the one hand, and from the inspiring story of Nobel Peace Prize winner Aung San Suu Kyi, on the other. We'll also meet one of the most famous investors of all time—the so-called Oracle of Omaha. As many fallen business leaders have learned, your reputation is like your share price on the talent stock market. It gives you tremendous power when it's high, but it doesn't take much misbehavior for it to crash, and the recovery period may require more time than you have.

Chapter 10 discusses the ebb and flow of power in organizations. Power doesn't exist in a vacuum. In organizations, power is a dynamic relationship among individuals, teams, and divisions, and the power each person or group has continually evolves as power is exercised, work gets done, people come and go, environmental conditions change, and people gain or lose power relative to each other. It's like a giant power grid with numerous power stations and transmission lines connecting them. Some forces work to maintain the status quo, while other forces work to change it.

Chapter 11 explores the power of will, the power that comes from within and can magnify every other source of power. This source is uniquely individual and is not culturally determined or biased. It stems from your passion and energy, dreams and commitments, from your restlessness and discontent with the status quo. It is the power that comes from fiercely saying no and defiantly saying yes. It comes from your drive and initiative, from creativity, from what you are compelled to build (and sometimes destroy). This power comes from your courage and persistence, from your unwillingness to be defeated, from the relentless quest for something else or something more. The power of will comes from authentic leadership, and it may be that nothing great was ever created except from this source of individual power. This chapter introduces some inspiring people who began with virtually nothing and created transformational enterprises out of the sheer force of their will.

> *There is no such thing as a great talent without great willpower.*
> —Balzac

The book concludes with chapter 12, which includes a Power Sources Self-Assessment to help you gauge the strength of your power sources. No matter who you are, what position you occupy, or what organization you belong to, you can build some (if not most) of your power sources and increase your leadership effectiveness and capacity to be influential. Unless you are among the very few to become the CEO of a major corporation, you may never have the power of a Jack Welch, a Bill Gates, or a Warren Buffett, but you can be more powerful than you are today—and you can have more impact inside and outside your company.

THE MAGNITUDE OF POWER AND ITS RELATIONAL NATURE

I find it helpful to think of power as a battery. Depending on how they are constructed, batteries contain any number of chemical cells that are their sources of power. Those cells convert chemical energy into potential electrical energy as measured in volts. The higher the voltage of a battery, the more electromotive force it is capable of delivering; and the greater the force, the more work the battery is capable of doing. A 100-volt battery can deliver much more electromotive force than a 1-volt battery, and a 1,000-volt battery can deliver much more electromotive force than a 100-volt battery. This is a useful metaphor for how power works in people. Like the cells in a battery, we have a number of sources of power. The more power we have, the more work (leadership or influence) we are capable of doing.

Consider the power difference between an army private and his platoon sergeant, and the difference between the platoon sergeant and her company commander, and then extrapolate all the way to the commander in chief. Each person in this chain of command has increasingly greater power and can exert increasingly more leadership and influence. In effect, each person up the chain has a battery with greater voltage. Or consider the difference between a struggling actor in New York, who waits tables to make a living while he hopes for that big break, and George Clooney, the award-winning actor, producer, director, and screenwriter. If Clooney wants to meet with other power brokers in Hollywood, he can be assured that they will take the meeting. If he wants to make a film, he can galvanize interest, attract partners, and find investors. For others, there's a conviction that if he is involved in a movie project it is likely to succeed. His power comes from his stature and successes (having won an Academy Award and two Golden Globes), knowledge of the business, and network of other influential people in Hollywood, not to mention his magnetic personality and good looks. In the domain of filmmaking, and compared to the struggling actor's AA battery, George Clooney is like the power grid for a major city.

Yet compared to Barack Obama, Nicolas Sarkozy, Vladimir Putin, David Cameron, Angela Merkel, and Wen Jiabao—all heads of state at the time of this writing—Clooney has relatively little power, at least in the domains in which heads of state operate. In Clooney's domain, however, he undoubtedly has more power than these politicians, and this raises an important point about power. Power is relational and dependent on the domain in which you are operating. The magnitude of my power depends on my relationships with others in my domain. I may have a lot of power in my own company but no power in Nastro Azzurro (an Italian beer company) or any number of other companies where I don't work, have never worked, and don't know anyone. I can be recognized and renowned in my own field and, as a consequence, have some degree of power— perhaps a lot of power—and yet be unknown, unappreciated, and uncared about in other fields and essentially powerless in them. The magnitude of my power depends, in part, on my relationships with others in my domain and whether they recognize me—my position, capabilities, successes, potential, and on so—and grant me power.

> Like the cells in a battery, we have a number of sources of power. The more power we have, the more work (leadership or influence) we are capable of doing.

Each of us has eleven sources of power (five *personal* sources, five *organizational* sources, and one meta-source, otherwise known as *will*), and these sources act like the chemical cells in a battery. Some of our power sources will be stronger than others, and they form, if you will, a mosaic of the power we can bring to bear in different situations. I may have very strong role and network power but be weaker in information and reputation power; stronger in knowledge and expressiveness, but weaker in attraction and history. In aggregate, my power sources, in their varying degrees of strength, determine how much influence or leadership I am capable of exerting in the domains in which I am operating. If I want to be a more influential leader, if I want to have more impact in my company, I need to understand these eleven sources of power and know how I can build mine.

POWER SOURCES AND POWER DRAINS

Each of the power *sources* can also act as a power *drain*, which means they can add power to me but also take power away. Character, for instance, can be a great source of personal power, but what makes it a source of power is not simply the fact that you have good character but that other people recognize it and hold you in higher esteem because of their perceptions of you. The *Washington Post*'s Katharine Graham is a good example. Born in 1917, she had a privileged childhood as the daughter of a financier who bought the *Washington Post* at a bankruptcy auction in 1933. While working at the *Post,* she met and married Philip Graham, who became publisher of the newspaper when her father left to become head of the World Bank.

For nearly two decades, she and her husband were an important part of the social scene in Washington, D.C. They were friends with some of the most important politicians and public servants of that era, including John and Jacqueline Kennedy, Robert McNamara, and Henry Kissinger. Her husband was especially close to Lyndon Johnson and is said to have had a major hand in convincing Johnson to become the vice presidential nominee in 1960. Philip Graham suffered from bipolar disorder and became increasingly ill. In 1963, after having a nervous breakdown and then experiencing major depression, he committed suicide, and Katharine Graham became CEO of the *Washington Post,* having no experience in management and no female role models in the publishing industry.

In her autobiography, Graham talked about how she overcame her lack of confidence as she took on that challenge: "I had very little idea of what I was supposed to be doing, so I set out to learn. What I essentially did was to put one foot in front of the other, shut my eyes, and step off the edge."[2] Proving to be a very agile on-the-job learner, she went on to become not only an outstanding manager but an admired and respected publisher. During her tenure at the helm, she transformed the *Post* from a mediocre city newspaper into one of the two most powerful, must-read dailies in the country. She also helped transform the image of what women can do. She said, "The thing women must do to rise to power is to redefine their femininity. Once, power was considered a masculine attribute. In fact power has no sex."[3]

Along with courage, honesty and journalistic integrity were hallmarks of her character. As she grew as a publisher, she became less comfortable with the kind of personal ties her husband had had with Lyndon Johnson. She came to believe that journalistic integrity demanded a more arm's-length relationship with those the newspaper had a duty to report on. So, in 1971, when the *Post* was debating about whether to publish the Pentagon Papers, a classified report on U.S. military involvement in Vietnam, she backed Ben Bradlee, the executive editor, and authorized publication, despite intense pressure from the highest government officials. Her decision, later vindicated by the U.S. Supreme Court, was considered an important victory for freedom of the press. In 1972, when operatives paid by the Committee to Reelect the President (Nixon) tried to bug Democratic National Committee headquarters in the Watergate office complex, she again withstood major heat from the government and supported *Washington Post* reporters Bob Woodward and Carl Bernstein in an investigation that led eventually to the indictments of more than forty members of the Nixon administration and Nixon's resignation from the presidency in 1974. Afterward, Graham said, "If we had failed to pursue the facts as

Newspaper publisher Katharine Graham.
Photo by Arnold Newman/Getty Images.

far as they led, we would have denied the public any knowledge of an unprecedented scheme of political surveillance and sabotage."[4]

As CEO and publisher of the *Washington Post* and as a wealthy woman, Katharine Graham had high role and resource power. She was also well networked, well educated, and well spoken—all sources of power. But what made her one of the most admired and powerful newspaper publishers of her era was her character, forged by courage, journalistic integrity, and honesty in her personal life. For Graham, character was an enormous source of power. In stark contrast is the tawdry tale of Jim Bakker, for whom character was initially a source of power but then became a classic power drain.

At the height of his career, Jim Bakker was one of the most successful televangelists in the United States, and whatever else we might think televangelism to be, it is certainly a business. In the 1970s, he and wife Tammy Faye Bakker originated the *PTL Club* (short for "Praise the Lord"), a television program that quickly grew in popularity, coverage, and donations—at one time it was carried by nearly 100 television stations with an average of more than 12 million viewers. By the 1980s, the Bakkers had built a successful theme park called Heritage USA and a satellite television network to distribute the *PTL Club* across the country twenty-four hours a day. At one point, their organization was earning more than $1 million a week in donations, and Jim and Tammy Faye were living a life of gushing excess. According to *Time* magazine, among their possessions were "six luxurious homes, complete with gold-plated bathroom fixtures and, famously, Tammy's air-conditioned doghouse."[5] Their largess, along with questionable fund-raising tactics and allegations of improprieties in the handling of PTL funds, attracted the attention of the Internal Revenue Service, federal prosecutors, and reporters. Later, a federal grand jury charged Jim Bakker with multiple counts of mail and wire fraud and conspiracy, and in the subsequent trial he was convicted on all counts.

However, to millions of Christian evangelical followers, his greatest moral transgression involved a sexual encounter with a single woman, church secretary Jessica Hahn. He said they had consensual sex; she said she was drugged and raped by Bakker and another man. Whatever the truth may be, it caused a scandal that disillusioned his viewers, many of whom had contributed money to his ministry. Part of Bakker's undoing, too, was the revelation that Hahn had been paid $279,000 by a Bakker crony to keep silent. Bakker resigned from PTL and later spent nearly five years in prison. Bakker's is a tale of a power source gained and lost. For a time, he built a followership based on a perception of piety and righteous-

Onetime televangelists Jim and Tammy Faye Bakker.
Photo by Scott Miliman/AFP/Getty Images.

ness. If followers learned of his lavish lifestyle, they apparently believed it was his due as the guiding light of the ministry. When his moral and fiduciary transgressions came to light, however, what had once been a power source for Bakker became a power drain. Just as he had gained power based on perceptions of his strength of character, he lost power based on perceptions of his character flaws.

Moral transgressions of leaders may be more repugnant when those leaders profess to be moral guardians like Jim Bakker, but character flaws have also brought down many business leaders. In 2005, Harry Stonecipher was forced out as Boeing's CEO after admitting to an improper relationship with a female executive. The following year, the business process outsourcing firm Keane, Inc. forced out its CEO, Brian Keane, son of the company's founder, after the fallout from two female employees accusing him of sexual harassment. In 2007, former Volkswagen personnel chief Peter Hartz received a suspended sentence and a fine of $855,000 for authorizing secret payments to a labor boss, Klaus Volkert, who reportedly used the money to finance pleasure trips, some involving prostitutes, for himself and other VW labor representatives. And in 2009 the one-man business venture named Tiger Woods lost many longtime sponsors and was forced to withdraw from the PGA circuit after news of Woods's many extramarital affairs hit the press.

Character flaws can cause a rapid fall from grace—and consequent loss of power. In fact, every source of power can also become a power drain. These various sources of power can enhance your capacity to lead and influence others, but they can also diminish it. In each of the following chapters on power sources, I show how that can happen.

Every source of power can also become a power drain. It can enhance your capacity to lead and influence others, but it can also diminish it.

THE SUSTAINABILITY OF POWER

How sustainable is the power base anyone builds? As the examples already discussed show, power, once gained, can be lost if it becomes a drain instead of a source. Power reversals of the magnitude of a Jim Bakker or Tiger Woods, however, generally depend on a significant event that tarnishes the leader's image or otherwise causes people to reevaluate their perceptions of him. Power is also lost when someone leaves a position in an organization and no longer has the formal authority granted to that position, or when someone who controlled important resources loses that control for one reason or another (an example might be a policy change in a company that reassigns responsibility for assignments and staffing from a human resources manager to someone else). Power can also be diminished when a leader is perceived to be a lame duck, as George W. Bush was during the final year of his presidency. Although he still had the responsibilities and the authority that came with being president, he was increasingly disrespected, disparaged, and disempowered by the press, the public, the opposition, and even some members of his own party as they tried to distance themselves from him in an effort to keep or gain Republican seats in Congress. When executives or politicians are leaving their positions, many members of the constituency look to the future and begin to align themselves and their thinking with the incoming leader. The stature and authority of the outgoing leader is invariably diminished, and this is particularly true if that leader is not held in the highest regard.

Power is a "use it or lose it" proposition. Consider knowledge power. This is a personal power source that people build by developing their knowledge, skills, and talents. But even the most knowledgeable and skilled people in the world would have no knowledge power unless other people were aware of what they know or what they can do. This is not to say that knowledgeable people should walk around spouting their knowledge, which would at best be a boorish and arrogant exercise, sure to alienate just about everyone. But if someone's knowledge and skills are never revealed in appropriate ways, or if others are not aware of them, then it's as if the person does not possess knowledge power. Similarly, the highest-voltage battery on earth essentially has zero voltage if it's not connected to anything. Knowledge power is based on other people's awareness of and respect for both the person and the knowledge and skills that person possesses. To sustain knowledge power, you have to show your knowledge. To sustain network power, you have to use your network. To sustain reputation power, you have to behave in ways that reinforce your reputation. To sustain expressiveness power, you have to continue communicating in powerful and expressive ways.

Finally, sustaining power may depend on timing, as Shakespeare adroitly observed in *Julius Caesar*. Near the end of the play, Marcus Brutus and Cassius are leading their forces in a civil war against the forces of Octavius Caesar and Marcus Antonius. Cassius, favoring a defensive strategy, says to Brutus:

> 'Tis better that the enemy seek us.
> So shall he waste his means, weary his soldiers,
> Doing himself offence, whilst we, lying still,
> Are full of rest, defence, and nimbleness.

Brutus disagrees, arguing that waiting will allow their enemy to grow stronger. He favors an offensive strategy:

> Our legions are brim-full, our cause is ripe.
> The enemy increaseth every day;
> We, at the height, are ready to decline.
> There is a tide in the affairs of men
> Which, taken at the flood, leads on to fortune;
> Omitted, all the voyage of their life
> Is bound in shallows and in miseries.
> On such a full sea are we now afloat,
> And we must take the current when it serves
> Or lose our ventures.[6]

Brutus is correct. Power can be sustained only if you apply it at the right moment in the right way. In a business meeting, for instance, it is best to offer a cogent summary when the group needs to reflect and refocus, to be the one to say that a conversation has run its course and it is time to move on, or to offer the stimulating alternative when everyone else is exhausting the one option no one can agree upon. But you squander your power of speech and interaction if you summarize too early or too late, miss the mark while urging people to move on, or don't think of the stimulating alternative until the meeting is over.

Power normally dissipates when a leader leaves his leadership role. Yet, while the capacity to actively exercise power ends with the influencer's death or departure, some power bases can be sustained even after the power holder is gone. Albert Einstein's monumental contributions to physics have given him an enduring legacy that continues to influence scientists. And, as any aspiring blues musician knows from listening to artists like W. C. Handy, Mamie Smith, Huddie Ledbetter, and Robert

Johnson, the effects of a person's influence may linger in the records and collective memories of the living for years to come.

THE MORALITY OF POWER

Does might make right, as the old saying goes? Or are people in power largely governed by the better angels of their nature? It would be difficult to argue that power is not immoral if you consider, in the same breath, the Turkish genocide of Armenians during and just after World War I; the genocide of 6 million Jews during World War II as part of the Nazis' Final Solution; the millions of Russians and Chinese killed by Stalin and Mao, respectively, as they consolidated power; the killing fields in Cambodia; the mass killing of Muslims in Bosnia; the genocide of the Tutsis by the Hutus in Rwanda; or the slaughter of innocents in Darfur. And these atrocities occurred just in the past 100 years of human history. In the early twentieth century, left-leaning American journalist and muckraker Lincoln Steffens argued that "power is what men seek, and any group that gets it will abuse it." At the other end of the political spectrum, James Madison, one of the Founding Fathers of the United States and its fourth president, said, "The essence of government is power, and power, lodged as it must be in human hands, will ever be liable to abuse." And Edmund Burke, the eighteenth-century British statesman and philosopher, warned that "the greater the power, the more dangerous the abuse."

Observers from all cultures and political persuasions have understood the corrupting nature of power and the potential for (if not certainty of) abuse if power is concentrated in too few hands with too few checks and balances. And the potential for abuse stems not only from political power but from every kind of power. The beatific view of human nature inherent in the Golden Rule is either distorted or corrected, depending on your degree of cynicism, by the more perverse version of this Rule: "He who has the gold makes the rules." There is a view that power, by its very nature, is immoral, and that whenever people have control over the lives of others, they will be led, like a hungry man at a banquet, to feast on that power to the point of gluttony. Unfortunately, we have had ample evidence in the past few years from Wall Street and elsewhere in corporate America that people in positions of power, no matter how smart they may be, can often not resist the siren's call of greed or the abuse of their positions.

In 1991, during his acceptance of the Sonning Prize,[7] Václav Havel,

> There is a view that power, by its very nature, is immoral, and that whenever people have control over the lives of others, they will be led, like a hungry man at a banquet, to feast on that power to the point of gluttony.

president of Czechoslovakia (a country that two years later was peacefully divided into the Czech Republic and Slovakia), spoke eloquently about the temptations of political power. He observed that the privileges and perks of high office, which are essential to the officeholder, have a devious allure, that a politician can become so used to them that he loses his perspective: "He becomes a captive of his position, his perks, his office. What apparently confirms his identity and thus his existence in fact subtly takes that identity and existence away from him. He is no longer in control of himself, because he is controlled by something else: by his position and its exigencies, its consequences, its aspects, and its privileges."[8] Noting that "there is something treacherous, delusive, and ambiguous in the temptation of power," Havel argues that politics requires pure people because "it is especially easy to become morally tainted."[9] If it is true, as Shakespeare said, that "the abuse of greatness is when it disjoins remorse from power,"[10] then it is essential for anyone who attains a position of power to resist the treacherous temptations of power and remain morally sensitive and alert to the self-delusions that can distort one's character. Sadly, this is easier to say than to do, particularly in environments where the exercise of power is uniformly Machiavellian. As Steve Forbes once observed, "As more money flowed through Washington and as Washington's power to regulate our lives grew, opportunities and temptations for graft, influence peddling, and cutting corners grew exponentially. Power breeds corruption."

Forbes was speaking about politics, but as we know, there are tremendous temptations in business to abuse power. There has been no shortage of con men and corrupt leaders in business whose aims were self-serving, whose victims often included close family members, and whose willingness to abuse the power entrusted to them ruined investors and damaged or destroyed the companies they led. To name a few: Dennis Kozlowski of Tyco, John Rigas of Adelphia Communications, Jérôme Kerviel of Société Générale, Enron's Jeff Skilling and Andrew Fastow, HealthSouth's Richard Scrushy, Texas financier Billie Sol Estes, and Wall Street's Bernard Madoff.

Unlike politicians, business leaders are often out of the public eye and shielded from effective scrutiny, particularly if their boards are inept and their influence extends to the people expected to be watchdogs for the public trust. The failure of corporate boards to exercise effective oversight of corporations led to the Sarbanes-Oxley Act of 2002.

Although Adam Smith believed that rational self-interest would create an efficient free market, as I write this book in early 2010, there is considerable debate in Washington over just how much new regulation of banks and investment houses is necessary to prevent the blind excesses (spurred by self-interest) that fueled the damaging recession that began in 2008. It seems clear that unbridled power in too few hands is a recipe for disaster, particularly when the people in power are more motivated by self-interest than the collective good.

Several decades ago, David C. McClelland and David H. Burnham studied the need for power in organizations and concluded that "the top manager of a company must possess a high need for power—that is, a concern for influencing people. However, this need must be *disciplined* and *controlled* [my emphasis] so that it is directed toward the benefit of the institution as a whole and not toward the manager's personal aggrandizement."[11] The challenge, then, is how to attain and use power wisely and in a disciplined way, and how to exercise power over others without abusing it or allowing its focus to be the elevation of oneself and one's interests. I am not convinced that power, in and of itself, is immoral, any more than a gun is guilty of homicide. It may be the instrument of evil but not the agent. Nonetheless, power can distort the power holder, especially when that power is absolute and unchecked, and it can lead a person to justify acts that, seen in the clear light of history and unbiased observation, are clearly immoral.

KEY CONCEPTS

1. People have five sources of organizational power (role, resources, information, network, and reputation), five sources of personal power (knowledge, expressiveness, attraction, character, and history), and one meta-source of power (will).

2. Power is like a battery. The higher the voltage of the battery, the more work it can potentially do. The more power people have, the more influence they are capable of exerting.

3. Power is relational and dependent on the domain in which a person is operating. You can have a lot of power in your own domain or organization but relatively little power in other domains.

4. The magnitude of your power depends, in part, on your relationships with others in your domain and on whether they recognize you (and your position, capabilities, successes, and potential) and grant you power.

5. Each of the power sources can also act as a power drain; they can give you power but they can also take power away.

6. Power can be diminished under a variety of circumstances, such as when an officeholder leaves the office. Also, power is a "use it or lose it" proposition. To sustain power, you have to wield it from time to time. In some cases, when a person of power has established an enduring legacy, his power can be sustained even when that person is deceased or no longer part of the company.

7. Power is not inherently immoral, but it can distort the power holder, especially when that power is absolute, and it can lead the individual to justify acts that, seen in the clear light of history and unbiased observation, are clearly immoral.

CHALLENGES FOR READERS

1. Reflect on the eleven sources of power. What are your strongest and weakest sources of power? Think about others in your organization or your life. What are their strongest and weakest sources of power? (Chapter 12 includes a Power Sources Self-Assessment that you can use to measure your sources of power.)

2. Identify the domains in which you operate. Examples might be your home, family, company, circle of friends, clubs, classes, schools, teams, and so on. In what ways does your power differ in each of these domains? What effect do your power differences in these domains have on your ability to lead or influence people in each domain?

3. In this introduction, I offered an example of character as a power source and as a power drain. Think about the people you have known or worked with. Have any of them had a power source that became a

power drain? What happened and what effect did that have on their ability to lead or influence others effectively?

4. The sustainability of power depends partly on timing. Have you ever seen a business leader or colleague lose power because he did not say or do the right thing at the right time? Has that ever happened to you? Why and how did it happen? Were you able to recover from the experience? What is the lesson learned?

5. The business press is replete with stories of bad bosses, most of whom abuse their power and authority in some way. Have you ever worked for a bad boss? How did that person abuse his power? What effect did it have on the people who worked for this boss?

6. Have you ever been in a position of authority and felt the power "going to your head"? What does that feel like? Were you able to discipline yourself and avoid abusing your power? If not, why not? What happened?

7. I have argued that power is not, in and of itself, immoral. Do you agree?

PART I

PERSONAL POWER SOURCES

Knowledge

Expressiveness

History

Attraction

Character

Where does power come from?

THE POWER TO LEAD AND INFLUENCE OTHERS EFFECTIVELY BEGINS WITH YOU—WITH YOUR KNOWLEDGE AND SKILLS, YOUR ABILITY TO COMMUNICATE, YOUR FAMILIARITY WITH OTHERS, YOUR APPEARANCE AND PERSONALITY, AND YOUR CHARACTER. THESE FIVE PERSONAL POWER SOURCES (*KNOWLEDGE, EXPRESSIVENESS, HISTORY, ATTRACTION,* AND *CHARACTER*) ARE THE PRICE OF ADMISSION WHEN YOU ENTER THE WORLD OF WORK. THEY ARE WHAT MAKE YOU AN ATTRACTIVE JOB CANDIDATE, AND THEY ARE THE FOUNDATIONS FOR SUCCESS IN YOUR WORK AND IN YOUR ELIGIBILITY FOR ADVANCEMENT. NO MATTER WHAT YOUR ROLE IS IN AN ORGANIZATION, THESE PERSONAL POWER SOURCES ARE CRITICAL TO HOW PEOPLE REGARD YOU AND HOW WILLING THEY ARE TO BE INFLUENCED BY YOU OR TO FOLLOW YOUR LEAD. THE CHAPTERS IN PART I OF THE BOOK EXPLORE THESE PERSONAL POWER SOURCES AND WHAT THE RESEARCH SAYS ABOUT THEM.

CHAPTER 1

SHAKESPEARE ATE BACON

The Power of Knowledge

IN THE 1960s, WHEN I WAS A SENIOR IN COLLEGE, SOME LITERARY SLEUTHS were debating whether William Shakespeare could actually have written the plays and poetry of, well, William Shakespeare. Called the Baconians, these sleuths had amassed some rather convoluted evidence that the real author of Shakespeare's works was Sir Francis Bacon.[1] On the night of my twenty-second birthday, a group of undergraduates rushed into my dorm room and carried me off to the showers, where they threw me under a stream of cold water, fully clothed. Along with a cold shower, their birthday gift to me was a button that read, "Shakespeare Ate Bacon." I am telling this story because it was Bacon, my namesake if not my ancestor, who wrote in 1597 that "knowledge is power" (from *Meditationes Sacrae*). In 1620, in *Novum Organum,* Francis Bacon presented an empirical method for determining the causes of natural phenomena. A scientist, as well as a statesman, philosopher, and author, he devoted much of his life to the study of knowledge and was instrumental in the development of the scientific method.

However, the idea that knowledge is power predates Francis Bacon. Proverbs 24:3–5 (Revised Standard Version) says, "By wisdom a house is built, and by understanding it is established; by knowledge the rooms are filled with all precious and pleasant riches. A wise man is mightier than a strong man, and a man of knowledge than he who has strength." These verses reflect the commonsense belief that knowledge is a platform for advancement, and that being well educated increases one's potential in work as well as life. People who are skilled, learned, and wise can open more doors and accomplish more than those who are simply strong. There must have come a time in human history, as our brains developed and we diverged from the beasts, when human beings recognized that what distinguishes us most from other creatures—our intelligence—enables us to defeat animals that are bigger, faster, and stronger than we are and allows us to master our environment. From that moment of collective self-discovery, we have understood that knowledge is power, enhancing not only our capacity to shape our environment and control other living things, but also our ability to lead and influence other people.

Knowledge is one of the most important of the personal power sources because it is classless and democratic. Although there are some areas of special knowledge only a select group of people can acquire (the combination for opening a vault in a particular bank, for instance), by and large, knowledge is available to virtually anyone with average mental abilities who has the desire to acquire it and/or access to teachers, mentors, libraries, the Internet, or some other source of knowledge. Most societies consider knowledge so important to the preservation and advancement of civilization that they require their children to devote years of their lives to education, and usually the more years of education people have, the more knowledgeable they are—and the more influence they can wield in society.

In this book, I am using the term *knowledge power* to refer not only to what people know but also to their skills—that is, what they can do. Broadly speaking, knowledge power includes people's skills, talents, and abilities, as well as their learning, wisdom, and accomplishments. Peyton Manning of the Indianapolis Colts may have considerable knowledge of American football, but it's his skill as a quarterback that gives him power. Yo-Yo Ma may know a great deal about the cello, but admirers don't go to hear him lecture on the cello; they go to hear him play. Master chef Joël Robuchon may be an expert on French cuisine, but what attracts people to him—and gives him power—are such delights as his cauliflower cream with caviar and potato puree. You build knowledge power as you gain knowledge but also as you acquire skills, develop your talents, and demonstrate your capabilities by enabling others to experience the fruits of your accomplishments.

> Knowledge power refers not only to what people know but also to what they can do. It includes people's skills, talents, and abilities, as well as their learning, wisdom, and accomplishments.

This last point is important because knowledge in a vacuum is impotent. Skills no one else knows you have might be self-satisfying, but they don't make you more powerful among others. Knowledge can give you power only when others *recognize* and *value* what you know and can do, and only if it *differentiates* you from other people, which implies that knowledge becomes power only when you use it—especially when you know something others don't. We can imagine a reclusive genius with a photographic memory who speed-reads thousands of books and has total recall of everything in them. But because she remains in self-imposed exile, never communicating with others, never sharing or using what she knows, she might as well know nothing. Her potential knowledge power is negated because others don't recognize it. Or we might imagine a more outgoing person who memorizes tens of thousands of arcane facts, like the average rainfall in regions around the world for the past fifty years. Wanting to share what he knows, he tells strangers on the subway that the average rainfall in March in Cayo, Belize, is two inches. Although he is using his knowledge, it's doubtful many people will value what he knows, so the knowledge gives him very little power (unless he happens to be speaking to someone who is about to travel to Cayo in March).

People generally admire others who are highly knowledgeable or skilled, but they won't give them knowledge power unless the knowledge or skill is relevant. Take the case of a sales representative for Xerox. She has in-depth knowledge of the product line she represents. She also knows the market in Ottawa, Ontario, which is her region. I am sitting next to her on a flight from Chicago to Toronto, and she tells me about Xerox's latest copiers. However, I don't buy copiers or use them in my business, and I don't care about her products. I may admire the fact that she knows so much about copiers, but she has less knowledge power in my eyes because what she knows is not relevant to me. On the other hand, if I work in a company that needs copiers, if we are unhappy with our current copiers, and if I will participate in the buying decision for new copiers, I may not only admire what she knows but recognize its value to me in potentially solving an immediate business problem. Her knowledge power increases substantially in my eyes because I value it highly and it is relevant to my work.

In another case, imagine ten software engineers competing for a single management position. They know their knowledge and performance matter, so they all study diligently, learn the same amount of information, develop the same skills, and accomplish the same amount in their current positions. Their knowledge may give them power when they are compared to new software engineers (who lack their knowledge and skills) or to others in their company (who can't do what they do), but among themselves they are undifferentiated. None of them has greater knowledge power than the others, so their employer has to use some criterion other than knowledge to make the promotion decision. Of course, in most software engineering groups, most of the engineers have special areas of expertise and accomplishment that give them differentiated degrees of knowledge power, even among their peers.

Finally, consider the 1973 film *The Paper Chase* or the subsequent television series based on it. It tells the story of a first-year student, James T. Hart, at Harvard Law School and focuses particularly on his classes with scholarly and intimidating Professor Charles Kingsfield Jr. Kingsfield has considerable role power, both as the professor leading the class and as the person who will judge the students' performance and give them grades. But Kingsfield's greatest source of power is his imposing knowledge of the law. Like any great teacher, he knows much more than his students, and he leads principally through the Socratic method, which reveals the depth of his knowledge and the relative lack of theirs. Hart's admiration of (and ultimately obsession with) his professor stems from his recognition that Kingsfield is an expert in contracts, a field of study Hart values because it is highly relevant to his studies. The knowledge differential between them is palpable, which gives Kingsfield a substantial amount of knowledge power in his domain.

Knowledge power is based on what you know or can do. The more you know, the greater your knowledge power—if others recognize it, if they value it, and if it differentiates you from them.

▶   PROFILES *in* POWER

BILL GATES

Time magazine called him one of the most influential people of the twentieth century as well as one of the 100 most influential people in 2004, 2005, and 2006. *Chief Executive Officer* magazine cited him as CEO of the Year in 1994. He has received numerous honorary degrees, been made an honorary Knight Commander of the Order of the British Empire, and received numerous other accolades as an entrepreneur, business magnate, and philanthropist. To top it all, he has been cited as the wealthiest person in America for the past sixteen years, as well as one of the wealthiest in the world, according to *Forbes*. His accomplishments are the result of a combination of luck (being in the right place at the right time), an astute

Photo by Chuck Nacke/Getty Images.

understanding of business, aggressive (some would say illegal) business practices, and a phenomenal amount of knowledge power.

William Henry Gates III was born in Seattle in 1955 to William H. Gates Sr. and Mary Maxwell Gates, upper-middle-class professionals who wanted their son to become a lawyer. As a child, he was a gifted student, a voracious reader, and intensely competitive. When he was thirteen, his parents enrolled him in Lakeside School, an exclusive prep school in Seattle, where he and fellow students, including Paul Allen, were given access to an ASR-33 teletype terminal and a block of time on a General Electric mainframe computer. Gates was immediately fascinated with the machine and devoted much of his free time exploring its possibilities. After learning the BASIC computer language, he created a program that played tic-tac-toe. Then he and three other students lost their computer privileges after they exploited bugs in the operating system to give themselves free computer time. They bartered their way back onto the system when they offered to find other bugs in the operating system. Now in stride, Gates wrote a payroll program for the company whose computer he had hacked and then a class scheduling program for his school. In 1970, when he was fifteen, Gates and Allen developed a program called Traf-O-Data that analyzed traffic patterns in Seattle, for which they earned $20,000.

Gates graduated from Lakeside in 1973 after scoring 1590 out of 1600 on the SAT. At his parents' urging, he enrolled in Harvard University on a path toward a law degree, but his passion had been and would always be computer programming. He got passable grades in his classes by cramming while he spent most of his time in the university's computer lab. His friend Paul Allen had gone to Washington State University but dropped out after two years and went to work for Honeywell in Boston. In 1975, Allen showed Gates an issue of *Popular Electronics* with a feature on the world's first personal computer, the Altair 8800 minicomputer. Gates marveled at the possibilities of personal computing and saw the business opportunity in creating software for PCs. They contacted the maker of the Altair (a company called Micro Instrumentation and Telemetry Systems, or MITS), and said they were creating a BASIC program that could run on the 8800. This was not true. They didn't have an Altair 8800 and hadn't done any programming for it in BASIC, but the company was intrigued and asked for a demonstration. So Gates and Allen worked day and night for two months writing the software and testing it in Harvard's computer lab. When they demonstrated it for MITS, it worked as well as they had promised it would. It was a case of chutzpah meeting genius and opportunity. Gates soon dropped out of Harvard and formed a company with Allen called Microsoft.

In those early days of personal computing, the ethic among computer hobbyists and early adopters was to freely trade programs and share code with each other, which Bill Gates the businessman felt was wrong because it did not reward programmers for the investment they made in creating the software. If people freely shared software, then there was no incentive for innovation. Although Gates's position rankled hobbyists, it paved the way for the prevailing business model in software today. Gates was also innova-tive in licensing software rather than selling the source code, and licensing the Microsoft Disk Operating System (MS-DOS) for PCs to IBM was the most important early move he made. More than anything else, that decision made Microsoft the software giant it is today.

You know the rest. Microsoft became and remains a software giant worldwide. Its Windows operating system and Microsoft Office suite are installed on the majority of personal computers around the world. The com-pany has faced numerous antitrust battles and defended itself against alle-gations of unfair business practices on many occasions. But it remains the dominant force in PC software and has an installed base that would be the envy of any company in any industry. All this began with a very smart, competitive boy with the right friends at the right school at the right time in the history of personal computing. He was fortunate to have been enrolled in a forward-looking school that could afford to give eighth-graders access to a computer. He was curious and talented enough to learn about operating systems and computer languages. He was driven to take his fascination with the machines to its logical conclusion. And he was savvy enough about business to turn his thirst for knowledge into a viable enterprise in an industry that was still in its infancy.

Today, Bill Gates is one of the most influential people in the world. As the cofounder and chairman of Microsoft and as the wealthiest person in the United States, he has extraordinary role and resource power. He has unparalleled access to information in his domain, a broad network of con-tacts inside and outside his organization, and a reputation as a shrewd and highly successful businessman. But it was his early mastery of computers, and the knowledge power that gave him, that propelled him to his later successes. He is an exemplar of how knowledge can catapult a gifted but otherwise unremarkable fellow into a position of exceptional power. To his credit, he is using his great wealth for philanthropy, and he has a sense of humor about himself. In 2007, while receiving an honorary degree from Harvard University and speaking at the graduation ceremony, Gates said, "I applaud the graduates today for taking a much more direct route to your degrees. For my part, I'm just happy that the *Crimson* [Harvard's daily stu-dent newspaper] has called me 'Harvard's most successful dropout.' I guess that makes me valedictorian of my own special class. . . . I did the best of everyone who failed."[2]

What We Can Learn from Bill Gates

1. *Applied knowledge has value.* Gates was fortunate to have developed special knowledge during the infancy of his industry, but there were other smart young people doing the same. He was driven, though, to apply his knowledge in ways other people valued. It was the practical application of his knowledge that built his knowledge power. Lesson number one: It isn't enough to know a lot about something. You have to apply that knowledge in valuable ways.

2. *Nothing builds knowledge power more than using it to get results.* His early attempts to demonstrate his knowledge—the tic-tac-toe program, the class scheduling program, the payroll program, Traf-O-Data, and BASIC for the Altair 8800—were all successful. Those early successes gave Gates the confidence and the track record to persuade others that he knew what he was doing. The lesson is a familiar one but worth repeating: Get results. Take the time, devote the energy, do what it takes to ensure that your efforts succeed.

3. *Technical knowledge alone is not sufficient.* Bill Gates also had an instinctive understanding of business. Although he was a brilliant programmer, he had equal or greater genius in the art and science of business. That's why Microsoft is what it is today. The lesson? Whatever else you bring to your company, whatever special knowledge you have, it is crucial that you also develop good business acumen. It's the combination of technical smarts and business savvy that helps build extraordinary knowledge power.

4. *The power of curiosity can lead us to many domains of knowledge.* Throughout his life, Gates has had an appetite for knowledge. He was especially open to and curious about advances in the rapidly growing world of information technology. He hasn't always invented what's new (Xerox PARC initially developed a graphical interface for users, which many people believe Microsoft "adopted" in its Windows operating system), but his fascination for what's new, coupled with keen insight into its application, drove a number of Microsoft's innovations. The lesson: Be insanely curious about advances in your field and other fields related to it—and explore how those advances might apply to your company's products and services.

DIFFERENT WAYS OF KNOWING

In his 1983 book *Frames of Mind: The Theory of Multiple Intelligences,* psychologist Howard Gardner proposed that people can be intelligent in different ways, an argument he elaborated upon in subsequent books. The eight intelligences Gardner identified were linguistic, logic-mathematical, musical, spatial, bodily-kinesthetic, naturalist, interpersonal, and intrapersonal.[3] Gardner's theory reflects earlier work on the structure of intellect by J. P. Guilford, who identified ninety intellectual abilities and thirty behavioral abilities,[4] and on differences in styles of thinking by Robert J. Sternberg.[5] These theories have a commonsense ring to them and are gaining acceptance among cognitive psychologists. It makes sense that Twyla Tharp, the renowned choreographer, would have greater bodily-kinesthetic intelligence than most other people; that Frank Lloyd Wright would have had greater spatial intelligence; and that Charles Darwin would have had greater naturalist intelligence. People can be smart in different ways. I have very little talent in foreign languages, whereas my daughter picks them up easily. I have more linguistic or word smarts but less spatial smarts. I don't have a talent for higher mathematics but am modestly gifted musically, although Carlos Santana appears to have much more musical intelligence than I do. And so on.

Similarly, there appear to be different ways of knowing, although purists might argue that there is only one way of knowing but different things to be known. It seems evident to me, however, that there are different ways of knowing. For instance, some people have a way of knowing that I would call *spiritual* knowing. They seem to have an understanding that transcends normal understanding. Shamans and ordinary people with great spiritual comprehension have a level of consciousness and awareness that other people don't seem to have; they have a connection to a mystical realm that people who lack spiritual knowing don't experience and may mock because of its apparent unreality. It is easy to dismiss spiritual knowing if you don't experience it, and it is easy to dismiss it when you see charlatans on television preaching spirituality so that they can raise money to buy another fancy car or mansion. But when you are in the presence of a person with authentic spiritual knowing, like the Dalai Lama, you appreciate that he has a level of awareness and a way of knowing the world that most people do not have.

I'm not going to attempt a complete taxonomy of the ways of knowing, nor will I offer scientific proof for what I'm describing. That's not my purpose. I simply want to suggest that what Twyla Tharp knows and the way she knows it differs from what the Dalai Lama knows and the way he knows it. There are different ways of knowing, and they help people build knowledge power in different ways.

It seems clear, for example, that there is also a *procedural* way of knowing. A qualified neurosurgeon knows how to perform a hypophysectomy, and a Navajo Hataali (medicine man) knows how to perform a Blessing Way ceremony for a Navajo soldier going to war, just as Twyla Tharp knows how to choreograph a dance, Pedro Almodóvar knows how to make a movie, and Lidia Matticchio Bastianich knows how to make mouthwatering Italian food. In well-run business operations, procedural knowledge is prized. People who understand those operations, and execute them well, develop the kind of knowledge power that companies value and reward. Procedural know-how protects their jobs during downturns and makes them attractive targets for other companies seeking to improve their operations by acquiring talent. Others value what they know because these people can get things done, usually more efficiently and effectively than anyone else can. They are not only problem solvers; they are problem avoiders. If you want a high-quality solution, you seek someone with tremendous know-how; those individuals who have this know-how build more knowledge power because of it.

Another way of knowing might be called *institutional.* This is knowledge about "who's who" and how an institution works: who makes and who influences decisions, how the informal network operates, how things get done (or not), how the institution's stated values differ from the values in practice, how the institution has evolved and what's changing now, and so on. Often, the people with the greatest institutional knowledge are those who have been there longest and been at the hubs of major activities or communications, although they may not be the highest ranking of the institution's members. In fact, often they are not. But the leaders of the institution know how valuable these people are in getting things done, particularly during times of crisis or change. Furthermore, smart executives who are hired into a company try to identify these people during their on-boarding process because those people have the kind of knowledge incoming executives need in order to quickly understand how the company actually works, how to get things done, and how to stay out of trouble.

Probably the most traditional way of knowing is *substantive,* which we might also call factual or content knowledge. Rote memorization of the periodic table would be an example of building substantive knowledge. People who excel at substantive knowledge are like walking encyclopedias; they are great in problem-solving sessions, where they can provide a lot of data, and good to have on your team during a trivia contest. It may sound like I'm trivializing the value of their knowledge, but I'm really not. Having a great deal of factual knowledge clearly builds a person's knowledge power. However, in this digital age, access to information is simpler and easier than at any earlier point in human history, so the value of substantive knowledge, although still great, is not what it used to be.

Another way of knowing might be called *artistic,* although it is more accurate to describe it as an alternative way of seeing. One of the most important ways people experience—and therefore comprehend—the world is through an artist's eyes. It's the way Katsushika Hokusai, reflecting the Shinto religion's reverence of nature, could look at the ocean and see an image of Mount Fuji in the foam suspended momentarily at a wave's crest. Or how Picasso could look at a woman and see fractured blocks, shapes, lines, and colors in her composition. Picasso's genius was to break down the dogmatic Renaissance way of depicting the world as realistically as the artist could render it and to, in effect, say, "No! There is a fundamentally different way to see the world." You may not truly appreciate the insanity of war until you read *Catch-22,* Joseph Heller's starkly irreverent, antiheroic sense of the madness of it all. And you may not appreciate emptiness until you look into the vacant gaze of Suzon, the Folies-Bergère barmaid, as painted by Édouard Manet, or appreciate the deadening monotony of institutions until you read Theodore Roethke's poem "Dolor," or feel utter rage against the machine until you hear e.e. cummings's "I sing of Olaf glad and big." Art and language give us both a modality and a voice for comprehending ourselves and the world we live in. Thus, they help shape what we know and how we know it, which can give an artist a tremendous amount of knowledge or perception power.

Still another way of knowing is *inter*personal and *intra*personal—that is, knowing other people and knowing ourselves, which are important ways of knowing for everyone but critically important for managers and leaders. Daniel Goleman was not the first person to write about this way of knowing, but he popularized it in his book *Emotional Intelligence.* According to Goleman, emotional intelligence is a greater predictor of success in life and work than intelligence quotient (IQ). Describing a study of star performers at Bell Labs, Goleman observes:

> The labs are peopled by engineers and scientists who are all at the top on academic IQ tests. But within this pool of talent, some emerge as stars, while others are only average in their output. What makes the difference between stars and the others is not their academic IQ, but their emotional IQ. They are better able to motivate themselves, and better able to work their informal networks into ad hoc teams.[6]

In their pioneering work on the identification and assessment of leadership competencies, Michael Lombardo and Robert Eichinger have also noted the importance of understanding others and understanding oneself. Their studies of executive competencies show, for example, that understanding others (which is part of a cluster of skills they called "managing diverse relationships") is a key to executive effectiveness yet among the most difficult skills to develop. Furthermore, among the "flame-out factors," or reasons for executive derailment, are "failure to build a team" and "insensitive to others."[7]

In my three decades as an executive coach and educator, I have seen thousands of executives who have exceptional business knowledge but very little "people smarts." They understand business. They know their products, markets, and industries well. They are superb technicians in the science of business but amateurs in the art of knowing people. So they blunder badly as they try to build teams, inspire people, create trust, manage conflict, and deal with people challenges. In the end, no matter how good they are as technical managers, they often either fail or underperform because organizations are social structures whose functions are carried out by human beings. Some executives can recover if they have a high degree of intrapersonal knowing, or self-insight. In other words, if they are aware that they lack people smarts and know it's important to develop this way of knowing, then coaching, education, and self-development can help them overcome the deficit. But for many of them this is a blind spot, and they don't have enough self-awareness to realize they need to develop themselves in this crucial area, so they risk derailment.

Finally, there is a cumulative way of knowing that is popularly called *street smarts*. Some people are remarkably savvy about the way the world works. Others may have profound book knowledge but are relatively naïve about life in the real world. Street smarts is about understanding how things *really* work, as well as being able to accurately assess both a situation and the risks and rewards of alternative courses of action. I referred to street smarts as a *cumulative* way of knowing because it appears to fuse procedural, institutional, and interpersonal/intrapersonal ways of knowing. Street-smart people know how things work, understand groups and how they behave, have an intuitive grasp of people, and know themselves well enough to know how best to respond to different situations. Warren Buffett, "the Oracle of Omaha," has phenomenal street smarts about investing. Like all street-smart people, he occasionally makes mistakes, but his record at Berkshire Hathaway is ample evidence that he is right more often than not.

Are there other ways of knowing? Probably. Hunters sense how their prey will behave; farmers have a feel for the soil, sun, rain, and growth of plants; and ships' captains understand the shifting patterns of ocean waves. There is the way Tiger Woods can look at the subtle topography of a green and know how to aim a putt, and know how much force to apply, and how to gauge the way the ball will travel. There is the way Robert F. Kennedy, on the night of Martin Luther King Jr.'s assassination in 1968, knew how to talk to a gathering of thousands of people in Indianapolis, some of whom were intent on violence, and persuade them to go home peacefully.

Whatever the complete taxonomy of the ways of knowing might be, it seems clear that there are different ways of knowing, all of which we may value in others depending on our needs and circumstances. When other people demonstrate a high degree of knowledge about something or skill in doing something, especially if their knowledge or skill is greater than mine, I recognize them for it and value it if it is relevant to me. If I am meeting with a business partner in Helsinki who demonstrates expertise in supply chain management, and if that is relevant to me and he obviously knows more than I do, then I will be likely to defer to his judgment on matters involving supply chain management. I may ask for advice, refer him to someone who is looking for a supply chain expert, or ask him to participate in problem solving on a supply chain issue. If his expertise is much greater than mine, then he may become the Professor Kingsfield to my James T. Hart. That is what gives him high knowledge power in my eyes.

▶ PROFILES *in* POWER

MAYA ANGELOU

In her book *I Know Why the Caged Bird Sings,* Maya Angelou wrote, "All knowledge is spendable currency, depending on the market." In those words, she said more eloquently than I ever could that knowledge has power if others value it. In her life, Angelou has been a cable-car conductor,

waitress, cook, teacher, writer, poet, singer, actress, dancer, director, producer, journalist, and civil rights activist. Since 1981, she has been the Reynolds Professor of American Studies at Wake Forest University, and in 1993 Bill Clinton asked her to read her poem "On the Pulse of Morning" at his presidential inauguration. However, she may be most renowned as a poet and autobiographer. Of the more than thirty books she has written, six are autobiographies, beginning with *I Know Why the Caged Bird Sings* (1969) and concluding, thus far, with *A Song Flung Up to Heaven* (2002). As her autobiographies suggest, much of her life has been a journey of self-discovery, and she is an exemplar of the interpersonal and intrapersonal ways of knowing.

Photo by Frederick M. Brown/Getty Images.

Born in St. Louis, Missouri, in 1928, her parents divorced when she was three, and she and her brother (who nicknamed her "Maya") were sent to live with her grandmother in Stamps, Arkansas, which was then part of the segregated South. She experienced firsthand legally sanctioned racial discrimination. When she was seven, while visiting her mother in Chicago, she was sexually molested by her mother's boyfriend, something she confided only to her brother. When an uncle later killed the molester, she felt responsible for his death because she had spoken up, and she fell silent, communicating only with her brother, until she was thirteen. She attended high school in San Francisco; dropped out; became a single mother; and, while working as a waitress and cook, developed her artistic talents. In her life's journey, she has performed in *Porgy and Bess,* studied dance with Martha Graham and Alvin Ailey, developed her writing talent with the Harlem Writers Guild, worked as a journalist in Egypt and Ghana, written the first screenplay by an African-American woman to be produced as a film (*Georgia, Georgia,* 1972), appeared as an actress on the television miniseries *Roots,* worked with Martin Luther King Jr. as northern coordinator of the Southern Christian Leadership Conference, won three Grammys, and received more than thirty honorary degrees.

A considerable part of Angelou's knowledge power derives from her versatility. It is rare for someone to excel as a poet, author, actress, dancer, singer, director, producer, and professor. Truly a Renaissance person, she is one of the most honored and respected people of her generation, whose power comes from an eventful life, enlarged by the people she has known, encouraged by those who believed in her, and enriched by introspection. Her grandmother wanted her to be a preacher, but that was not her path. "It has devolved to me," she once said in an interview, "to write about morals, about hope, about desolation, and pain and ecstasy and joy and triumph in the human spirit. So it seems to me, that is my calling. And I write about it for all of us, because I know that human beings are more alike than we are unalike."[8] In the book that brought her fame, Angelou said that a caged bird doesn't sing because it has an answer; it sings because it has a song.

In her life, Angelou has lain on both the rock and the pillow and has been thoughtful and eloquent in communicating her experiences. Her greatest sources of power are her expressiveness, character, attraction, and knowledge—knowledge of herself, knowledge of others, and knowledge of the human spirit and the tragedies and triumphs that shape it.

What We Can Learn from Maya Angelou

1. *The value of versatility.* Throughout her life, Angelou has explored many facets of herself and has been able to integrate her perspectives to form a truly unique view of life and human experience. The lesson for businesspeople: Don't become too narrowly focused as you develop your knowledge and skills. You can magnify your knowledge power by developing mastery in multiple domains. Moreover, one of the keys to

innovation is the ability to draw upon perspectives and concepts from multiple fields in order to see what those who are too narrowly focused don't see. You are more likely to be innovative—and be known for it—if you have developed knowledge power in a spectrum of fields. Don't be too narrow.

2. *The value of introspection.* In her life and through her art, Angelou has taken a deep look inside herself, and the honesty with which she communicates what she's learned makes her insights potent and meaningful. Much of her power comes from being an authentic leader. The lesson? An important part of the knowledge you need to develop as a leader is self-knowledge. Daniel Goleman considers it an essential part of emotional intelligence. You are unlikely to develop an authentic leadership voice and perspective if one of your blind spots is you.

3. *The value of spirituality.* At the heart of Angelou's life and work is a deep sense of connectedness with the world and other human beings. She communicates the spirituality of being without insisting that it be religious. The lesson for the rest of us: Business does not exist in a vacuum. Business operates in a human sociocultural web. An important way of knowing is to appreciate the interconnections between your company and its products, your customers and their customers, your suppliers and their suppliers, your mission and values and those of every culture in which you operate, and your processes and by-products and our global environment and its sustainability. Your knowledge power increases with your sensitivity to and knowledge of the holistic context in which you and your company operate.

THE SYMBOLS OF KNOWLEDGE POWER

In 2008, Françoise Barré-Sinoussi shared in the Nobel Prize in Medicine for her part in the discovery of the human immunodeficiency virus (HIV). She has a doctorate in virology, has authored or coauthored hundreds of articles for scientific journals, and is director of the Regulation of Retroviral Infections Unit at the Institut Pasteur in Paris. If that's not impressive enough, she was also named France's Woman of the Year in 2008. Even if you don't know her and have not read her articles or heard her speak, from my brief description alone you would surmise that she has tremendous knowledge power in her domain. Why? Because she is surrounded by symbols of knowledge power. Her degree, title, position, publications, and awards all communicate that this is a person with a significant capacity to lead and influence others because of her knowledge.

Symbols are a form of shorthand. They allow us to communicate a great amount of information quickly. In addition to saving time, symbols help establish respect. If I go with a friend to a restaurant in Paris and he introduces me to "Françoise Barré-Sinoussi," I will be polite but not necessarily impressed. If he introduces her as "Dr. Barré-Sinoussi," I will know that she has earned a doctorate, which is impressive, and I will treat her as someone who is an expert in some field. Beyond signifying authority, titles such as "doctor" often imply a degree of knowledge that surpasses that of people who have not attained the title. If, however, he introduces her by saying, "May I present Dr. Françoise Barré-Sinoussi, who won the Nobel Prize in Medicine in 2008 for her part in discovering HIV," I will feel honored to have met her and will immediately grant her the respect she has earned. Those symbols (her doctoral degree and Nobel Prize) are evidence of the knowledge power she has established. Of course, if I have traveled to Paris to find a semiconductor supplier for my new mobile phone manufacturing facility in Lyon, her knowledge power will probably not be helpful to me because semiconductor manufacturing is outside of her domain of expertise, but I will nonetheless be impressed by what her symbols represent. Here are just a few examples of the thousands of global symbols of knowledge power:

TITLES: Doctor, professor, judge, archbishop, imam, reverend, rabbi, minister, chairman, president, prime minister, king, prince, sultan, emir, duke, baron, general, marshal, ambassador, mahatma

POSITIONS: Chief technology officer, chief financial officer, chief of surgery, vice president of research and development, John H. and Elisabeth A. Hobbs Professor of Cognition and Education at the Harvard Graduate School of Education, Fulbright Distinguished Chair, Walt Whitman Distinguished Chair of American Culture

AFFILIATIONS: Mensa, Cerebrals Society, Intertel (societies for people with high IQs); Harvard, Yale, Stanford, University of Chicago, Université Paris Sorbonne, Oxford, Cambridge, Imperial College London, MIT, Caltech (prestigious academic institutions)

DEGREES: Ph.D., EdD, JD, MFA, MBA, MD (the tangible symbol of knowledge power is usually a diploma)

CERTIFICATIONS: CFM (certified in financial management), CLU (chartered life underwriter), RN (registered nurse), CPL (commercial pilot license), BJCP (beer judge certification program)

AWARDS: Pulitzer Prize, Nobel Prize, Fields Medal (mathematics achievement), Olympic Medal, Academy Award, Grammy Award, Ballon d'Or (European Footballer of the Year)

HONORS: National Honor Society, Sports Illustrated Sportsman of the Year, Poet Laureate, Chef of the Century

These symbols are offered as proof of knowledge and skill. They differentiate between those who have them and those who don't. They are a shorthand way of communicating that the person bearing the symbols has evidence of accomplishment. So when we read them on someone's résumé, we understand both the kind and extent of the knowledge power the person claims to have.

Is it possible to overuse these symbols of knowledge power? Yes, of course. It would be ludicrous to imagine Françoise Barré-Sinoussi walking around Paris wearing her Nobel Prize medal around her neck. In most parts of the world, such displays would be considered not only crass but laughable. In an informal culture, like Australia, a public display of one's accomplishments would drain power more than enhance it. However, in more formal cultures, like Austria, referring to someone by his title (e.g., Doktor Schmidt) is considered appropriate and polite. Generally speaking, people with high knowledge power don't need to display the symbols of that power publicly, although they typically list them in their résumés or biographies. If they have a doctorate, they may include "Ph.D." or another appropriate designation on their business cards. Or they may have others cite their accomplishments for them. If you are invited to give a keynote presentation at a conference, for instance, a summary of your credentials usually appears in the program and someone else introduces you by citing your bona fides.

KNOWLEDGE POWER IN ORGANIZATIONS

Businesses run on know-how. They thrive when they can bring the most innovative products to the marketplace, and they compete with one another in the ongoing war for talent to attract and retain the top performers. Indeed, knowledge development and deployment has become one of the central themes in business strategy in this postindustrial era. Rather than discuss knowledge management per se, which is an enormous topic that's been addressed in-depth elsewhere, I wish to examine how people in organizations build and use knowledge power.

Consider two hypothetical extremes. Annika has been with her company for ten years. She not only knows how to do her job, she also has a great deal of procedural knowledge about many aspects of the company's operations. Furthermore, she has considerable institutional knowledge. She understands how things work, what the lines of communication are, who has formal and informal power and authority, and how to get things done. People are aware of Annika's deep knowledge about the company and come to her when they need help, advice, or contributions to problem solving. The contrasting extreme is Zoe, who does a satisfactory job in her position but still makes mistakes now and then and often has to ask for help. She doesn't have much know-how and seems naïve about how things really work in the company. She's one of the last people you would go to if you need information or guidance. Since power is the capacity to influence others, Annika's superior knowledge will make her considerably more influential in the company than Zoe, assuming all things are equal. (Zoe, of course, could have other power sources that make her more influential than Annika. Zoe could be the daughter of the company's founder, for instance. Or she could be well connected with one of the company's key customers.)

It is tempting to conclude that people of higher rank in organizations have more knowledge power, and to some extent this is true because their positions in the hierarchy give them greater access to privileged information. The senior vice president of research and development has access to information the average researcher does not have. However, within the researcher's domain (her field of expertise, her projects, her peer group), she will likely have more knowledge power than the SVP, unless the SVP is also a specialist in her field and knows her projects well. In organizations where knowledge is a strategic imperative (e.g., Europe's CERN or NASA's Jet Propulsion Laboratory in the United States), individual contributors who are experts in their field are prized for their knowledge and usually paid well for it, and they develop considerable knowledge power even though they are not necessarily managers of others.

Although it is important to recognize pockets of special expertise in organizations, to some extent every person in every position in an organization uses knowledge and generates or refines knowledge as work is done. Knowledge building can be formal and explicit, as occurs in research laboratories, engineering and design groups, product development teams, and problem-solving task forces. But it is often informal and unplanned, as occurs when a field technician discovers a better way to inspect and replace control modules on a power generation unit or when an executive assistant develops an improved way to arrange multicountry conference calls. Knowledge building is a continuous by-product of the process of work, and smart leaders and companies find ways to capture and share that knowledge.[9]

KNOWLEDGE AS A POWER DRAIN

The dream of plentiful, cheap energy seemed to have been realized with the stunning announcement on March 23, 1989, that a pair of scientists had discovered a process for producing cold fusion. Nuclear fusion normally occurs at temperatures found at the center of stars (and nuclear bombs). It occurs when two or more like-charged atomic nuclei fuse to form a heavier nucleus, a process that releases energy. Clearly, fusion is not economically feasible for your average power generation company, and it is exceedingly dangerous (kids, don't try this at home!). So, when Stanley Pons and Martin Fleischmann announced at a press conference that they had achieved cold fusion (fusion at room temperature) in their laboratory at the University of Utah, it sent shock waves through the scientific world. If it were true, then it seemed possible for humanity to harness a safe, inexpensive, and plentiful source of energy. Prior to this announcement, Pons, who was chairman of the chemistry department at the university, and Fleischmann were respected electrochemists. Purportedly, they wanted to publish their findings in a scientific journal first but were pressured by university officials to make a grander public announcement. We can speculate that this was done to establish academic bragging rights, as well as to secure precedence on any patents to follow.

Scores of scientists and laboratories around the world tried to replicate the Pons-Fleischmann results—and few were able to do so. Gradually, enthusiasm and hope for this discovery faded as more and more scientists found fault with their work after failing to reproduce what Pons and Fleischmann had claimed. The coup de grace came when scientists at the Massachusetts Institute of Technology (MIT) examined the gamma-ray spectra Pons and Fleischmann submitted as proof and found it faulty. Subsequently, the U.S. Department of Energy examined their work and declared that cold fusion had not occurred. The University of Utah, which

Cold fusion researchers Martin Fleischmann (left) and B. Stanley Pons
(right). Photo by Diana Walker/Time Life Pictures/Getty Images.

had moved ahead to create a cold fusion research center, ultimately aban-
doned its plans when the earlier results could not be replicated. Pons and
Fleischmann left the university to continue their work in a private laboratory in France, but this work, too, was eventually halted, after expenditures
of millions of dollars, when the dreams of cold fusion could not be realized.[10]

It's easy to imagine the accolades these two unfortunate scientists
would have received had their cold fusion experiment yielded replicable
results. It would have given them a tremendous boost in knowledge power.
Instead, the damage done to their reputations, both at large and within the
scientific community, created a knowledge drain. Their story illustrates the
impact on knowledge power when you turn out to be wrong. It can happen
on a much-less-spectacular scale when friends are playing a game like Triv-
ial Pursuit and one person continually guesses the wrong answers. Eventually, no one trusts him. And it can occur in business if someone keeps
getting the facts wrong, doesn't have the answers to legitimate questions,
or keeps proposing unworkable alternatives. Eventually, colleagues lose
faith in the person's ability to get it right, and this constitutes a serious

power drain. So the lesson is this: Get it right much more often than you get it wrong. Do your homework and know what you are talking about. This is how you build knowledge power in the workplace.

WHAT THE RESEARCH TELLS US ABOUT KNOWLEDGE POWER

How powerful is knowledge power? In my research, I compared the people who rated highest on knowledge power with those who rated lowest. In each case, I asked respondents to identify how influential each leader was compared to all the other leaders the respondents had ever known. I discovered that the people rated highest on knowledge power are more than three times more likely to be perceived as role models than people whose knowledge power was rated low. Knowledge power was second only to expressiveness in the impact it has on a person's capacity to lead and influence others.

Knowledge is an extraordinary source of power. People find knowledgeable people inspiring. We want to emulate them—and learn from them. Knowledgeable people also score significantly higher in two key skill areas: taking the initiative to show others how to do things and supporting and encouraging others. Consequently, they are far more likely to be sought after as teachers, mentors, and coaches.

The research shows that people high in knowledge power are very logical and rational in their approach to leadership and influence. Not surprisingly, they rate significantly higher in cognitive and analytical skills, namely, logical reasoning, finding creative alternatives, analyzing and displaying data visually, and asking insightful questions. They lead from a base of knowledge or skill and are credible as leaders based on their superior knowledge and expertise.

What's somewhat surprising, however, is that people with high knowledge power also excel at engaging others, making connections, and asking provocative questions. Their knowledge and skill apparently give them insights that enable them to ask the right questions and engage others in the dialogue. Highly knowledgeable people are more likely to form alliances with others and to work collaboratively to increase their impact within organizations. Their expertise and capabilities make them attractive alliance partners who excel at *building consensus*. They are skilled at bringing disparate points of view together and at gaining agreement among people who may initially disagree.

Operating from a position of knowledge and skill gives leaders a substantial advantage—in credibility, respect, trust, and influence over others. Without question, one of the best ways to become a more powerful leader is to build your knowledge and skill.

GLOBAL DIFFERENCES IN KNOWLEDGE POWER

Of course, knowledge is an important source of power in every culture. However, my research indicates that knowledge is a greater or lesser source of power in particular countries. Two caveats are important here. First, knowledge power is a personal power source and is highly individualized. In any culture, there will be people with very high and very low knowledge power. Consequently, the rankings of countries are indicative only of how knowledge power is viewed in the culture as a whole. Second, the power source rankings are relative to each other. In Venezuela, for example, knowledge power may (on average) be relatively less important to the culture than another source of power, even though it could be extremely important in a particular organization in that culture (Bolivar Banco Venezuela, for instance), or a particular group, or a particular individual. That said, here are the countries ranked in the top tier, middle tier, and bottom tier according to the relative importance of knowledge power in their culture. The countries are listed alphabetically.

COUNTRIES WHERE KNOWLEDGE POWER IS HIGHER

Austria, Belgium, Colombia, Czech Republic, France, Germany, India, Ireland, Italy, Netherlands, Portugal, Singapore, South Korea, Spain, Switzerland

COUNTRIES WHERE KNOWLEDGE POWER IS AVERAGE

Brazil, China, Denmark, Greece, Hungary, Indonesia, Japan, Malaysia, Norway, Pakistan, Poland, Russia, Taiwan, United Kingdom, United States of America

COUNTRIES WHERE KNOWLEDGE POWER IS LOWER

Argentina, Australia, Canada, Chile, Finland, Hong Kong, Israel, Mexico, New Zealand, Peru, South Africa, Sweden, Thailand, Turkey, Venezuela

As these rankings indicate, there are few discernible patterns in how knowledge power is valued, on average, across the regions of the world. Nonetheless, it would be fair to say that in organizations in Austria and Germany, for instance, knowledge is a more important source of power than it would be in organizations in Peru and Venezuela—*relative to other sources of power.* The difference in average scores for the Czech Republic (highest rated on knowledge power) and Peru (lowest rated) is nearly one full point on a seven-point scale, which is a significant difference. That said, having high knowledge power is advantageous in every one of the world's cultures.

For more information on our global research on power and influence, and in-depth profiles of each of the forty-five countries studied, see www .kornferryinstitute.com, www.theelementsofpower.com, or www.terryr bacon.com.

KEY CONCEPTS

1.   Knowledge is one of the most important of the personal power sources because it is classless and democratic—available to virtually everyone with the desire to pursue it.

2.   Knowledge power refers not only to what people *know* but also what they can *do.* It includes people's skills, talents, and abilities, as well as their learning, wisdom, and accomplishments.

3.   Knowledge can give you power only when others *recognize* and *value* what you know and can do, and only if it *differentiates* you from other people.

4.   There are different ways of knowing: procedural, institutional, substantive, spiritual, artistic, interpersonal, and intrapersonal.

5.   There are various kinds of symbols of knowledge power, including titles, positions, affiliations, degrees, certifications, awards, and honors—all of which are shorthand ways of communicating knowledge power.

6.   Knowledge power can become a knowledge drain if the knowledge a person claims to have is wrong. Getting it wrong, especially repeatedly, destroys people's confidence and trust in what you claim to know.

7. Leaders with high knowledge power are more than three times more influential than leaders with low knowledge power. Knowledge is a significant source of power in every culture.

CHALLENGES FOR READERS

1. Reflect on your own knowledge power. How much knowledge power do you have and in what domains? Who would consider you knowledgeable? About what? Who wouldn't consider you knowledgeable?

2. In what ways do you use knowledge power to lead or influence others? How effective are you at using your knowledge? How could you be more effective?

3. In your culture or in your organization, who has the greatest amount of knowledge power? Why do they have it? How do they use it to lead or influence other people?

4. In this chapter, I referred to the movie *The Paper Chase*. Think about your educational years. Did you ever have a teacher or professor like Charles Kingsfield? What effect did that experience have on you? How did it change you? How did your Kingsfield influence you?

5. What symbols of knowledge power do you have? When and how do you use them? Have you ever met people who overused their symbols of knowledge power? What effect did that have on you?

6. Knowledge power can become a knowledge drain. Have you ever seen this happen? How did it happen? Was the person able to recover?

7. Have you ever been wrong about something and felt that it cost you some knowledge power in the eyes of others?

8. Take a moment to review the lessons that businesspeople can learn from the two people, Bill Gates and Maya Angelou, profiled in this chapter. Which of the lessons are most meaningful or relevant for you? And what can you do to act on the lessons learned?

CHAPTER 2

MR. OBAMA GOES TO WASHINGTON

The Power of Eloquence

IN FRANK CAPRA'S CLASSIC FILM *MR. SMITH GOES TO WASHINGTON* (1939), A naïve and idealistic junior senator from a Midwestern state goes to Washington, D.C., where he fights for change against the corrupt political establishment that has been subverting American values. Late in the film, defamed, disillusioned, and discouraged, but not yet defeated, he visits the Lincoln Memorial and is heartened by reading the closing words to the Gettysburg Address. Then, in the climactic scene of the film, he stages a one-man filibuster in the Senate chamber, and his rousing, nearly twenty-four-hour-long speech gains him the admiration of fellow senators, as well as the public, and influences his corrupt rival to confess.

Jefferson Smith, played by Oscar-nominated James Stewart, is home-spun, his speech filled with the cadences and homilies of a more innocent time and place in the American imagination, but his gifted speech making and naïve idealism are reminiscent of a real junior senator from the Midwest who came to Washington promising change.

In 1981, when he was a student at Occidental College in Los Angeles, nineteen-year-old sophomore Barack Obama participated in a student rally aimed at convincing the college's trustees to divest any institutional investments the college had that supported South Africa and its system of apartheid. He prepared well and delivered a speech that changed his life, because he (and those listening to him) discovered that he had a rare gift for public speaking. One of his classmates later said, "He was so composed in his arguments that I think after that speech a lot of people wondered, 'Who is that guy and why haven't we heard more from him?'"[1] They would hear much more from him.

Whether or not people supported him in his bid for the American presidency, most people would agree that Barack Obama is an eloquent speaker. What is remarkable about his victory is that his credentials for the job were not nearly as good as those of John McCain, his Republican opponent, nor of his principal Democratic opponent in the primaries, Hillary Clinton. Both opponents and pundits faulted Obama for his lack of experience, and they were right. But what made him a powerful candidate, what made him the *successful* candidate, is his power of speech. As a candidate, one of Obama's most potent sources of power was his expressiveness. Consider this passage from the speech he gave in Grant Park in Chicago after being declared the victor in the 2008 presidential election. His thesis was that America can change. The evidence was his victory—the first African-American elected president of the United States. But his focus in this part of his speech was 106-year-old Ann Nixon Cooper:

She was born just a generation past slavery, a time when there were no cars on the road or planes in the sky, when someone like her couldn't vote for two reasons—because she was a woman and because of the color of her skin. And tonight, I think about all that she's seen throughout her century in America—the heartache and the hope, the struggle and the progress, the times we were told that we can't, and the people who pressed on with that American creed:

Yes, we can.

At a time when women's voices were silenced and their hopes dismissed, she lived to see them stand up and speak out and reach for the ballot.

Yes, we can.

When there was despair in the dust bowl and depression across the land, she saw a nation conquer fear itself with a New Deal, new jobs, a new sense of common purpose.

Yes, we can.

When the bombs fell on our harbor and tyranny threatened the world, she was there to witness a generation rise to greatness, and a democracy was saved.

Yes, we can.

She was there for the buses in Montgomery, the hoses in Birmingham, a bridge in Selma, and a preacher from Atlanta who told a people that "We Shall Overcome."

Yes, we can.

A man touched down on the moon, a wall came down in Berlin, a world was connected by our own science and imagination. And this year, in this election, she touched her finger to a screen, and cast her vote, because after 106 years in America, through the best of times and the darkest of hours, she knows how America can change.

Yes, we can.

America, we have come so far. We have seen so much, but there is so much more to do. So tonight, let us ask ourselves: If our children should live to see the next century, if my daughters should be so lucky to live as long as Ann Nixon Cooper, what change will they see? What progress will we have made? This is our chance to answer that call. This is our moment. This is our time, to put our people back to work and open doors of opportunity for our kids, to restore prosperity and promote the cause of peace, to reclaim the American dream and reaffirm that fundamental truth: that, out of many, we are one; that while we breathe, we hope.

And where we are met with cynicism and doubts and those who tell us that we can't, we will respond with that timeless creed that sums up the spirit of a people:

Yes, we can.

One of Barack Obama's rhetorical gifts is understanding the power of that simple, short, repeated phrase: "Yes, we can." His supporters chanted it with him, and doing so engaged them in his speech and his movement. In 2008, none of Obama's opponents were as gifted a speaker as he, and none were so powerfully expressive.

As I am using the term, *expressiveness* refers to a person's ability to communicate powerfully and effectively in written and oral form. People who are more expressive generally have a greater ability to lead and influence others. Why? Because people who are more expressive:

- Communicate more frequently—so they have greater visibility in groups compared to those who are less expressive.
- Make others more aware of their ideas, feelings, reactions, and proposals, so they create greater "mind share" than less expressive people.
- Are often more skilled at expressing their thoughts and feelings because they practice it more often. And, as the saying goes, practice makes perfect.
- Are often more assertive and therefore tend to be more dominant in groups.
- Are perceived to be more competent and influential than people who take up less airtime.

Researchers at the University of California-Berkeley have studied which people in groups are most influential, and they discovered that dominant people consistently have higher levels of influence. The people who emerge as leaders of a group appear to be more competent because they are heard first and more frequently, even though their contributions are often no better than those of less dominant contributors—and are sometimes worse! To make this assessment, the UC Berkeley researchers observed meetings and noted which people made which verbal contributions. Then they assessed the quality of those contributions, identified the people they thought were most influential, and then asked the meeting participants to do the same. What they discovered is startling. The most influential people did not dominate by intimidating or bullying the others; they simply took more airtime and made more suggestions.[2]

Expressiveness power comes from a person's ability to communicate powerfully and effectively in written and oral form.

The simple fact is that people develop greater expressiveness power, in part, because they capture more of our attention. We hear them more often, notice them more often, and interact with them more often. Their visibility alone makes them more influential, but if their ideas or suggestions move us, intrigue us, or enlighten us, then we are even more likely to be influenced by them. Moreover, highly expressive people who are also eloquent—like Barack Obama—are usually more skilled at motivating and inspiring people, at firing people's imaginations and causing them to react emotionally to what they are hearing. Of course, eloquence alone does not necessarily make someone a better leader. As I write this, a year into Obama's presidency, it is unclear whether he can deliver on his lofty promises, and some pundits are complaining about the "inspiration gap" between Obama's talk and his walk. However, this doesn't detract from his power as a speaker. Whether he turns out to be a poor, mediocre, or great president, eloquence is one of his primary sources of power.

Aristotle was the first person to study the art of public speaking as a means of influencing others. In *Rhetoric*, his treatise on the art of persuasion, Aristotle described rhetoric as a key element of philosophy, along with logic and dialectic. Rhetoric concerned building arguments and proofs to reach scientific certainty, while logic and dialectic dealt with a way for philosophers to test hypotheses in order to learn the truth. Aristotle considered rhetoric the more practical art of persuading audiences of the truth of a proposition. His treatise on rhetoric, written between 367 and 322 BC (probably in the form of notes to his lectures), laid the foundation for all subsequent study of the art of persuasion and is considered the most significant rhetorical work in Western thought.[3]

Plato called rhetoric the art of enchanting the soul—and not necessarily in a positive sense. He and Aristotle were initially skeptical of rhetoric because they felt that it (and poetry) could be used to manipulate people by playing on their emotions and ignoring facts. Their discomfort with eloquence and their fear that it may manipulate more than enlighten lingers today. George Will, a conservative columnist for *Newsweek* and himself an eloquent writer, complained after Barack Obama's speech in Berlin in 2008 that his eloquence "is beginning to sound formulaic and perfunctory," that an eloquent politician can become "inebriated with the exuberance of his own verbosity," and that one of Obama's advisers should warn him about "rhetorical cotton candy that elevates narcissism to a political philosophy."[4] The suspicion that we might be deceived by someone's silver-tongued eloquence is reasonable, given that it has happened frequently enough not to be exceptional, but it is important to distinguish between an earnest person with the gift of speech and someone who is glib and conniving.

THE BASIC REQUIREMENTS FOR POWERFUL EXPRESSION

To be powerful, expression must meet three requirements: It must be substantive, concise, and correct. First, you must have something to say that other people value. So your ideas must be interesting, insightful, illuminating, or provocative. They have to advance the line of thought in a team meeting, help drive the team toward a conclusion, produce a meaningful step forward in the dialogue, or offer a thoughtful summary of what's been discussed. To be powerful, your thoughts must be relevant to others and move them intellectually or emotionally. The quality of your thoughts is more important than the quantity of them. Blathering about something inconsequential is a power drain rather than a power source.

Next, powerful expression is concise. It has no empty words, no fillers, and no verbal pauses ("ah," "uh," "umm," "like"). Abraham Lincoln ended his first inaugural address by saying, "We must not be enemies.

Though passion may have strained it must not break our bonds of affection. The mystic chords of memory, stretching from every battlefield and patriot grave to every living heart and hearthstone all over this broad land will yet swell the chorus of the Union, when again touched, as surely they will be, by the better angels of our nature." Imagine if he had started this passage with: "It's, like, really important that we are not enemies. You know? Although all the ill will and anger and stuff caused by this civil war that just started may have strained our feelings for one another, umm, we must not let that permanently destroy, ah, our bonds as fellow country-men." Okay, that's silly. I know. But it makes the point. Good writing and speaking are crisp and clean. Josh Billings, a nineteenth-century American humorist, said, "There's a great power in words, if you don't hitch too many of them together."

Finally, powerful expression is grammatically correct. Effective writers and speakers know the language well (whichever language they are communicating in). They know the rules of usage and abide by them. It is jarring when we hear speakers, especially people in powerful roles, misusing the language. They appear ignorant and lose our respect. Former American Vice President Dan Quayle once said, "Republicans understand the importance of bondage between a mother and child." (Of course, he meant to say "the bond between." *Bondage* is something else entirely.) On another occasion, he said, "Quite frankly, teachers are the only profession that teach our children." Quayle's incorrect use of the language, coupled with a marginal grasp of logic, strained his credibility in the public eye but made him a rich source of material for comedians.

Because expressiveness can be a huge source of power, people who are shy, quiet, or introverted face a particular challenge. If they don't speak up, if they don't contribute enough of their voice to the discussion, they forfeit some of their capacity to lead and influence others. On the other hand, speaking too much and saying nothing is a power drain rather than a power source. The art is in the balance. It is better to speak a little and say much than to speak much and say little. People with high expressiveness power communicate valuable thoughts, and they express themselves concisely and correctly. But even this won't give them the expressiveness power of a Barack Obama or a Winston Churchill. The most charismatic speakers and writers have additional qualities in their expression—they use images and metaphors that resonate in people's minds, and they invoke poetry and music in their use of language.

It is better to speak a little and say much than to speak much and say little.

CHARISMATIC EXPRESSION: THE MUSIC AND POETRY OF ELOQUENCE

Charisma comes from the Greek word χάρισμα ("kharisma"), which means "divine favor" or "gift from the gods." The ancient Greeks believed that when the gods favored particular people they would bestow upon them a special gift, such as beauty, charm, grace, or magnetism. These gifted people would have an enhanced effect on others because of their uniquely attractive qualities. One of those qualities is persuasive communication. In chapter 4, I discuss the qualities of charismatic people that make them more attractive (and thus give them attraction power). Here, I want to talk about how the use of language can have a charismatic effect.

Sir Francis Bacon believed that the duty of rhetoric was to apply reason to imagination for the better moving of the will. Of course, another way of expressing "the better moving of the will" would be "influencing others." Central to Bacon's concept of influencing is the fusion of reason (logic, facts, evidence) and imagination (emotion, dreams, values), as may occur when you are presenting a logical argument but include metaphors and images to paint pictures in people's minds. This fusion of reason and imagination gained credence after French physician Pierre Broca and German physician Karl Wernicke discovered that some brain functions (speech production and language comprehension) occurred in specific areas of the brain, which led to the theory that the left hemisphere of the brain is objective, rational, and analytical, whereas the right hemisphere is subjective, intuitive, and holistic. A thick bridge of nerves called the corpus callosum connects the two hemispheres and allows them to communicate, so the human brain is not either rational or intuitive. It is both. When speakers use images or metaphors, they invoke both sides of the brain and create a greater effect than could be achieved without that connection.

The human brain also loves patterns and repetition. When a word or phrase is repeated, it restimulates the neural pathway just stimulated, which produces a pleasant connectedness, the memory of a lyric just past, like a refrain in music. One of the great speakers of the twentieth century was Winston Churchill. Figure 2-1 analyzes a passage from his first speech

Figure 2-1. Imagery, reflection, and repetition in Churchill's May 13, 1940, speech.

I have nothing to offer but **blood, toil, tears, and sweat**.

We have before us an ordeal of the most grievous kind.

We have before us many, many long months of struggle and suffering

You ask, what is our policy? I can say:

It is to wage war by sea, land, and air

With all our might

And with the strength that God can give us

To wage war against a monstrous tyranny

Never surpassed in the dark, lamentable catalogue of human crime

That is our policy.

as prime minister, made to the British House of Commons on May 13, 1940.

He begins this passage with a memorable string of four images: *blood, toil, tears,* and *sweat*. These images are the visceral manifestations of the string of four related concepts that follow: *ordeal, grievous, struggle,* and *suffering*. He says their policy is to wage war by *sea, land,* and *air*—and we can envision total war being waged on every front. And Churchill uses a number of parallel constructions: The phrase "we have before us" is repeated; he asks, "What is our policy?" and then states, "That is our policy"; "with all our might" is followed by "with the strength"; and he twice states the policy itself, "to wage war." The impact he achieves is through image, reflection, and repetition. The next part of Churchill's speech makes even greater use of repetition and parallel constructions, as analyzed in figure 2-2.

In the first part of the passage, he asked, "What is our policy?" and here he asks, "What is our aim?" The answer is hammered home: "Victory." For without victory, there is no survival. These are powerful

Figure 2-2. Parallelism in Churchill's May 13, 1940, speech.

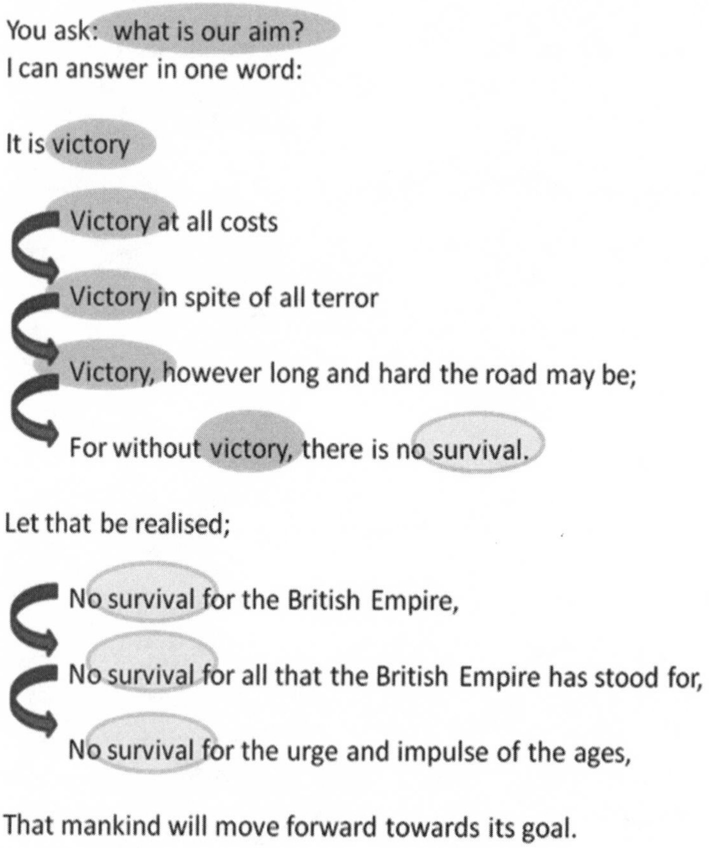

You ask: what is our aim?
I can answer in one word:

It is victory

  Victory at all costs

  Victory in spite of all terror

  Victory, however long and hard the road may be;

  For without victory, there is no survival.

Let that be realised;

  No survival for the British Empire,

  No survival for all that the British Empire has stood for,

  No survival for the urge and impulse of the ages,

That mankind will move forward towards its goal.

thoughts, delivered during a moment of crisis and apprehension. This speech is widely credited with uniting the British people and raising morale and resolve against the "monstrous tyranny" they faced from Hitler's armed forces.

One of the greatest speechwriters who ever lived was a humble, largely self-educated lawyer from Illinois who became America's sixteenth president. Abraham Lincoln's speeches use repetition of words, grammatical structures, and themes to mimic the lyrical patterns of poetry. The repetition of "we can not" in the opening of the Gettysburg Address (shown in figure 2-3) emphasizes the futility of the living to do more than the dead have already done.

Figure 2-3. Gettysburg Address, passage 1 (reiteration).

But in a larger sense

We can not *dedicate*

We can not *consecrate*

We can not *hallow*

this ground

Then Lincoln uses more repeated words (*dedicated, devotion*) to emphasize what the living must do to complete the unfinished work "these honored dead" have "thus far, so nobly, carried on" (see figure 2-4).

One of the most famous speeches in American history ends with four parallel clauses followed by another series of three parallel prepositional phrases (see figure 2-5).

Throughout this speech, Lincoln connects the *living* and the *dead* and the *nation,* and his theme of the rebirth of the nation through the noble sacrifice of the dead is strongest in his closing—that *we here* [the living]

Figure 2-4. Gettysburg Address, passage 2 (more reiteration).

It is for us, the living,

rather to be dedicated here

to the unfinished work which they have, thus far, so nobly carried on.

*It is **rather for us to be here dedicated***

to the great task remaining before us

*That from these honored dead **we take increased devotion***

*To that cause for which **they here gave the last full measure of devotion***

Figure 2-5. Gettysburg Address, passage 3 (parallelism).

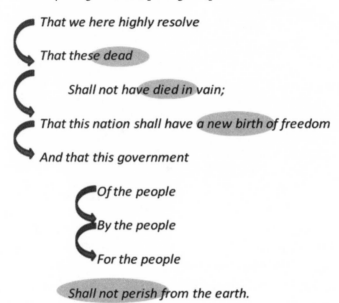

That we here highly resolve

That these dead

Shall not have died in vain;

That this nation shall have a new birth of freedom

And that this government

Of the people

By the people

For the people

Shall not perish from the earth.

highly resolve that these dead shall not have died in vain; that this nation shall have a new birth of freedom. . . . Life. Death. Rebirth. And the resolve that this government will not only be reborn but "shall not perish from the earth." Those are powerful sentiments, written like poetry.

Rod Serling, Hollywood scriptwriter and creator of *The Twilight Zone,* once commented on the difference between writing for radio and writing for television. He observed that when you write for radio and say, "There was a castle on a hill," listeners instantly imagine a million castles on a million hills. But when you say the same thing in a television script, a set director shows up and says, "Okay, what's this castle look like? How big is it? How many turrets?" and so on. Image words are powerful because they engage listeners' minds. Churchill chose words—"blood, toil, tears, and sweat"—that gave his listeners a gritty and personal sense of the dark reality of their struggle and the sacrifices each individual may have to make.

In 2005, researchers at California State Polytechnic University and Claremont McKenna College set out to discover whether there was a direct connection between charisma and a speaker's use of metaphors. They compared the rated charisma of thirty-six U.S. presidents and how frequently they used metaphors in their inaugural addresses. Their charisma ratings were based on work by Professor Dean Keith Simonton of the University of California-Davis.[5] In comparing speeches by seventeen high-charisma presidents and nineteen low-charisma presidents, the researchers discovered that those rated high in charisma used nearly twice as many metaphors in their inaugural addresses as did those rated low in charisma. They also discovered that the density of metaphors was highest in those parts of the speeches that were deemed most inspirational.[6] The most effective speakers fill their speeches with images and metaphors that create pictures in their listeners' minds.

Of course, the total effect depends not on the words alone but also on the speaker's delivery. Charismatic speakers are enthusiastic and passionate. They often use bold, definitive gestures to make their points. They speak with their whole instrument—mouth, face, hands, arms, and body—the way Joe Walsh of The Eagles plays his guitar. They are demonstrative and engaged, conveying a total commitment to their topic. They are vibrant and inclusive, speaking often of "we" and less of "they." And whatever else they are, they are not boring.

> The most effective speakers fill their speeches with images and metaphors that create pictures in their listeners' minds.

Maya Angelou once said that words mean more than what is set down on paper. It takes the human voice to infuse them with deeper meaning. What people sense in listening to a charismatic speaker—whether it's Winston Churchill, Martin Luther King, Abraham Lincoln, or Barack Obama, on the one hand, or Jack Welch, Lee Iacocca, or Steve Jobs, on the other—is that these leaders are communicating from their core, that they are speaking authentically about what they believe rather than what they think people want to hear. There are, of course, cynics who distrust charismatic speakers and doubt their authenticity, but the vast majority of people who listened, say, to Martin Luther King's "I have a dream" speech have no doubt that King believed every word of what he said, that it came from an authentic place deep inside him, and that what you saw and heard of King was not a mask—it was his real face. That speech was a bravura moment in human history, but it was not a performance.

MARTIN LUTHER KING JR.

In 1963, on the steps of the Lincoln Memorial, he said, "I have a dream that my four little children will one day live in a nation where they will not be judged by the color of their skin but by the content of their character." The man whose power of expression would change a nation was born in Atlanta,

 Georgia, in 1929, the son of the pastor of Ebenezer Baptist Church and grandson of one of the founders of Atlanta's NAACP chapter. He studied theology at Crozer Theological Seminary in Pennsylvania and received a doctorate in theology from Boston University in 1955—the same year Rosa Parks refused to give up her seat on a bus in Montgomery, Alabama. Inspired by her example, King led a successful boycott of Montgomery's bus system, which lasted 385 days and resulted in the desegregation of that system. During the 1950s, he also helped establish—and was the first president of—the Southern Christian Leadership Conference and toured India, where he studied the nonviolent protest philosophy and methods of Mohandas Gandhi.

In the early 1960s, King organized "Freedom Rides" to protest segregation that persisted in the transport system of the Deep South and helped mobilize African-American support for John F. Kennedy's presidential bid. He organized and led numerous marches and protests to end racial discrimination and, in 1963, argued in his "Letter from Birmingham Jail" that it was his moral responsibility to disobey unjust laws. Later that year, he delivered his famous "I have a dream" speech in Washington. The following year, he became the youngest person to receive the Nobel Peace Prize for his nonviolent civil disobedience in the cause of racial equality. In 1965, he organized and led the mass march from Selma, Alabama, to Montgomery that built national support for voting rights legislation. Then, in 1968, while supporting a garbage workers' strike, he was assassinated at the Lorraine Motel in Memphis, Tennessee.

Martin Luther King's power was built on foundations of knowledge and character—from the moral certainty that his cause was just, from the religious traditions that were his roots, and from the courageous examples of Gandhi and other civil rights leaders whose feet had worn down the path on which he walked. But one of his greatest sources of power was his expressiveness. His command of the language and powerful delivery, amplified by his public presence and the millions of people who heard him speak, enabled him to influence hundreds of millions of people and change the world.

Photo by Rolls Press/Popperfoto/Getty Images.

What We Can Learn from Martin Luther King

1. *The power of inspiration.* Although from humble origins, King became one of the most inspirational speakers in recorded history, and his impact was profound. The lesson for business leaders? Don't underestimate the power of inspiration or your own ability to be inspirational. The best way to move large groups of people toward a common purpose is to appeal to their emotions and values. If your company is emerging from a difficult period and you need to reenergize the members of your workforce, speak from your heart about your confidence in them and your certainty that "we" will come out of this crisis better and stronger than ever before. Don't bore them with facts and announcements. Engage them with your deepest feelings, connect with what they value most, and communicate with pride and passion. If you shy away from inspirational speaking because you don't think you are good at it, you'll never become good at it. And if you can't muster the energy and passion to speak inspirationally, you will erect boundaries around your effectiveness as a leader.

2. *The value of repetition.* Near the end of his "I have a dream" speech, King repeated the phrase "Let freedom ring" ten times. That repeated phrase echoed in the minds of his listeners. It was a mesmerizing theme not only because it appealed to his audience's deepest values and yearnings, but because they kept hearing it, and hearing it, and hearing it. When he finished his speech, that phrase kept ringing in their ears, much as Barack Obama's "Yes, we can" became a mantra for his candidacy. Eloquent speakers often find the simple phrase that will echo their primary theme and then repeat it over and over. The lesson for the rest of us? In your speeches to employees or customers or any other group, find the one simple phrase that expresses the heart of your message—and then repeat it, over and over.

3. *Practice makes perfect.* Like all great speakers, Martin Luther King was not born with the gift of eloquent speech. He studied it, learned from previous great speakers, and practiced until he had perfected the skill. The lesson is obvious: If you want to build your expressiveness power, you have to devote the time and energy necessary to make it seem artful but effortless to those listening to you. Expressiveness is a strong source of power precisely because so few people truly master it. So when people hear an expressive and eloquent speaker, they take notice. Communication is one of the most powerful skills a business leader can possess. Don't neglect it, take it for granted, or assume it's not important just because you work for a technology company, or a mortgage broker, or chain of shoe stores. Eloquent speech is extraordinarily powerful in every domain and every kind of business.

A final, very important aspect of charismatic speech is that it must resonate with its intended audience. Even the most eloquent speaker may not have a charismatic effect on people if those people cannot connect with the message. Martin Luther King had a profound effect on people in the United States and around the world whose minds were open to the message of inequality and injustice. It's not that he was telling them what they wanted to hear; rather, he was saying what they already believed or were able to take into their hearts if they hadn't believed it already. No doubt, the people who opposed King did not find him so charismatic. When an eloquent speaker delivers a discordant message, people's adverse reaction to the message obscures the eloquence of the speaker, and rather than finding the speaker charismatic, they find him dangerous.

AMPLIFYING THE VOICE

Besides being an eloquent speaker, Barack Obama has very high expressiveness power because, as president of the United States, he occupies a *bully pulpit*. Today, the word *bully* usually refers to a person who browbeats or intimidates others, someone who is cruel or mean, so bully pulpit may mistakenly be thought to be a pejorative term. In fact, it refers to any prominent public office that affords the officeholder a platform for expressing his views to a large audience. To Theodore Roosevelt, who originated the term, *bully* meant "great" or "wonderful," and he knew the presidency gave him a tremendous forum for expounding his opinions. When he spoke as the president, people listened. Heads of state around the world obviously have bully pulpits, at least in their own domains but often more broadly. So, to a lesser extent, do CEOs, board chairs, company presidents, and other senior executives, as well as prominent actors, celebrities, writers, sports figures, religious leaders, and others whose formal positions or access to the media, in effect, amplify their voices.

An eloquent but unknown person may have relatively high expressiveness power within her circle of friends and acquaintances, but that power is amplified many times over if she publishes a book that is widely read, or becomes a television news commentator, or is elected to public office, or runs a popular blog, or is featured on a popular YouTube video, or otherwise attracts media interest and gains public attention. Television exposure and other media coverage can amplify a person's expressiveness power—*if* that person is eloquent and expressive. The "if" part is crucial, because an inarticulate person appearing on television does not necessarily gain expressiveness power. We have all seen relatively inarticulate people being interviewed on CNN or some other network and we may be informed, perhaps, but not moved.

However, an eloquent speaker, especially a charismatic speaker, not only can gain considerable expressiveness power but can also attain near-mythic status. This is one of the reasons Martin Luther King Jr. became a modern-day icon, even before his assassination elevated his status further by orders of magnitude. Beyond his moral stature as a civil rights leader, Nobel Peace Prize winner, and ordained minister, he spoke up—publicly, passionately, and often. He understood the power of the media to advance his cause, and his eloquent, impassioned voice was heard the world over. His 1963 speech on the National Mall in Washington, D.C., was recorded and has been seen countless times by millions of people since. The playing and replaying of this speech has amplified his power of expression. Similarly, Barack Obama's eloquence as a speaker, amplified by his candidacy for the presidency, by an extraordinary amount of media exposure, by his writings, and by his public appearances, gave him so much expressiveness capital that he was able to influence a majority of the American electorate to vote him into the highest public office in the land. I'm not arguing that his success was due entirely to his eloquence, but it played a major role. None of the other candidates from either party were remotely as eloquent as he was, and his eloquence, while boosting his own power, effectively limited theirs by comparison.

This phenomenon—amplifying the voice—happens to a lesser degree with every capable speaker who gains a public forum. Lee Iacocca, former CEO of Chrysler, gained that forum when he appeared in television commercials for the automaker, as did George Zimmer in his commercials for Men's Wearhouse, and Victor Kiam for Remington ("I liked the shaver so much, I bought the company!"). Donald Trump gained a forum on his TV show The Apprentice. Richard Branson (Virgin Group) and Herb Kelleher (Southwest Airlines) gained it with their publicity stunts and flamboyant public appearances. If you are a capable communicator in an organization, you can increase your expressiveness power by finding the means to amplify your voice—through papers, articles, or books that are widely distributed; through powerful speeches or presentations that many people hear; through audio or video recordings that are circulated throughout and perhaps beyond the organization; and through blogs, Facebook, LinkedIn, YouTube, and other means of reaching across the Web.

EXPRESSIVENESS AS A POWER DRAIN

Like all the sources of personal power, expressiveness can be a power drain as well as a power source. Expressiveness becomes a drain when a writer or speaker blunders, factually or grammatically, in some obvious or ridiculous way. Vice President Dan Quayle lost expressiveness power because of his verbal missteps. As the second-highest-ranking executive in the land, Quayle also had a bully pulpit, but news accounts of his blunders—and the mocking he received at the hands of comedians—amplified his verbal incompetence and thus diminished his expressiveness power.

German Chancellor Angela Merkel is also not known for her expressiveness. She seems to be most effective when she follows a script but is a less capable speaker extemporaneously. In 2009, Kurt Kister of the German newspaper *Süddeutsche Zeitung* complained about her lack of expressiveness. Reporting on an interview Merkel did with another journalist, Kister said Merkel "ignored the questions that didn't suit her." What people wanted was a chancellor "ready to argue, ironic, well prepared, witty, convinced, and convincing." But that was not what they saw. "We want a chancellor," he wrote, "who gives the impression that she can explain the economy and has a master plan to fix it, someone with strong convictions that can lead us out of despair. Unfortunately, that's not the chancellor we've got."[7]

If you are (or aspire to be) a leader or executive in an organization and you are not a capable speaker, it would pay to build your public speaking skills, join Toastmasters, and devote time to studying the writings and speeches of eloquent communicators. Otherwise, you risk losing power when you take up a pen, sit at a keyboard, or open your mouth.

▶ PROFILES *in* POWER

GEORGE W. BUSH

George W. Bush hardly needs an introduction. The forty-third president of the United States, he was born in 1946 to a rich and powerful Texas family. His grandfather, Prescott Bush, was a U.S. senator from Connecticut, and his father, George H. W. Bush, was the forty-first American president.

George W. graduated from Yale University in 1968 (where he characterized himself as an average student) and later earned an MBA from Harvard Business School. He worked in his family's oil business in Texas, was part owner of the Texas Rangers baseball franchise, and was elected governor of Texas in 1994. In 2000, he became president of the United States in a controversial election in which his opponent, Al Gore, received more than half a million more votes than Bush did, but Bush won three more electoral votes.

After his election, Bush had broad support from the American people, particularly after the terrorist attacks on 9/11. Patriotic fervor spread through the country after those attacks, and people saw Bush as a leader who would punish their enemies and defend America against further terrorism. He won reelection in 2004 by a wide margin, although his decision to invade Iraq, and the mounting cost of that increasingly unpopular war, began to erode his support. By the time he left office in January 2009, Bush's approval ratings had dropped to record-low levels, and he was viewed by many people as one of the nation's most incompetent leaders.

George W. Bush's power sources were considerable. As a nation's chief executive, he had tremendous role and resource power. He also had a broad network of allies and supporters and had access to a great deal of information. For a time, he also had high reputation power and continued to the end of his time in office to enjoy that power among those faithful to him. His organizational sources of power were extraordinarily high. Many of those who have known him would argue that he also had some strong personal power sources, including character, attraction, and history. He can be an engaging person, warm and friendly, and seems sincere and well-intentioned. But what became evident during his term in office—painfully evident sometimes—and what eroded his power base was his lack of expressiveness. Bush misspoke on so many occasions that a new term was invented ("Bushisms") to label his non sequiturs and other verbal gaffes.

In January 2009, he said, "One of the very difficult parts of the decision I made on the financial crisis was to use hardworking people's money to help prevent there to be a crisis." In 2008, while speaking to the president

Photo by Brendan Hoffman/Getty Images.

of Liberia, he said, "Yesterday, you made note of my, the lack of my talent when it came to dancing. But nevertheless, I want you to know I danced with joy. And no question Liberia has gone through very difficult times." Following Hurricane Katrina, he remarked, "The people in Louisiana must know that all across the country there's a lot of prayer—prayer for those whose lives have been turned upside down. And I'm one of them." The list could go on and on. A search on Amazon.com for books including the term *Bushisms* yields 375 results. Whatever else he did as president, he created a cottage industry in books capitalizing on his misstatements.

Because of these kinds of mistakes, expressiveness became a power drain for Bush. It detracted from his stature as the president and made him an object of ridicule. Some authors questioned whether it was an oxymoron to use "George W. Bush" and "intelligence" in the same sentence.[8] His misstatements allowed his critics to discount him, even when he may have been right, and probably contributed to the widespread opinion, voiced after Barack Obama had been elected president in November 2008, that it was a shame the country had to wait until January 2009 for Bush to step down.

What We Can Learn from George W. Bush

1. *There's a price to pay for verbal gaffes.* George W. Bush may have been a competent and effective chief executive in every other respect, but his verbal gaffes diminished his effectiveness and gave his opponents license to ridicule him. The lesson for business leaders? You risk undermining your authority and others' respect for you if you cannot speak logically, clearly, and correctly. In business, people assume a basic level of communication competence that includes writing effectively, speaking clearly, and listening well. There are higher expectations for business leaders. Essentially, the higher you are in the hierarchy, the more people expect of you. CEOs (or those who aspire to be CEOs) should ensure that they are not only competent communicators but very powerful ones.

2. *Beware of overusing homespun inflections.* For the most part, President Bush used his Texas accent to good effect. It made him appear more human, more "down home," more "one of us." The common man. A good ole boy. This image worked well for him with many of his constituents—but not all. For some Americans, Bush's homespun inflections made him appear comical and even incompetent. They didn't want to be led by a good ole boy; they wanted to be led by someone who was above the fray, not part of it. However, in contrast, Obama's closer-to-perfect diction and preciseness of speech convey the image of the cold, distant, learned professor (which he was). Obama may not convey enough warmth, while Bush came across as too cozy and even goofy. The lesson for business leaders? Most people want leaders who are role models, who speak and act in ways they admire and aspire to be like. Beware of homespun inflections in your speech that may marginalize you in the eyes of employees, but also don't

appear too cold, distant, or academic. The right balance is a voice, hopefully authentic, that conveys the images of competence, professionalism, caring, optimism, and aspiration.

WHAT THE RESEARCH TELLS US
ABOUT EXPRESSIVENESS POWER

Of all the power sources I discuss in this book, expressiveness has the greatest potential leverage. That is, the gap between the overall influence ratings for those who score highest and lowest in expressiveness is wider than for any other power source, which means that developing your ability to express yourself—in speaking and writing—is the most important step you can take to increase your power. People who score high on expressiveness power are more than three times more influential than those scoring low on this power source. Eloquence is power.

My research also shows a very strong correlation between expressiveness power and three other key power sources: character, attraction, and reputation. People who are highly expressive may or may not actually have stronger character. Bernard Madoff, for instance, was well educated and very articulate. Many con artists are effective in part because they have the gift of speech—and that gift persuades many people to trust them. People who have high expressiveness power are also perceived to have higher character and to be more likeable or attractive than people with low expressiveness power. These are probably among the halo effects of eloquence. If you speak well, people will tend to think more highly of you in many other regards, which may also explain the high correlation between expressiveness and reputation. Whatever the case may be, if you are highly expressive and eloquent, you are also likely to be thought of highly in your organization.

Highly expressive people also tend to have larger and better networks than inexpressive people. This is probably true because highly expressive people are more communicative and persuasive. Consequently, they are better at attracting people to their networks and sustaining those connections through more frequent and effective communication. Networks grow and thrive only when you nurture them, and inexpressive people appear to be less effective at the nurturing. Other notable findings about highly expressive people:

► They are significantly more effective at logical persuasion. They are better at framing arguments, presenting evidence, and making a compelling case.

► They are much better at stating directly what they want or believe and leading others by making assertive statements.

► They are considerably more self-confident than people who lack expressiveness. Moreover, as we might expect, they have better command of their voice and body while communicating. They are substantially more skilled at using a compelling tone of voice, using assertive nonverbal cues (gestures, facial expressions, appropriate eye contact), and conveying energy and enthusiasm as they speak. These tools help them be more influential and more effective as leaders.

However, highly expressive people are not just more effective in formal speaking situations. They are also significantly more skilled at speaking conversationally and building rapport and trust with others. They are better at asking insightful questions, building consensus among people who may initially disagree, and resolving conflicts and disagreements among others. In short, their expressiveness power gives them a substantial boost in the skills that involve managing interactions among other people—and this is partly what makes them more effective leaders and managers.

GLOBAL DIFFERENCES IN EXPRESSIVENESS POWER

In the research on global power and influence, I examined how people from different cultures rated on their expressiveness power. Of course, expressiveness is a highly individual power source, and there will be people with high and low expressiveness power in every culture. Nonetheless, expressiveness is more highly valued in some cultures than in others. Following are the countries ranked in the top tier, middle tier, and bottom tier based on the aggregate rankings of expressiveness power in each culture. Within each tier, the countries are listed alphabetically.

COUNTRIES WHERE EXPRESSIVENESS POWER IS HIGHER

Argentina, Australia, Brazil, Canada, France, Germany, Greece, Ireland, Italy, New Zealand, Pakistan, Spain, United Kingdom, United States of America, Venezuela

COUNTRIES WHERE EXPRESSIVENESS POWER IS AVERAGE

Austria, Chile, Colombia, Denmark, India, Israel, Mexico, Netherlands, Peru, Portugal, Singapore, South Korea, Switzerland, Taiwan

COUNTRIES WHERE EXPRESSIVENESS POWER IS LOWER

Belgium, China, Czech Republic, Finland, Hong Kong, Hungary, Indonesia, Japan, Malaysia, Norway, Poland, Russia, Sweden, Thailand, Turkey

An important caveat is that this research was conducted with a bias toward the English language, although the survey instrument does appear in German, Spanish, French, Japanese, and Chinese. Respondents had the option of completing the survey in languages other than English, but English was nonetheless the dominant language respondents used. So it may not be surprising that the top tier of countries (those with the highest aggregate scores) includes the countries with native English speakers, whereas the bottom tier has all the Slavic or Eastern European countries, as well as many Asian countries.

With that caveat in mind, however, another interesting observation is that some countries in the first tier have highly expressive cultures— Ireland, Brazil, Italy, Pakistan, Spain, and Venezuela—whereas the bottom tier includes cultures that are, by comparison, more reserved—Finland, China, Czech Republic, Hungary, Japan, and Thailand. Ireland was ranked highest on expressiveness, while Thailand ranked lowest, and it would be evident to most people who have traveled to both countries that the Irish, on the whole, are a more expressive lot than the Thais.

For more information on our global research on power and influence, and in-depth profiles of each of the forty-five countries studied, see www .kornferryinstitute.com, www.theelementsofpower.com, or www.terryr bacon.com.

KEY CONCEPTS

1. Expressiveness is a person's ability to communicate powerfully and effectively in written and oral form.

2. People who are more expressive create more airtime for themselves, make others more aware of their thoughts, are often more skilled at

expressing themselves because they have more practice, are often more assertive in groups, and are perceived to be more competent and influential than people who use less airtime.

3. To be powerful, expression must meet three requirements: It must be substantive, concise, and correct.

4. To be powerful, your thoughts must be relevant to others and must move them intellectually or emotionally.

5. Because expressiveness can be a huge source of power, people who are shy, quiet, or introverted face a particular challenge. If they don't speak up, they may forfeit some of their capability to lead and influence others.

6. Charismatic speakers use more images and metaphors in their communications than uncharismatic speakers. They also use repeated words, structures, and themes.

7. Charismatic speakers also tend to be enthusiastic and passionate about their subjects. They use bold, definitive gestures and speak with their whole instrument. They are demonstrative and engaged, vibrant, and inclusive.

8. The finest communicators speak from their core, and their ideas resonate with their audiences.

9. When eloquent speakers have a public platform upon which to express their ideas, it amplifies their voices. Television, print, and other media, such as the Internet, can amplify a person's voice if that person is eloquent and expressive.

10. Expression can be a power drain instead of a power source if the communicator is inarticulate, inaccurate, or blunders while speaking.

11. Highly expressive people are perceived to be better role models. People are more attracted to them and consider them to be more inspirational than people who have low expressiveness power.

12. Among all the power sources, expressiveness has the greatest potential leverage. That is, being highly expressive and eloquent can raise your capacity for influencing and leading others more than any other power source, which is a strong reason for devoting time and energy to developing your speaking skills.

1. Make a list of the most eloquent people you have heard speak. What made them so eloquent? What effect did their speeches have on you and others?

2. When we reflect on eloquent speeches, we usually think of great speakers such as Martin Luther King Jr. or Abraham Lincoln. But think about some of the better speakers you have heard in your company, school, or organization. Even if they lack the stature of a great speaker, what makes them effective—in their use of language, in how they speak or present themselves, in how they connect with an audience, and in how they demonstrate their passion or commitment?

3. How would you assess your own expressiveness? What do you do well when you speak publicly? What could you do better? What training or education have you had in public speaking? What more could you do to improve your speaking skills?

4. This chapter focuses mainly on oral expressiveness, but written expressiveness can also be powerful and give leaders and influencers higher expressiveness power. Identify some writings that have had a profound effect on you. What caused that effect? What made the writing powerful? What techniques did the writer use?

5. I did not discuss Adolf Hitler in this chapter, but he was undeniably a powerful speaker. One of his earliest and greatest sources of personal power was his expressiveness. It should be clear from his example that high expressiveness is morally neutral. The power of speech can be used for good or evil. In fact, many of the most notable con artists, psychopaths, and despots in world history have been accomplished communicators; it's part of what made them successful—at least for a time. Have you known anyone with the "gift of gab" who used that gift to manipulate people? What made those people effective? How can others defend themselves against their expressiveness power?

CHAPTER 3

PEOPLE ARE STRANGE

The Power of Relationships

LEGEND HAS IT THAT JIM MORRISON—POET, SONGWRITER, SINGER, AND 1960s rock icon—met fellow bandmate Robbie Krieger one afternoon at the latter's house, and the two of them went for a walk on Lookout Mountain above Laurel Canyon to watch the sun set. Morrison was depressed, and his mood and the California vista inspired him to write the lyrics to what would become one of The Doors' signature songs. This song about loneliness and alienation reflects a fundamental truth about human nature: We are social creatures. We need connection with other human beings. And an interesting fact about us is that when we form those connections—when we establish a *history* with other people—we are more likely to be influenced by them, and they by us. Our relationships and connections with other people are therefore another source of personal power.

In his groundbreaking book on the psychology of persuasion, Robert Cialdini, a professor of psychology and marketing at Arizona State University, said, "Few people would be surprised to learn that, as a rule, we most prefer to say yes to the requests of someone we know and like."[1] When we get to know people, particularly if we get to know them as fellow members of a group we identify with, we develop an affinity for them, a bond that, no matter how slight, makes us more inclined to go along with them and perhaps agree to their requests. Stronger bonding, of the type that occurs between family members and friends, creates even more relationship history power. Yet, as we will see in this chapter, almost any type of relationship with another person can increase the power each person in the relationship has to influence the other, and this is particularly true in business, in social clubs, on sports teams, and in other organizations where cooperation is the social norm.

Generally speaking, your capacity to lead and influence others increases with the length and strength of your relationship with them. Consequently, people who are more skilled at building close relationships with others tend to be more influential than those who are less skilled at building close relationships. In my research on power and influence, I found that people who excelled at building close relationships with others were viewed as significantly less threatening and intimidating. They were rated nearly twice as effective in their use of leadership and influence techniques and were perceived to be nearly three times more influential than people who were not as adept at building close relationships. The findings were similar for people rated highest in history power, the subject of this chapter.

One of the fundamental requirements of an interpersonal relationship is reciprocity. If you and I are friends or colleagues, we each expect reciprocity in our relationship. If I am cooperative with you, I expect you to be cooperative with me. If I do a favor for you, I expect you to return the favor—or at least be willing to do so if asked. All enduring human relationships among equals assume reciprocity, which means that if I can influence you, then I must be willing to be influenced by you in return. Ethical influence is consensual and often bilateral. So if we both do favors for each other, we will feel more affinity for each other based on our experience of mutual cooperation. However, if you fail to reciprocate, especially over a lengthening period, then your history power with me will erode as I realize that you are a taker but not a giver.

I am using the term *history* power as shorthand for "history with the other person"—the follower, direct report, colleague, friend, or influencee (a term I'll use to describe a person you are attempting to influence). This is the power derived from shared experience, from mutual familiarity and trust, and it is unique as a power source because it exists only between two people in a relationship—the leader and the follower, the influencer and the influencee. A history between people develops as they get to know each other, as they each disclose more information about themselves, and as they have positive experiences that reinforce the bond. Imagine that I am a technical support person in the company you work for. You are in customer service, and I am sent to diagnose a connectivity problem with your iPhone or BlackBerry. As I'm working on the problem, we get to know each other a little bit. On your desk is a photo of you and your dog. I have a dog, too, and we talk about our pets. I fix your device and tell you to call me if you have any other problems. You're happy to be connected again and thank me for helping you. The next time you have a technical issue, you remember how helpful I was last time and you decide to call me. I remember your photo of your dog, and this time I bring a photo of my dog, and we talk about our dogs while I'm solving your computer problem.

Sometime later, another friend e-mails you some funny dog photos, and you forward them to me.

> History power is derived from shared experience, from mutual familiarity and trust, and it is unique as a power source because it exists only between two people in a relationship—the leader and the follower, the influencer and the influencee.

This is how a history between two people might develop. It may or may not evolve into a friendship. Maybe we'll always think of each other as colleagues, acquaintances, or just friendly members of the same company. In any case, we nonetheless know each other better than people we've merely been introduced to but haven't worked with, and we might respect or even like one another. Because we have a history, when we interact with each other in the future, each of us will recall that history, and the bond that history has created will increase our ability to influence one another—as long as our regard for each other is positive. If you say to me, "Hey, I read a review of some interesting new online customer service software," I will be more inclined to look into it because I know you, because we've made a personal and professional connection. You will have influenced me.

Likewise, if we see each other in the company cafeteria and I say hello to you, and you don't acknowledge me, I will feel slighted, and my regard for you will diminish. The next time you call with a computer problem, I might see if someone else can go help you—or I might lose your request in the shuffle. History power is sustained by the positive regard that results from cooperation, helpfulness, and friendliness. We don't necessarily have to develop strong liking for each other, but we should find each other credible, accepting, and predictable. This is another thing that sustains history power. As we get to know people, we learn how they normally behave. We learn whether an experience with them is likely to be pleasant or helpful. We discover whether they are reliable, interesting, funny, provocative, thoughtful, and accommodating. The longer we know them, the more certain we become of our ability to predict their behavior, and being able to predict their behavior makes them safer to be around, assuming they are stable and benign. This is why it's so disturbing to us when someone we know does something that seems completely out of character (as many of Bernard Madoff's friends were bewildered when he turned out to be a master swindler). Puzzled, we might say, "I didn't think she was capable of that!" or "I thought I knew him!" On the other hand, we may discover that someone who sometimes acts normally can also be spiteful, erratic, volatile, difficult, or uncooperative. Those negative experiences typically reduce the other person's history power with us and make us less susceptible to that person's influence or leadership attempts.

One of the most fascinating aspects of history power is that our affinity toward other people extends even to people we don't know and have never met—*if* we identify with them in some positive way. Sports team fans are a great example. The Arsenal Gunners are one of the most successful English professional football clubs in the Premier League, having won thirteen league championships and ten Football Association Challenge Cups (known as FA Cups), and having the longest unbeaten sequence in league history (forty-nine matches). Arsenal has more than a hundred fan clubs around the world and a fan base estimated at more than 27 million people, many of whom refer to themselves as "Gooners."

Arsenal fans at Waterloo Station (1932).
Photo by S. R. Gaiger/Topical Press/Getty Images.

No matter where I might be in the world, if I am wearing a red-and-white Arsenal T-shirt and I see another guy wearing an Arsenal shirt, I will feel an immediate affinity with him even though we've never met. If we catch each other's eye, we might shake hands and introduce ourselves, and if he suggests that we go have a pint and talk about the club, I will be more inclined to say yes—because of our mutual fondness for the Arsenal Gunners—than I would be if a complete stranger asked me to share a pint. My identification with a fellow Gooner would act as an accelerator of relationship history, and this effect applies to every kind of social affiliation—families, clans, tribes, clubs, sects, teams, communities, neighborhoods, regions, and nations. It's why a German traveling in India is likely to feel closer to fellow Germans she might meet—and be more influenced by them. It's why Sunni Muslims are more likely to associate with other Sunni Muslims—and be more influenced by them. It's why an American member of the Harley Owners Group (HOG) touring in Japan is likely to feel a bond with Japanese HOG members—and be more influenced by them than by Japanese people who are not affiliated with HOG.

New hires in companies are not likely to be highly effective in their jobs for some period of time, no matter how qualified they are for a position, because they don't have a relationship history with their coworkers. People will grant them some trust because cooperating with one's colleagues is the social norm in business. Moreover, existing employees will assume that new hires are reasonably well qualified (or they wouldn't have been hired) or at least have good potential. Until those new hires have built a relationship history with their colleagues they will be less capable of influencing them. History power builds gradually as people get to know each other better and establish a track record of mutual cooperation, respect, and the bonding that generally comes with increasing self-disclosure.

THE PROPINQUITY EFFECT

In the 1950s, psychologists Leon Festinger, Stanley Schachter, and Kurt Back studied the formation of friendships among people living in graduate housing.[2] They discovered that people who lived closer together were more likely to become close friends, and this was true even among people living in the same building. People were more likely to become friends with people living on their floor than with people living on other floors. Other studies have confirmed what these psychologists called the propinquity effect. The more we interact with people, and the closer they are to us in proximity, the more likely we are to develop closer relationships with them. The propinquity effect works simply because we are exposed to them more often and because they are closer to us. Both of these factors matter—frequency of interaction and proximity.

> History power builds gradually as people get to know each other better and establish a track record of mutual cooperation, respect, and the bonding that generally comes with increasing self-disclosure.

History power will therefore be strongest with those people we are physically closest to and interact with most frequently. Assuming all else is equal, I will have greater history power with:

- My next-door neighbors (assuming I get along with them) compared to more distant neighbors
- Colleagues I work with in my local office every day compared to colleagues who work in other offices
- Friends I have known longest and kept in touch with compared to friends I no longer see
- A fellow guitarist I jammed with last Saturday compared to guitarists I've heard but not jammed with
- An Arsenal Gooner I regularly sit next to at matches compared to other Gooners I know but who sit farther away

The propinquity effect occurs because the more exposure we have to a stimulus (such as another person), the more familiar it becomes, and the more familiar the stimulus becomes, the more we tend to like it. The exception to this effect occurs when we find the stimulus unpleasant, and then more exposure to it can cause greater irritation than normal (like a song that plays over and over in your head to the point where you hate it). Many comedians have used this effect in their routines ("Take my wife . . . please!") and many voters have experienced it with their elected officials. You can enhance the propinquity effect by simply paying more personal attention to the people you interact with. As good salespeople know, small, personal touches, like remembering an executive assistant's name, go a long way toward making people more cooperative. Calling people by name usually has a pleasant effect on them. It's a simple and effective way to build affinity and history power.

THE POWER OF VIRTUAL HISTORY

Emmy Award–winning actor Robert Young was best known for two American television roles. From 1954 to 1960, he appeared in *Father Knows Best* as Jim Anderson, the wise and compassionate head of the archetypal American family of that era. Then from 1969 to 1976, he appeared as the title character, a wise and compassionate physician, in *Marcus Welby, M.D.* After the second series ended, Young became the spokesman in an aspirin commercial wearing a white lab coat, reminiscent of the lab coat he wore as Dr. Welby, and he began the commercial by saying, "I am not a doctor, but I play one on TV." Although this line has been parodied many times since, when the commercial originally ran it was an effective opening to a successful television ad. The question is: Why did it work? The answer is that Robert Young, in the guise of the wise and compassionate Dr. Welby, had developed great *virtual* history power with multiple millions of viewers. We felt we knew him. We felt we could trust him. If he (in his white lab coat) was confident in and endorsed this product, then it must be good medicine.

History power is based on the strength of the relationship between two people. When that history is virtual, it means we don't actually have a relationship with the real Robert Young, but we feel like we know him. We've seen him on television for years. He's come into our homes through that little screen, and we've been comforted by the caring he showed for his television show patients and the wise mentoring he gave to his brash, young colleague (played by James Brolin). Over several decades on television, Robert Young became very familiar to us, and he was credible as an authority figure, both as the caregiving Dr. Welby and as the paternal Jim Anderson (whose credibility was reflected in the title of the show—*Father Knows Best*). But, of course, we didn't know the real Robert Young. We only knew our fantasy of him, shaped by his paternal appearance, soft-spoken voice, and the sympathetic characters he played. (The real-life Robert Young may not have lived up to our fantasy. In fact, Young was haunted by the same demons that haunt many other people. He suffered from depression and alcoholism and attempted suicide in 1991.)

Part of the power of celebrity is the virtual history power celebrities

Robert Young as Dr. Marcus Welby.
Photo by ABC Television/Courtesy of Getty Images.

develop as a result of their public exposure and fame. We become familiar enough with their images and on-screen personas that we feel like we have a history with them. If a celebrity we are familiar with walked up to us and asked for a favor, we would be more inclined to say yes because of that person's virtual history power. That's why celebrities are hired as spokespeople for everything from television and print advertising to pleas for donations to charitable causes. It's why Jerry Lewis has been so successful doing telethons for the Muscular Dystrophy Association. It's why Snoop Dogg was hired to do a German TV commercial for VybeMobile (he comes out of a refrigerator wearing a tuxedo and starts singing) and why Japanese sake maker Takara hired Madonna to put on a kimono, raise a glass of its product, and announce, "I'm pure."

Virtual history is powerful because people are so influenced by what is familiar. But virtual history has a dark side for the celebrities themselves, as any of them who've been hounded by paparazzi or stalked by obsessed fans will attest. The curse of celebrity is that celebrities can hardly go out in public without attracting the unwanted attention of scores of people who feel like they know them—some of whom demand the ego buzz of actual contact.

LET'S FACEBOOK IT, MYSPACE IS ALL ATWITTER

Everyone knows by now that the Internet has changed the world in dramatic and unpredictable ways, and the pace of Web-driven evolution is accelerating so fast that the developments talked about here are likely to be outdated by the time this book is published. One of the most fascinating emergent phenomena from the Internet is social networking. The first online social network was Friendster, founded by Jonathan Abrams in 2002 both as a way for friends to keep in touch as and a way to meet new people. As the utility and promise of online social networking became apparent, other services were created, including MySpace, LinkedIn, Plaxo, Twitter, and currently the most popular of them all—Facebook.

I discuss the networking aspects of social media sites in chapter 8, but what is important here is how these sites enable the building of real and virtual history power among users connected to one another. When you join Facebook, for instance, you complete a personal profile that includes your name, gender, birthday, hometown, and relationship status; the type of person you are interested in (male/female); your political and religious views; your activities, interests, favorites (music, television, movies, books, quotations), contact information, education and work history; and other personal information you might want to enter. People who fill in all of the blanks in their profile are posting a significant amount of information about themselves online, and services like Facebook contend that they own this information, which opens up many possibilities for data mining, marketing, and research. Indeed, one of the continuing issues with these sites is member privacy and the potential for abusive use of the information. Another issue is truth. Members enter their own information, which is nearly impossible to verify, so they can lie about themselves and pretend to be someone they're not. Sexual predators have used such sites to scout for victims, and it's not clear that the services themselves can ever successfully eliminate sex offenders from their sites.

Potential abuses aside for the moment, social networking sites have enabled people to connect with scores of other people they might never have known and to develop closer relationships with the people they choose to. My stepdaughter in Colorado, for instance, has developed a much stronger relationship with one of her cousins who now lives in New York. Had they not found each other on Facebook and spent that time networking, they would not have had the opportunity to interact with each other and build the relationship. On the other hand, I have a friend whose fifteen-year-old daughter began connecting on one of these services with a guy in a nearby city, believing him to be a high school student like herself. It turned out that he was a much older married man trying to persuade her to meet him. My friend discovered what was happening and put a quick stop to it, but, tragically, this is not always the case, as some bereaved parents have learned.

Internet predators take advantage of the fact that they can hide behind false identities and build virtual history power with unsuspecting victims. By the time victims discover the truth about these pretenders, they have often identified so much with them that they discount reality and cling to the fantasy of the person they thought they were corresponding with. Such can be the grip of strong virtual history power. It is important to remember that virtual history is built on one's fantasy of the other person, not on who they really are. Still, online social networking is mostly benign—with friends and colleagues staying in touch; professionals networking beyond the reach of their own organization or location; and members of numerous societies, clubs, and associations better able to meet other members and communicate across geographies in ways that were not possible before the Internet. In each case, the connection may build the relationship or increase people's sense of familiarity with each other, which increases history power and the capacity for each person to lead and influence the other.

▶   PROFILES *in* POWER

XU JINGLEI

Although not yet well known outside of her native China, Xu Jinglei is a dynamo: actress, singer, screenwriter, director, producer, and celebrity. Born in 1974, she graduated from the Performance Institute at the Beijing Film Academy in 1997 and is considered by Chinese media as one of the Four Small Flowers—the quartet of leading Chinese female film stars (along with Zhang Ziyi, Zhao Wei, and Zhou Xun). In 2003, she won multiple acting awards: Best Actress for *Spring Subway* at the Popular Cinema Hundred Flowers Film Awards, Best Actress for *Far from Home* and *I Love You* at the Huabiao Film Awards, and Best Supporting Actress for *Far from Home* at the Chinese Golden Rooster Awards. That year, she also was honored as Best New Female Director at the Chinese Film Media Awards for *My Father and I.* In 2004, she was named Best New Director and Best Actress for *My Father and I* at the Chinese Film Media Awards and that year also won the Silver Shell for Best Director for *A Letter from an Unknown Woman* at the Donostia-San Sebastián International Film Festival in Spain.

The acclaim she has achieved in her short film career continues, but she may be even better known as one of China's most active and successful bloggers. She started blogging in October 2005. The following year she published a book based on her blogged articles. In 2006, Technorati (a blog search engine) reported that Xu's blog was the most popular one in the world as measured by the most incoming links of any blog in any language on the Internet. In July 2007, her blog had logged 100 million page views in 600 days, according to the *Beijing News.*[3] She is an attractive young actress in a country that treasures celebrity, but her popular blog is based on more than that. She is intelligent and has a reputation for integrity and wholesomeness, and she writes about her daily life in ways that invite her young fans to know her as a person. Here is one passage from her blog dated February 6, 2007:

> Sitting on the bed in the mountain hotel. Time's passing second by second. The heater's giving out a "hua hua" sound. I haven't seen

Photo by Carlos Alvarez/Getty Images.

the fluorescent lamp in a long time. The small yellow light from the wall lamp is still warm. I haven't spent my life like this. The voices of the people outside are noisy and confused. If I stay for a bit everything fades out. I'm really bored. Thoughts are flashing across my mind. I'm recalling the past. I'm missing my family. I'm feeling regretful. I'm feeling rejoiceful. These are the themes of my days.[4]

Xu Jinglei's power base is built on knowledge (particularly her skills as an actress, director, and writer), expressiveness (she is well spoken), attraction, and character. But her greatest source of power may be the virtual history power she has built through her popular blog. Xu is a modern diarist, a chronicler of life, and she is gifted at making observations that are more revealing about herself and her state of mind than the pedestrian posts usually appearing on social networks. People who read her blog regularly feel like they know her, and the history power she therefore develops increases her capacity to influence them.

What We Can Learn from Xu Jinglei

1. *The power of social networking.* Xu Jinglei has built a huge fan base and following through her adroit use of social networking. Consequently, she has increased her marketability and attractiveness as a performer as well as a spokesperson for products. Social networking has helped this enterprising young woman build the brand called Xu Jinglei. The lesson for business leaders? If career advancement is important to you, don't overlook the importance of building your personal brand or the role social networking can play. You may not aspire to be a world-class blogger like Xu Jinglei, but LinkedIn, Plaxo, and other work-oriented social networks can be an excellent way to build virtual history power with hundreds (potentially thousands) of other professionals, managers, and leaders in the Web sphere. Joining a site like LinkedIn and taking full advantage of the networking possibilities is an excellent way to make yourself known. If you have the time and inclination, creating a blog is an even better way to extend your Web presence. Millions of blogs already exist, including many by working professionals who appreciate the power of the Web to help build their personal brand.

2. *The power of being known, even if only virtually.* Xu Jinglei has developed a greater capacity to lead and influence people because so many of her blog readers feel like they know her. She's built virtual history power with them, and they would be more inclined to say yes to a request from her as long as it was reasonable. The lesson? There is power in familiarity. Remember that people are more inclined to say yes to the requests of people they know and like. To the extent that others know you—or feel they know you—you will be more successful in leading or influencing them. However, the number of people you can

actually know will be finite. To extend your influence, make yourself known to a broader audience.

3. *The power of appropriate self-disclosure.* Xu Jinglei's blog reveals something about who she is. Xu has a knack for revealing information about herself and her feelings and perceptions that leaves her readers wanting to know more. The art is to disclose enough to make yourself sound interesting and human but not so much that people will cringe when they read it. The lesson? You won't build history power if you build a wall around yourself and never reveal who you are as a person. But don't self-disclose too much when blogging or posting on a social network. Be interesting but not arrogant or self-indulgent. To find the right balance, read some blogs and study the ones where the author seems real, interesting, and insightful. Notice what the author does—and then emulate that style in your own postings.

HISTORY AS A POWER DRAIN: YOU TALKIN' TO ME?

In *Taxi Driver,* one of the classic American films of the 1970s, Robert De Niro plays Travis Bickle, an alienated, unstable veteran whose feelings of powerlessness and isolation lead him to the brink. He buys handguns and, in one of the film's most iconic scenes, stands in front of a mirror practicing his quick draw while threatening an imaginary antagonist, "You talkin' to me? You talkin' to me?" In the increasingly demented personal space he has created for himself, Bickle is rehearsing a violent response to a world he cannot successfully enter, and when his psychosis is fully formed, he sets out to assassinate a senatorial candidate. Although this violent film fantasy depicts an extreme response to the invasion of personal space, it does reflect to some degree how we all react to an unwanted personal intrusion.

We all have a sense of the appropriate pace at which relationships should develop, and our sense of relationship pacing is in part culturally determined. Americans, for instance, tend to move at a faster pace. In general, they are more open, make acquaintances faster, and build friendships quicker than Europeans do, especially northern Europeans. And it's easy for both sides to make judgments about the other. I have heard Europeans fault Americans for being "superficial" and Americans fault Europeans for being "distant and standoffish." Neither judgment is accurate.

People simply have a different pace at which relationships are established and people grow closer, and this is true of business as well as personal relationships. When relationship building with another person is pushed too quickly, history can become a power drain instead of a power source.

In the early 1970s, psychologists Irwin Altman and Dalmas Taylor developed social penetration theory, which proposes that when people interact, each person weighs the costs and benefits of a relationship with the other and determines whether it is favorable to proceed.[5] Initially, communication is shallow and limited to relatively impersonal areas, but gradually it deepens and becomes more intimate as trust develops. People tend to self-disclose in reciprocal ways, revealing information about themselves to about the same extent as the other person is willing to reveal information, but even then most people have an internal governor that regulates the amount of self-disclosure they are willing to do. When people are unwilling to reciprocate in self-disclosure, at least to an appropriate extent, the budding relationship will likely die on the vine. On the other hand, if someone reveals too much, the other person might cry, "Too much information!" and back away. The art in building relationships is to match the pace at which the other person seems comfortable communicating information that can deepen the relationship. But if you reveal too much about yourself too soon—or ask the other person to reveal more than he is comfortable doing—then the history power you've been building can quickly become a power drain. If you are working cross-culturally, it is imperative that you understand the social norms in the culture in which you are working and adapt to those norms.

A different approach to understanding human relationships is called relational dialectics.[6] According to this theory, relationships are not static; they are constantly evolving in push-pull fashion according to a dialectic process involving the tension between opposing forces, such as the need for autonomy versus the need for connectedness, the need for transparency versus the desire for privacy, and the need for novelty versus the need for stability. Consider a marriage. The husband and wife are autonomous beings, but they form a relationship based on each person's need for connectedness. As their relationship evolves, there will be changing tension between those needs, and each person will evolve according to his or her psychological dynamic. At some point, one person's need for autonomy may outweigh the need for connectedness and force tension in the relationship that may or may not be resolved through compromise or negotiation. Now consider the history power each partner has with respect to the other. If the husband's desire for autonomy comes to outweigh the wife's need for connectedness, then the wife's history power with her husband may diminish and she may become less capable of influencing his behavior in ways she wants (or vice versa). History or relationship power is not static. It increases or decreases depending upon people's attitudes, feelings, and needs toward one another.

Does familiarity breed contempt, as the old saying goes? We have all probably experienced this phenomenon, although the research on it is inconclusive. There is some evidence that early in a relationship we interpret ambiguous information about the other person favorably; as we learn more about the person, we may be let down by what we discover and like the person less. History power does not require admiration of the other, but it does require acceptance, and history power can quickly become a power drain if one person learns something disturbing or repugnant about the other, as may happen if a customer learns that a supplier has not been truthful with her or if a company discovers that a celebrity it is sponsoring has done something contrary to the image the company wants to project, as happened when Accenture and AT&T dumped Tiger Woods or when the Kellogg Company dumped Michael Phelps, the 2008 Winter Olympic swimming star, after a photo appeared in a British tabloid of Phelps smoking dope.

As I said at the outset, history power is unique among the power sources because it is based entirely on the relationship between two people. So this power source can become a power drain when a divorce is not amicable, when business partners have a falling-out, when lovers cheat on each other, or when a person learns something about the other person in the relationship that makes him not want to be around her anymore. It can also become a power drain if one person makes an inappropriate or outrageous request of the other. That would happen if a colleague asked me to hide evidence of his unethical behavior or asked me to help him embezzle money from the company. Or if he revealed that he's having an affair and wants me to tell his wife that he and I were together on an evening he was actually with his paramour. Or if he asks for anything else that violates my sense of ethics or propriety. History power assumes that there is an implicit agreement between two parties to be influenced by each other that's reciprocal and consistent with each party's values. It is sustained by each person's acceptance of the other and the confidence that each person can predict the other's behavior. In short, history power is built on familiarity and sustained by trust.

History power can become a power drain if one person makes an inappropriate or outrageous request of the other.

WHAT THE RESEARCH TELLS US ABOUT HISTORY POWER

NBA Hall of Famer Larry Bird once said of Magic Johnson, "He's the one person I could call day or night if I had a problem, and I know he'd be there for me." These longtime pro basketball rivals (Bird played for the Boston Celtics and Johnson for the Los Angeles Lakers) were initially standoffish with each other. But these two men developed a powerful friendship and deep bond of brotherhood that is sustained by the extraordinary history they share and their mutual feelings of liking and respect. Maybe you have some relationships like this. There may be certain people for whom you would do anything if they needed you, and vice versa, even if you don't see each other very often. These kinds of personal relationships are a testament to history as a source of power. Yet research shows that history has less potential leverage than most other sources of power (e.g., expressiveness, knowledge, reputation, attraction, character, and network).

Why? Probably because history power, although potentially strong, has relatively little reach because of the limited number of people the average person considers close. In another research study I conducted in 2005 on what people want from their workplace relationships, I asked more than 500 people to estimate how many close friends they have, including family members. The results are shown in figure 3-1.

Figure 3-1. How many close friends do people say they have?

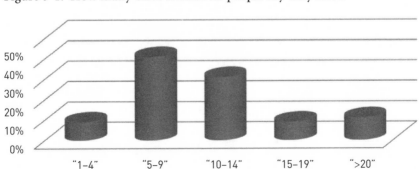

The majority of people estimate that they have between five and nine close friends (41 percent of those surveyed) or between ten and fourteen (31 percent). History is a strong source of power, but it doesn't reach very far, and if we were to narrow down the number of "best friend" relationships most people have, the total would likely be considerably lower.

The strongest power correlations for people who have strong history power are character, attraction, and reputation. When we feel close to someone, we typically also believe the individual to be of sound character, to be highly likeable or attractive, and to have an excellent reputation. I'll elaborate upon the reasons in the next chapter, but the likely cause is the "halo effect" that occurs with the people we like best and know well: We tend to ignore or excuse their faults and elevate their good points. Part of this response is self-serving (although unconsciously so) because if we associate with good, honest, likeable people, then we must also be good, honest, and likeable. In short, we choose our friends according to how we construct our own self-image.

Interestingly, the strongest power correlations for people with low history power are role, resources, and information (all organizational power sources). So when we don't know people well, we tend to believe that they are powerful largely because they play a key role in the organization, control essential resources, and/or have excellent access to and control of information. However, we don't see them as having notable *personal* sources of power. Moreover, they are generally perceived to be more assertive, persistent, and direct, even blunt about getting what they want. And they are perceived to be far more willing to ask people for favors than to do favors for others. They are takers, not givers.

Conversely, people who are highly rated in history power are also highly rated at a range of interpersonal skills: building rapport and trust, supporting and encouraging others, listening, showing genuine interest in others and sensitivity to others' feelings and needs, and building close relationships. For every one of these skills, people with high history power received significantly higher scores than people low in history power. This is not unexpected, but it does indicate the extraordinary premium you receive when you build a close or even friendly relationship with another person.

GLOBAL DIFFERENCES IN HISTORY POWER

History power is a unique power source, based as it is on the relationship between two people. Clearly, individuals anywhere in the world can have stronger or weaker sources of power based on their histories with the people they seek to lead or influence, depending on the strength of their relationships. Nonetheless, my research shows which countries have, on average, higher or lower history power scores, with the findings probably reflecting the relative importance of personal relationships in those cultures. The gap between the countries rated highest (Pakistan, 6.00) and lowest (Austria, 5.52) was only 0.48 on a seven-point scale, which is a significant difference but much less so than the gaps between the highest- and lowest-rated countries for all other power sources. This indicates that history power is relevant in every culture, with only slight degrees of cultural difference. The following lists are arranged alphabetically.

COUNTRIES WHERE AGGREGATE HISTORY POWER IS HIGHER

Australia, Brazil, Canada, Chile, Colombia, India, Ireland, Israel, Malaysia, New Zealand, Pakistan, Peru, South Africa, Taiwan, United States of America

COUNTRIES WHERE AGGREGATE HISTORY POWER IS AVERAGE

Argentina, Belgium, China, Czech Republic, Denmark, Mexico, Norway, Portugal, Singapore, Spain, Sweden, Switzerland, Thailand, United Kingdom, Venezuela

COUNTRIES WHERE AGGREGATE HISTORY POWER IS LOWER

Austria, Finland, France, Germany, Greece, Hong Kong, Hungary, Indonesia, Italy, Japan, Netherlands, Poland, Russia, South Korea, Turkey

For more information on our global research on power and influence, and in-depth profiles of each of the forty-five countries studied, see www .kornferryinstitute.com, www.theelementsofpower.com, or www.terryr bacon.com.

KEY CONCEPTS

1. History power is shorthand for history with the person you are trying to lead or influence. This is the power derived from familiarity and

trust, and it is unique as a power source because it exists only between two people in a relationship—a leader and a follower or an influencer and an influencee.

2.   Research shows that we prefer to say yes to the requests of people we know and like. Our affinity for them, no matter how slight, makes us more inclined to go along with them and agree to their requests.

3.   Generally speaking, your capacity to lead or influence others increases with the length and strength of your relationship with them. However, enduring relationships are based on reciprocity. For you to influence someone else you know, you must also be willing to be influenced by him in return. Ethical influence is consensual and often bilateral.

4.   The propinquity effect indicates that people are most likely to develop relationships with other people they are physically closest to and interact with most frequently.

5.   As I will explain in the next chapter, we tend to like people who are similar to us. Furthermore, we tend to become more like each other over time. Consequently, we develop greater history power with people who are similar to us.

6.   History power can be virtual—that is, it can be built with a person we have seen (on television, for instance) but don't actually know in real life. Celebrity-based advertising succeeds because of the effects of virtual history power.

7.   Social networking sites like Facebook, MySpace, and LinkedIn can also create virtual history.

8.   History can become a power drain if you try to push the relationship toward greater closeness or intimacy too quickly, or if you make inappropriate or outrageous requests of the other person.

9.   History power does not require admiration of the other, but it does require acceptance, and history power can quickly become a power drain if followers learn something disturbing or repugnant about the leader.

CHALLENGES FOR READERS

1.   Think about your closest relationships—with family members, friends, or colleagues. Do you have strong history power with them,

and vice versa? Have you asked them for favors in the past? How readily did they comply? Have they asked you for favors? How readily did you comply? Why did you or they comply?

2. People sometimes say, "I would do anything for that person." Have you ever felt that way about someone in your life? What is the basis for your feelings? If you have felt this way, and understand that the feeling derives from your history with this person—in other words, with the length and strength of your relationship—then you understand history power.

3. Are you a member of any of the social networking sites, such as Facebook, MySpace, Twitter, LinkedIn, or Plaxo? Do you feel like you've gotten to know anyone on those sites even though you've never met in real life? If that person asked you for a favor, would you be more inclined to say yes because you have connected with the person online?

4. Have you ever had a family member, friend, colleague, customer, or business acquaintance do or say something that surprised or shocked you? If so, did you become more distant from that person? Did you become less inclined to cooperate with the person? Have you experienced any other situations in which a history power source became a power drain?

CHAPTER 4

YOU LIKE ME! YOU REALLY LIKE ME!

The Power of Attraction

IN 1985, SALLY FIELD WON BOTH A GOLDEN GLOBE AND AN ACADEMY AWARD for Best Actress for her portrayal of Depression-era Texas widow Edna Spalding in *Places in the Heart*. During her acceptance speech for the Academy Award (the second in her career), she said, "I haven't had an orthodox career, and I've wanted more than anything to have your respect. The first time I didn't feel it, but this time I feel it, and I can't deny the fact that you like me, right now, you like me!" She has often been misquoted as saying, "You like me! You really like me!" (I misquoted her again in the title of this chapter, but what she actually said was too long for a title. Sally, forgive me.) Undoubtedly, there is something profoundly pleasing about being liked. It is a wonderful affirmation of your worth as a human being—and it makes the people who like you more inclined to say yes to your ideas and requests. In other words, it increases your power to lead or influence people.

I refer to this as *attraction* power, where attraction is defined as your ability to attract others by causing them to like you. Attraction power differs from history power (see chapter 3), which is based on the power derived from an existing relationship between two people. Attraction power can exist even with people you don't know or have just met. Attraction power is why, even before you develop a history with someone, you may instantly like them, admire them, or find them attractive in some way. My grandfather often told the story of meeting my grandmother for the first time. He said the moment he laid eyes on her he knew he was going to marry her. That's how instantly attracted he was to her. Most of us probably haven't had that intense a reaction when first meeting someone, but at one time or another we have probably all been introduced to someone and immediately liked the person. Some people have that effect on us—and the attraction we feel for them increases their capacity to influence us.

In their essay on the bases of social power, John French Jr. and Bertram Raven referred to the personal liking of one person for another as *referent power*, which they believed derived from one person identifying with or wanting to be like the other.[1] They noted that referent power does not require a direct relationship between the two people. We can be attracted to a person we've only read about in a book or seen in a photo. Attraction is a power source in and of itself, but it can also amplify all the other power sources. For instance, if I have a good working relationship with a colleague, Gretchen, she and I will have some history power with each other. If I also find Gretchen very attractive in some way (not necessarily based on her appearance, but perhaps her sense of humor, wit, knowledge, or warmth), she will also have attraction power with me, and I am likely to value our relationship even more. Because of her high attraction power with me, I will seek opportunities to work with her, will want to continue our relationship, and will therefore be more susceptible to her influence attempts.

Attraction power is the ability to attract others by causing them to like you. This is a power source in and of itself, but it can also amplify the effect of all the other power sources.

It is natural to assume that attraction is based on physical appearance, and to some extent this is true. But attraction power is based on much more, as we will see. It can be based on genuineness or authenticity. Many people are attracted to others who are manifestly themselves, who don't wear masks, who are unafraid to be themselves and reveal who they really are.

Attraction may also be based on commonality of values, attitudes, or beliefs. Or it can be based on someone having a sincere interest in others and being friendly and open. We could define attraction as the ability to make friends, but it is more than that, too. It is also the ability to cause others to be drawn to you—for whatever reason.

Of course, what people around the world find attractive in others varies considerably—not only from culture to culture but from person to person. Views on attractiveness have also varied through time and depend on context. As I said, attraction power is not just about appearance (although that contributes to it), and it's not just about personality (although that also contributes to it). It is also about similarities and liking between people. And when we like someone, we are more apt to say yes to them. Attraction typically increases with familiarity, which is why we may not instantly like certain people upon first meeting them but become more attracted to them as we get to know them better. Some of the qualities we like about them may take time to reveal themselves, but familiarity itself can increase our liking of people. And, to be perfectly honest, so too can beauty.

BEAUTY IN THE FLESH

Florenz Ziegfeld was a Broadway producer in the late-nineteenth and early-twentieth centuries. Creator of the Ziegfeld Follies, he was known as the glorifier of the American girl. It should not be surprising, then, that he once said, "Beauty in the flesh will continue to rule the world." Was Ziegfeld right? Does beauty in the flesh rule the world? Or, as I would rephrase it for this book, is physical appearance the primary source of attraction power? The answer is no, but it is a strong component of attraction power for many people. The sad reality (for those of us who weren't born looking like Robert Redford in his prime) is that beautiful people have numerous advantages in life simply because their appearance gives them greater inherent attraction power than less attractive people. Here is a summary of some of the major research on physical attractiveness:[2]

1. The bias toward attractive people begins in childhood. Schoolboys whom adults considered to be unattractive were less well liked than their more attractive classmates. Furthermore, their classmates were more likely to label the unattractive boys as antisocial and aggressive.

2. Adult women, asked to view photos of attractive and unattractive children and make judgments about them, felt that the unattractive children were more likely to be dishonest.

3. Teachers, asked to view photos of attractive and unattractive children, voted that the attractive children were more likely to be well adjusted with their classmates and have parents who were interested in their education. Moreover, teachers believed that the attractive children were more intelligent and more likely to go to college.

4. Among college students, the most important determinant of popularity is physical appearance. In studies of blind dates, the more attractive the woman, the more her date liked her and the more likely she was to be asked on another date. Intelligence and personality, on the other hand, appeared to have no effect on whether the woman was better liked or asked out again.

5. Asked to rate people on a number of characteristics, respondents felt that the people who were more attractive were more sensitive, kind, interesting, strong, poised, modest, sociable, outgoing, and exciting than those who were less attractive. As these findings indicate, attractive people are considered to have more socially desirable traits, and they are expected to be more successful in life. In a number of studies, physical attractiveness has been found to correlate positively with higher social skills, career success, and income. One study, for instance, found that attractive people, on average, earn 12 percent more than their unattractive counterparts.

It is natural to assume that men are more preoccupied with physical appearance than women, and that's largely true, but studies have also shown an attractiveness bias on the part of women, too. In one study, women who were about to interact with an attractive man were more likely to shift their opinions to match his, but this was not the case when they anticipated meeting with an unattractive man.[3] The women modified their self-presentation in an apparent attempt to make themselves more socially desirable to the attractive men they were about to meet. This finding is hardly surprising, but it does confirm the effect of physical attraction.

These research findings reflect a common cognitive bias in all cultures: the belief that what is beautiful is good, and that attractive people have other socially desirable characteristics, such as being more honest, sociable, kind, and intelligent. This "halo effect" means that we have a higher, mostly unconscious appraisal of beautiful people that goes well beyond their physical appearance. Consequently, we tend to give beautiful people advantages that others have to work harder for. Compounding these cognitive biases are the multibillion-dollar global fashion, cosmetics, entertainment, and media industries, which bombard us with images of the rich and beautiful and reinforce the desirability of physical attractiveness. Finally, research also shows that attractive people are more self-confident, and self-confidence is another factor in liking.

The reality is that most people feel better and are more confident when they look better, and most of us would like to look as successful, happy, and desirable as the gorgeous or handsome models shown in fashion and cosmetic ads. Looking good opens doors (the media keeps telling us that). It has many advantages (we can see that for ourselves). And whether or not we would admit it, we unconsciously assume that beautiful people are better than everyone else. The net effect is that physical attraction is a strong component of attraction power, and beautiful people therefore have a great deal of attraction power that allows them to influence others, which is why advertising agencies hire beautiful people to appear in their ads. It's why the spokespeople companies choose to appear in their booths at industry conventions (such as car shows) are usually attractive and either well dressed or provocatively dressed. It's why television networks hire attractive people as news reporters and anchors. Despite the stereotype about gorgeous airheads, research shows that attractiveness is more persuasive than the alternative.

Having made my point about beauty, I want to end with a quotation from someone most people would not consider physically attractive, but who had one of the most beautiful souls in the world and was profoundly influential in other ways (and whom I profile in chapter 5). Eleanor Roosevelt said, "Beautiful young people are accidents of nature, but beautiful old people are works of art."

▶ PROFILES *in* POWER

BRAD PITT AND ANGELINA JOLIE

They are two of the most famous beautiful people in the world and hardly need an introduction. Brad Pitt was born in Shawnee, Oklahoma, and attended Kickapoo High School and the University of Missouri before heading to Los Angeles to study acting. In 1987, he began doing guest roles on television and made his first feature film in 1988 (*The Dark Side of the Sun*). Since then, he's been nominated for numerous acting awards, including two Oscars, and won a Golden Globe Award for his performance in *Twelve Monkeys*. He was twice named the Sexiest Man Alive by *People* magazine

Photo by Robyn Beck/AFP/Getty Images.

and has appeared on *Forbes* magazine's Celebrity 100 list and *Time* magazine's list of the 100 most influential people in the world.

Angelina Jolie was born in Los Angeles and was destined to be in the film industry. She studied acting at the Lee Strasberg Theatre and Film Institute and at age 14 began modeling and appearing in music videos. An early role that gained her a lot of attention was 1995's *Hackers,* which has become a cult favorite. Nominated for many acting awards, she won the Academy Award for Best Supporting Actress for *Girl, Interrupted*; two Screen Actors Guild Awards for *Gia* and *Girl, Interrupted*; and three Golden Globe Awards. In 2006, *People* magazine named her the most beautiful woman in the world, and Britain's Channel 4 named her the greatest sex symbol of all time. Like Pitt, she has appeared on the *Forbes* Celebrity 100 list and ranks among *Time*'s 100 most influential people in the world.

Brad Pitt and Angelina Jolie are wealthy supercelebrities, among the most recognized people in the world. Unfortunately, the glare of celebrity often obscures their talent as actors. Their primary power sources are reputation, network, knowledge (acting skill), history (within their domain, they know numerous people), and exceptionally high attraction. In fact, it would be difficult to find two more beautiful people who also possess a great deal of likeability. But another great source of power for both of them is character. Jolie was named a Goodwill Ambassador for the United Nations High Commissioner for Refugees (UNHCR) and has made numerous trips to refugee camps around the world. She has been a vigorous and visible supporter of human rights causes globally. For his part, Pitt has been active in the fight against AIDS, poverty, and genocide, most notably in Darfur. Following Hurricane Katrina, he founded the Make It Right Foundation to build new homes in the decimated Lower Ninth Ward of New Orleans. Together, Pitt and Jolie have contributed millions of dollars to humanitarian causes around the world.

Both suffer from the curse of celebrity and are subjected to merciless speculation in the tabloids about their private lives. Nonetheless, together and separately, they are among the most influential people in the world, and they have achieved that distinction due in no small part to the extraordinary power their attractiveness has given them, amplified by genuine caring for others less fortunate than they are. Critics might argue that their attraction power stems largely from people's fantasies about them, rather than who they actually are. But it hardly matters. They remain examples of attraction power at the far end of the bell curve.

What We Can Learn from Brad Pitt and Angelina Jolie

1. *There's a high premium for attractiveness.* Pitt and Jolie are at the far end of the attractiveness spectrum, and they have both used their looks to great advantage in their careers, arguably without the narcissism and arrogance that infects some nice-looking people. The lesson for business leaders? If you have it, use it. But beware of flaunting your looks or assuming that attractiveness makes you better than everyone

else in every other regard. In my years of coaching, I have met some attractive businesspeople who dressed inappropriately for a professional setting in order to display their assets, and it made them more appalling than appealing. Those who let their attractiveness go to their heads usually fall into the category of competent jerks. Unassuming beauty in someone who is also highly competent is most appealing.

2. *Likeability and attractiveness are a powerful combination.* Pitt and Jolie are not only attractive, they are highly likeable, which opens a lot of doors for them, particularly when they want to build support for one of their causes. The lesson for the rest of us? High likeability in the workplace makes you a more desirable work partner. Whether or not you are physically attractive, it is important to build attraction power. Attractiveness might be based on your personality, social skills, competence, and work ethic. Being an attractive person to work with—or work for—will open a lot of doors for you.

3. *Character plays an important role in attraction.* Part of what makes Pitt and Jolie attractive is their commitment to helping people less fortunate than they are. The lesson? The content of your character is as important as how you look, how you dress, and how much people like you. In fact, attraction without character is more likely to be a power drain than a power source.

THE EYE OF THE BEHOLDER

In 2008, the winner of the world's ugliest dog contest was Gus, a hairless, one-eyed, three-legged Chinese crested mutt whom his owner loved, despite his world-class ugliness. Fortunately for Gus, beauty is in the eye of the beholder. Physical attraction may be a strong component of attraction power, but what people like about others is not one-dimensional. In fact, the whole spectacular panorama of humanity allows us to find others attractive for reasons we might not even comprehend. Remember that attraction power comes from people's ability to cause us to like them. You may find a singer attractive because of his songs; a writer attractive because of how she tells a story; a teacher attractive because he taught you something meaningful; a colleague attractive because she's enjoyable to work with; and a friend attractive because he's insightful, loyal, colorful, mystical, or just plain goofy.

I may like someone because of his knowledge or skill. I like a particular colleague because he's a whiz at Sudoku, and when I'm stuck he helps me out. I like another colleague because she's a walking encyclopedia on our

> The whole spectacular panorama of humanity allows us to find others attractive for reasons we might not even comprehend.

company's products, and I always learn more when I work with her. I like a neighbor because she's a theater buff, and it's enjoyable to talk to her about plays. Or I may like someone because of his personality or behavior. I like a particular customer because he always returns my calls. I like my boss because she has a great sense of humor. I like a person I used to work with because he was a good listener and problem solver—and he was a great guy to brainstorm with whenever we shut ourselves in a room with a whiteboard and a pot of coffee.

I may like someone because we shared an experience. We pulled an all-nighter working on a proposal, and he did a good job. He carried his weight and contributed much to the finished product. I respect him for that and would work with him again. I like the boss I used to have because during a long business trip to Japan he gave me some useful career coaching. I like the people on my work team because we had a grueling four-month-long project with a demanding client, and everybody pulled together. Tempers flared now and then, but we learned how to work through the conflicts and finished with an outstanding solution. Of course, liking may depend on a successful process and outcome. If my work team experience had gone badly, minor irritations could have flared into lasting dislikes.

What we find attractive in other people depends partly on who we are and who they are, and partly on the context in which we interact with them. Nonetheless, there are patterns to what people find attractive in others. In September 2009, I conducted an informal Internet survey that asked about 1,000 people what attracted them to another person. The top ten responses were:

1. A sense of humor

2. Intelligence

3. A great smile

4. Physical attractiveness

5.   Personality; charm

6.   Kindness; caring; a good heart

7.   Honesty

8.   Thoughtfulness, politeness; respectfulness

9.   Wit; a good conversationalist

10. Passion; affection; warmth

Other responses included self-confidence, authenticity, compassion, loyalty, sweetness, neatness, athleticism, creativity, friendliness, generosity, humility, sensitivity, strength, and ambition. These characteristics focus more on personal than work relationships, but a purely work-focused list would likely be similar.

TROPHY WIVES AND BOY TOYS

Vickie Lynn Hogan's life was like one of those aerial fireworks that rocket into the night sky on New Year's Eve or Independence Day—glimmering and booming, showering the darkness with radiant color in glowing streamers that spiral and smoke and fade too soon but leave the residual image of spectacle in our eyes long after the fireworks have gone. Vickie was born in Harris County, Texas, in 1967, an only child, and was shuffled between caretakers. She left high school during her sophomore year and worked in a fried chicken joint. When she was seventeen, she married a sixteen-year-old fry cook and had a child. Divorced shortly thereafter, she worked at Wal-Mart and then Red Lobster before becoming an exotic dancer. Then she discovered *Playboy* magazine, and they discovered her. She first appeared in *Playboy* in 1992 and became a popular model, often christened the new Marilyn Monroe, and in 1993 she was named Playboy Playmate of the Year under the name Anna Nicole Smith.

I won't recount the whole sad saga of her life, which ended when she was found dead in a hotel room in Hollywood, Florida, of what the coroner called "combined drug intoxication." What is of most interest here is her marriage to oil billionaire J. Howard Marshall in 1994, when she was twenty-six and he was eighty-nine. It's not difficult to imagine what attracted him to her, but it is intriguing to imagine what attracted her to him. She claimed she didn't marry him for his money, and I'll let you decide whether you believe that. Regardless, Anna Nicole Smith may have been one of the best examples of a trophy wife, but there are many others. The phenomenon of rich men marrying beautiful women young enough to be their daughters (or, in Anna's case, conceivably even a great-granddaughter) raises the question about what the attraction might be.

The cynic's view is that wealthy older men want to display those beautiful young wives as evidence of their material success—like cavemen wearing the biggest bear claw around their neck as if to proclaim, "My club is bigger than your club." And the young woman marries the older—and often not physically attractive—male because she doesn't want to wait for the good life. She wants it while she's still young enough to enjoy it, and she likes being admired by her husband's friends and congratulated by her girlfriends. Although I'm focusing here on trophy wives, the syndrome would also apply to boy toys of older, wealthy women.

But the source of the attraction may be more complicated than cynics contend. Psychologist Virginia Lashbrooke believes there may be an evolutionary basis for this source of attraction.[4] These young women, she says, are attracted to the best hunter, the male who will be the best breeder and provider for her children. So they are attracted to strong men, not just men with money, but men who are strong in other ways (e.g., star athletes, renowned artists, powerful politicians, and powerful businessmen). The price these women often pay, says Lashbrooke, is that they must give away power to the man because his part of the bargain is to be the dominant and controlling person in the relationship. So the women have little real authority. The men feed off their dominance of the women and feel more powerful because they have their trophies to show off to the world.

Sometimes, people are attracted to someone because that other person feeds some deficiency within themselves. Typically, according to Lashbrooke, that deficiency is rooted in their upbringing. A man who grew up being highly rational may not have evolved his emotional and intuitive side. So he may be attracted to an overly intuitive and emotive woman who has in abundance what he lacks—and this is how opposites may attract. In essence, she becomes his emotional side. When he needs to express an emotion, he provokes her and she expresses it for him, which eases the internal tension he can't release himself. This might be called compensatory attraction, and it's not healthy for him, her, or the relationship.

Cult leaders like Jim Jones of the Peoples Temple understand this dynamic very well. Jones was the megalomaniac who led his followers to a compound in Guyana known as Jonestown, where more than 900 of them died on November 18, 1978, by drinking cyanide-laced Flavor Aid. Jones preached an odd fusion of self-reliance, socialism, and religion and spoke out against racism, capitalism, and traditional religious practices, which attracted many followers in the socially disruptive America of the 1970s. But he was also accused of having sex with various Temple members, and he became increasingly paranoid as authorities began to question his group's nonprofit status. Moving en masse to Guyana was an attempt to escape scrutiny from authorities, and the inevitable confrontation occurred when a delegation led by Congressman Leo Ryan flew to Guyana to investigate reports of human rights abuses. Temple gunmen killed Ryan and four others before the Jonestown group committed mass suicide.

Why did people join the Peoples Temple? What was it that attracted them to Jim Jones? Only his followers could answer that, and no doubt their reasons varied, but it seems clear that he represented something they desperately needed—perhaps escape from the unjust society some felt they were living in. Or perhaps he represented the authority figure they lacked in their lives, or the radical path they would not have had the courage to take themselves. Some people need a leader who will make their decisions for them (and Jones was willing to do that), even if it means drinking the poison and forcing 276 children to drink it, too.

It is important to recognize that when you like someone, when you are attracted to him—for whatever reason—you enhance his ability to lead or influence you. The more attracted you are to him, the more influencing power he has with you. And that's okay, but it's wise to be aware of what you are getting in exchange for the power you are giving up. It would have been healthier for members of the Peoples Temple to examine why they were attracted to Jim Jones and to have said, when he was passing out the Flavor Aid, "Wait a minute. What is he asking us to do?" (In fairness to those who did question his actions, Jones had stationed armed men around the group to ensure that everyone drank from the poisoned well. But I contend that they should have questioned his authority sooner.)

When you like someone, when you are attracted to him, you enhance his ability to influence you. The more attracted you are to him, the more influencing power he has with you.

THE LAW OF SIMILARITY

Another basis for attraction is similarity. The law of similarity says that we are attracted to people who are similar to us in some way. When Aristotle was lecturing to his students—perhaps at Plato's Academy or at the Lyceum, his own school in Athens—he observed:

> Since everything like and akin to oneself is pleasant, and since every man is himself more like and akin to himself than anyone else is, it follows that all of us must be more or less fond of ourselves. For all this resemblance and kinship is present particularly in the relation of an individual to himself. And because we are all fond of ourselves, it follows that what is our own is pleasant to all of us, as for instance our own deeds and words. That is why we are usually fond of our flatterers, [our lovers,] and honor; also of our children, for our children are our own work.[5]

This is a law of similarity. Robert Cialdini also said it well: "We like people who are similar to us. This fact seems to hold true whether the similarity is in the area of opinions, personality traits, background, or lifestyle. Consequently, those who wish to be liked in order to increase our compliance can accomplish that purpose by appearing similar to us in any of a wide variety of ways."[6]

As the old saying goes, "Birds of a feather flock together." We like people who are similar to us and tend to associate more with them because they provide social validation for our values, beliefs, and attitudes. Moreover, we tend to like the people who seem to like us and dislike the people who seem to dislike us (this is called the reciprocity effect). In 1984, researchers at the University of Maine found, for instance, that men had greater liking for women who gave them nonverbal liking cues—even when those women disagreed with the men on important issues. Moreover, the men rated these women as more similar to themselves, despite their substantive disagreements, than they did to a control group of women who did not give nonverbal liking cues.[7] Thus, the notion that opposites attract has not been shown conclusively in psychological research and may be more a myth than a reality (the marriage of James Carville and Mary Matalin notwithstanding).[8]

Research on social bonding also shows that people who associate with each other tend to become more similar to each other over time. We tend to talk like them, think like them, and perhaps even dress like them. For example, in the 1960s, hippies adopted similar dress and grooming styles, despite their professed nonconformance, and today's Goths think and act alike, dressing in black, applying black cosmetics, and listening to the same music. Not that I'm picking on these groups. Every group in every culture tends toward similarity as members seek to conform to the group's social norms, which validates both their belonging and their own identity. One of the consequences of the law of similarity is that it builds attraction power among the people who feel similar to others. So, if I feel a connection with another person, I am more likely to agree with him. If I perceive that a woman likes me, I am more inclined to say yes to her requests. And, as Robert Cialdini observed, people who want something from me can use this power to influence me, which is why salespeople are taught to call potential customers by their first name, to find some similarities with the customer, to make it personal.

Liberals tend to be more attracted to fellow liberals than to conservatives (and vice versa). People with strong religious convictions tend to be more attracted to others who share their convictions. And people who belong to particular clubs or associations tend to like other members of those groups (the exception is Groucho Marx, who once said he would not want to belong to any club that would have him as a member). We prefer to associate with and have greater liking for others who share our interests, values, attitudes, and beliefs because they reinforce the wisdom of our choices and validate our self-worth. Conversely, we assume that people who disagree with us have negative personality traits.

ATTRACTION POWER IN THE WORKPLACE

Attraction power obviously matters if your employability depends on your appearance—if you are a model, an actor, or a spokesperson for a product, for instance. But does attraction make a difference in the vast majority of jobs and organizations where beauty and likeability are not requirements for success? Does it help a petroleum engineer working for Exxon if she is attractive? Or a manager for Cisco Systems if he is handsome? Or lawyers, physicians, salespeople, and clerks if they are nice looking? The answer is an unqualified yes. In a study published in 1994, professors Daniel Hamermesh and Jeff Biddle revealed that, on average, plain-looking people earn less than average-looking people, who in turn earn less than good-looking people.[9] Surprisingly, the earnings gap was somewhat greater for men than it was for women, and the type of organization or industry did not matter. Attractive people in the workplace do receive a "beauty premium."

A later study by Harvard's Markus Mobius and Wesleyan University's Tanya Rosenblat concluded from a controlled laboratory experiment that there are three reasons beauty matters in the workplace:

1. Physically attractive workers are more confident, and employers recognize and reward higher levels of confidence.

2. Employers of attractive workers wrongly assume that they are more competent (the halo effect I spoke of earlier).

3. Physically attractive workers have greater communication and social skills that enable them to perform better in organizations.[10]

It appears that physical attractiveness is a self-fulfilling prophecy. Attractive people receive preferential treatment as children and are more desirable as playmates, so they have more opportunity to learn and practice their social skills, which increases their attractiveness and self-confidence, which makes them appear to be more competent, which increases their appeal to employers, and so on.

However, attraction power in the workplace is not based solely on appearance. In 2005, professors Tiziana Casciaro and Miguel Sousa Lobo published a study on likeability at work. They noted that "in most cases, people choose their work partners according to two criteria. One is competence at the job (Does Joe know what he's doing?). The other is likeability (Is Joe enjoyable to work with?)."[11] They divided workers into four categories: lovable stars (high in likeability and competence), incompetent jerks (low in both), competent jerks (low likeability/high competence), and lovable fools (high likeability/low competence). As we would expect, everyone wants to work with the lovable stars, and no one wants to work with the incompetent jerks. However, when they have to choose between working with a competent jerk or a lovable fool, people usually choose likeability over competence. "Generally speaking," the authors conclude, "a little extra likeability goes a longer way than a little extra competence in making someone desirable to work with."[12] As these studies show, attraction power is as important in the workplace as it is in the rest of life. People who have natural good looks and/or a warm personality have an inherent advantage at work, but even if you don't have these advantages, you can build attraction power considerably (see chapter 12 for suggestions).

ATTRACTION AS A POWER DRAIN

By definition, what is attractive to us is a source of power and can't be a power drain, unless you are one of those rare people who are attracted and repelled by the same thing simultaneously. However, more often than not, we will dislike some things even about the people we are most attracted to. Likewise, the people most attracted to us will dislike some things about us. We will continue to have attraction power with them as long as the positives (or attractors) outweigh the negatives, although the balance between the two may shift over time. If I were to catalog all the people I've known in my life and indicate on a chart those who were most attracted to me, on one side of the scale, and those who were least attracted to me, on the other, I would probably see a broad spectrum and discover that most people fall somewhere in the middle, as in a normal bell curve. Hopefully, more people would be listed on the positive side, which means I would have some attraction power with many of the people I've known.

Occasionally, someone's attraction power can be diminished substantially when he does something so contrary to our expectations and values that what had been attractive about the person is replaced in our mind's eye with what is repulsive. For many people in my generation, such a person was Jane Fonda. A beautiful and talented young actress, she was the daughter of a movie icon, and many young men found her attractive—for her looks, her abilities, her charm, and her views against the Vietnam War (which an increasing number of people shared). Then, in 1972, she visited North Vietnam, made propaganda broadcasts on Radio Hanoi, and allowed herself to be photographed looking through the sights of an anti-aircraft gun emplacement. For most Americans, even those who opposed the war, her behavior was treasonous, and decades later many Vietnam veterans have still not forgotten what she did nor forgiven her for it.

► PROFILES *in* POWER

ANN COULTER

By most measures, Ann Hart Coulter is an accomplished person. Born in New York City, she graduated cum laude from Cornell University and received a law degree from the University of Michigan Law School, where she was an editor of the *Michigan Law Review.* She clerked for the U.S.

Court of Appeals, worked for the U.S. Senate Judiciary Committee, and was a litigator for the Center for Individual Rights. But her fame (or notoriety) comes mainly from her writings and her television and radio appearances as a far-right political commentator. She is a controversial syndicated columnist and the author of seven best-selling books critical of liberals.

Ann Coulter is intelligent, articulate, and accomplished, which, by itself, would create a considerable amount of attraction power, but most people would also consider her physically attractive. Tall and slender, she has the look of a classic blue-eyed blonde beauty. She knows how to carry herself, has an inviting smile, and can be flirtatious when she wants to be. Moreover, she knows she is attractive and uses it to her advantage. On many book covers she is shown wearing a basic black dress, cut low to reveal a hint of cleavage, her blonde mane spread on her shoulders, her penetrating gaze staring at potential book buyers as if to say, "I'm opinionated and gorgeous. Buy me."

For many people, however, the attraction ends there. Her opinions are so radically right-wing and so filled with invective that she offends many people, including some religious conservatives. After 9/11, she wrote that America should invade Islamic countries, kill their leaders, and convert the people to Christianity. She wrote in 2005 that the U.S. government should spy on Arabs in the United States, televise torture as a spectator sport, drop carpet bombs throughout the Middle East, and send liberals to the Guantanamo Bay prison. She called a group of 9/11 widows "witches," mocked a disabled Vietnam veteran on television (which got her fired from MSNBC), referred to Jews as "imperfect Christians," argued that women should not be allowed to vote, and said she regretted that Timothy McVeigh hadn't targeted the *New York Times* building.

Her rhetoric is often incendiary, extreme, insensitive, and belligerently divisive, and the words people have used to describe her include mean, cruel, shameless, arrogant, intolerant, inflammatory, nasty, disgusting, and mistress of malice. On the Internet, she has been labeled "a self-loathing transsexual plagiarist" and a "fascist Barbie doll." No doubt, Coulter doesn't care what she's called. Her inflammatory words spark a reaction, and she gets the attention she appears to crave. She plays to a conservative

Photo by Rob Hill/FilmMagic.

constituency that numbers in the tens of millions, including many prospective book buyers. Is she aware of the ire she provokes? Susan Estrich says of Coulter, "She knows exactly what she is doing. And she is scary as hell because of it."[13]

People who agree with Coulter's views are drawn to her because she's an attractive attack dog for radical conservatives. But those who find her hateful and soulless are repelled by her views, and for them her attraction is not a power source; it's a power drain. Her deliberate polarization of people is a weapon for advancing her views—and making money in the process—but she would likely be more effective in promoting political conservatism (if, indeed, that's her aim) if she were less hateful, less inflammatory, and less divisive. As it is, she comes across as a pretty face with an empty heart, and that drains her of the power to truly be a force for change.

What We Can Learn from Ann Coulter

1. *There are pros and cons of being outspoken.* Ann Coulter has built fame and fortune by being provocative and polarizing. If achieving her kind of notoriety is your goal, then she's a good roadmap. For most business leaders, however, she is a lesson on the dangers of being outspoken. I've met people in the workplace who believed that "shooting from the hip" and being unapologetically candid was a virtue. They often say things like, "I am who I am," or "What you see is what you get." Honesty is unquestionably a virtue, but so are tact and diplomacy. In business, being provocative is more likely to be a power drain than a power source, particularly if you are perceived to be reckless and irresponsible. It's best to avoid extreme positions or pronouncements and avoid antagonizing your peers, employees, and customers. Of course, Ann Coulter's goal is to provoke, and she is a public figure, so we hold her to a lesser standard than we would the average business leader.

2. *Wearing a smart, tailored suit will make you more attractive, but not if the suit is dirty.* You will lose what attraction power you have if your personality and leadership style are arrogant, condescending, dismissive, self-serving, or petty. Your appearance, demeanor, manners, and personality represent the total package, which is what your employees, direct reports, peers, superiors, and customers have to deal with. If some part of that total package is flawed in their eyes, you can lose attraction power.

ATTRACTION POWER AND CULTURAL NORMS

Dictionary.com defines *ugly American* as "a pejorative term for Americans traveling or living abroad who remain ignorant of local culture and judge everything by American standards." Although this stereotype has typically been applied to Americans, it could be applied to anyone who travels to or works in another culture and does not try to understand and adapt to the social norms of that country. If you are working in another culture, you will be more attractive to the people there if you behave according to the social norms of their culture and you'll be less attractive (ugly) if you don't. In other words, you gain or lose attraction power in other cultures according to your willingness and your skill in adapting your behavior to reflect an awareness of and respect for local customs and protocols.

Australia, for example, is an informal, egalitarian culture. Mutual respect and equality are important. It's bad form for someone to stand out, so you could be perceived as arrogant if you make too much fuss about your academic credentials or achievements. A boastful foreigner in Australia will lose attraction power quickly. At the same time, Australians appreciate humor, and good-natured teasing is something of an art form there, especially among mates. But there are cultural protocols about how it's done. Teasing a bloke when he is present is okay, but joking about him in his absence is not. When Australians have accepted you, they'll insult you in a good-natured way, and you are expected to take it in stride and dish it back. They call it "taking the piss." If you can do that, you'll build attraction power, but if you are easily offended and can't dish it back, you'll lose attraction power.

In Australia, as in every other part of the world, your ability to adapt to the country's cultural norms is a matter of character (judgment, humility, authenticity), social skill (openness, friendliness, warmth), and respect. The more you can demonstrate awareness of and respect for the social conventions and protocols of the culture, the more attraction power you stand to gain.

ATTRACTION POWER MAGNIFIED

What do Mary Kay Ash, Charles Manson, Albert Schweitzer, Adolf Hitler, and George Washington have in common? To their followers, each of these leaders possessed an extraordinary amount of attraction power. They drew some people to them as though they were human magnets. In short, they had charisma. Max Weber (1864–1920), one of the founders of sociology, was among the first to define charisma: "The term charisma," he wrote, "will be applied to a certain quality of an individual personality by virtue of which he is set apart from ordinary men and treated as endowed with supernatural, superhuman, or at least specifically exceptional powers or qualities."[14] Weber believed that charisma was of divine origin and not available to ordinary people. The contemporary view of charisma is that ordinary people can learn to be more charismatic, although the *most* charismatic leaders seem to have been born with innate qualities that make them extraordinarily attractive to other people.

Charismatic people are usually described as being positive, charming, self-confident, energetic, eloquent, and assertive. Other words to describe them include graceful, poised, likeable, enthusiastic, sincere, and authentic. In business, they are likely to be knowledgeable and credible, focused, determined, visionary, and inclusive. Sometimes, they have physical characteristics that enhance their charisma. They are often taller than average, have resonant or penetrating voices, and present themselves well. Their dress and bearing command respect and attention. Despite these laudable traits, truly charismatic leaders are not full of themselves. What makes them charismatic is that they don't convey themselves as though they are above everyone else (as an arrogant person would). Instead, they appear to be accessible while exemplifying an ideal that everyone else identifies with and aspires to. Because of their great attraction power, they can be extraordinary role models.

Although most people admire charismatic leaders, there is some skepticism about them, too. After all, Adolf Hitler was a charismatic leader. So were Jim Jones, David Koresh, and Charles Manson—at least to their cult followers. Charismatic leaders have an abundance of attraction power, and they can use it for good or evil. My purpose here is not to promote or defend charismatic leaders, but rather to highlight that their extraordinary attraction power can make them extraordinarily influential. It is important for people drawn to charismatic individuals to remain aware of whether such charismatic leaders are asking them to go in a positive and healthy direction or asking them to drink the Flavor Aid.

WHAT THE RESEARCH TELLS US ABOUT ATTRACTION POWER

In this chapter, I cited a number of studies that show that being attractive (physically and otherwise), being likeable, and especially being charismatic are huge sources of influencing power, and my research confirms those findings. Being likeable—having high attraction power—more than triples your capacity to lead and influence others. Being attractive—being able to cause others to like you—can give you extraordinary leverage in your interactions with others.

The halo effect was evident in my research. The most highly correlated power source with attraction is character power, so people who are perceived to be highly attractive or likeable are also perceived to have significantly higher character, to be more honest and more trustworthy, for instance. Furthermore, there is a strong correlation between attraction and history power. People tend to believe that the other people they have the longest and strongest relationships with are highly likeable and attractive. The strongest correlations between attraction power and skill demonstrate a similar bias. Those with high attraction ratings are also perceived to be significantly more effective at speaking conversationally, building rapport and trust, supporting and encouraging others, showing genuine interest in others, being friendly and sociable with strangers, building close relationships, listening, being sensitive to others' feelings and needs, building consensus, and having insight into what others value. On *every* interpersonal skill we measured, people with high attraction power were rated significantly higher than those with moderate or low attraction power. This finding may not be surprising, but it illustrates the extraordinary effect emotional intelligence and interpersonal skills have on someone's capacity to lead and influence others.

In contrast, people rated low on attraction power were perceived to derive their leadership and influencing power from role and resource power—from their position in their organization and the important resources they command and control. In short, they have to rely on formal authority and organizational structure to get their way. Moreover, they were seen as significantly more threatening, intimidating, manipulative, and passive-aggressive. One final interesting finding was the correlation between attraction power and listening. People who were considered poor listeners were also rated low on attraction power. They were perceived to have low character and a negative reputation, and to be insensitive to others, ineffective at building consensus, more manipulative in their approach to other people, and significantly less influential than good listeners. Part of what makes someone attractive to others is that she listens well. You pay a steep penalty for poor listening.

GLOBAL DIFFERENCES IN ATTRACTION POWER

Although attraction power is a personal power source, and particular individuals within every culture may have high or low attraction power with other people, our research shows that attraction is a more important power source in some cultures than in others. The following lists show, for instance, that attraction is an especially important power source in South America. It is less important in central and eastern Europe and in many Asian countries. The lists are arranged alphabetically.

COUNTRIES WHERE ATTRACTION POWER IS HIGHER

Argentina, Australia, Brazil, Canada, Colombia, Ireland, Italy, Mexico, New Zealand, Pakistan, Peru, Taiwan, Thailand, United States of America, Venezuela

COUNTRIES WHERE ATTRACTION POWER IS AVERAGE

Belgium, Chile, China, Denmark, France, India, Israel, Malaysia, Netherlands, Norway, Portugal, South Africa, Spain, Sweden, United Kingdom

COUNTRIES WHERE ATTRACTION POWER IS LOWER

Austria, Czech Republic, Finland, Germany, Greece, Hong Kong, Hungary, Indonesia, Japan, Poland, Russia, Singapore, South Korea, Switzerland, Turkey

Countries where attraction power rates highest are typically highly social countries—where socializing among business associates before meetings is the norm, where the culture values and celebrates beauty, where how you look and how you present yourself are important elements in others' acceptance of you. For more information on our global research on power and influence, and in-depth profiles of each of the forty-five countries studied, see www.kornferryinstitute.com, www.theelementsof power.com, or www.terryrbacon.com.

KEY CONCEPTS

1. Attraction power is the ability to attract others by causing them to like you. This is a power source in and of itself, but it can also amplify the effect of all the other power sources.

2. Physical attractiveness is one component of attraction power, but attraction can also be based on authenticity; commonality of values,

attitudes, or beliefs; personality; character; wisdom; shared experiences; and many other factors.

3. Sometimes, people are attracted to someone because that other person feeds some deficiency within themselves. This type of "compensatory attraction" may explain why people join cults or follow leaders like Jim Jones, David Koresh, or Charles Manson.

4. When you like or are attracted to someone, you enhance that person's ability to lead or influence you. The more attracted you are to them, the more power they have with you.

5. We like people who are similar to us and tend to associate more with them because they provide social validation for our values, beliefs, and attitudes.

6. Attraction is culture dependent. You gain or lose attraction power in other cultures depending on your ability to adapt your behavior to reflect an awareness of and respect for local customs and protocols.

7. Charisma is attraction power magnified. Charismatic leaders have an abundance of attraction power and can use it for good or evil.

CHALLENGES FOR READERS

1. How much attraction power do you have? Reflect on the characteristics that make you more or less attractive to others (remembering that attraction is not based on physical attraction alone).

2. What could you do to increase your attraction power? What would help make you more attractive to a greater number of people? Reflect on the "top ten" list of the attributes people said attracted them to others. Which of these attributes are strengths for you?

3. Think about the people who are attractive to you (again, not just physically, but in every way). What makes them attractive to you? Likewise, think about the people you find unattractive, for whatever reason. Brainstorm two lists: First, write down what you find attractive about people, and second, write down what you find unattractive about people. What do those lists tell you about what you value in others? And in yourself?

4. Think about how you use your attraction power with others. Do you find it easier to influence the people with whom you have a lot of attraction power? What makes it easier?

5. Now think about someone you know who doesn't find you attractive. Is it more difficult for you to influence that person?

6. Your ability to adapt to other cultures is crucial in developing attraction power in those cultures. If you have lived or worked in another culture, how effective were you at adapting? How long did it take you to build some attraction power with the people you interacted with? What would you advise someone else traveling to or working in another culture?

CHAPTER 5

A DIAMOND SCRATCHING EVERY OTHER STONE

The Power of Character

CHARACTER IS A SIGNIFICANT SOURCE OF PERSONAL POWER. BEING RECOGnized as a person of character enhances your capacity to lead and influence others because they trust your intentions, are more confident in your leadership, and see you as a person worth emulating. Even if they disagree with you, they know you are an honorable advocate. Character is a crucial power source for executives, professionals, diplomats, teachers, parents, and everyone else in a position of responsibility—but it can also be a substantial power drain if people believe your character is flawed.

In his book *John P. Kotter on What Leaders Really Do,* John Kotter observes that "the more a person finds a manager both consciously and (more important) unconsciously an ideal person, the more he or she will defer to that manager. Managers develop power based on others' idealized views of them in a number of ways. They try to look and behave in ways that others respect. They go out of their way to be visible to their employees and to give speeches about their organizational goals, values, and ideals."[1] What Kotter says applies to leaders of every kind. Children need to see their parents as role models. Believers need to see their ministers, priests, rabbis, and mullahs as models of piety and devotion. Students need to see their teachers as models of erudition and judgment. Whether or not you manage others, your character is a substantial part of your credibility as a human being and underlies all other sources of personal power. If you are a leader, your character is the core of the magnet that draws followers to you.

People long for that idealized person in the guise of their leader because they seek validation of their own values and beliefs—which the leader symbolizes—and confirmation that they have made the right choices. It is as if they say to themselves: "I am only as good as the person

I follow." They want someone to look up to, someone who objectifies their aspirations. Seeing their leader as an ideal confirms their urgent need to believe that there are people who embody, as Abraham Lincoln put it, "the better angels of our nature." It tells them that courage, hope, integrity, and trust are possible even in a world filled with disappointments and doubts. This is why people feel so disheartened and deflated when a person they have respected falters. They despair about losing that idealized vision of humanity, especially when that person is tarnished by flaws in his character that threaten to unravel the whole fabric of their basis for respecting him.

Cyrus Agustus Bartol, a nineteenth-century author and minister, wrote that "character is a diamond that scratches every other stone." Character is the only source of power that can add or subtract from every other source. You can be knowledgeable, eloquent, and attractive (in every respect), and have existing relationships with the people you are trying to influence, but if people perceive that your character is flawed, your power to lead or influence them will be greatly diminished. That's why character is so important.

THE ELEMENTS OF CHARACTER

At various times in human history, people have believed that a person's features were a window into his soul. In *Prior Analytics,* for instance, Aristotle wrote that "it is possible to infer character from physical features."[2] This notion, called physiognomy, fell out of favor after the Greeks but enjoyed a rebirth in popularity in the eighteenth and nineteenth centuries. One of its most ardent advocates during that period was Johann Kaspar Lavater, a Swiss poet, mystic, and pastor renowned for his passionate oratory. He argued that "actions, looks, words, and steps form the alphabet by which you may spell character." Lavater believed that the shapes of people's faces, and their facial resemblance to animals, revealed the secrets of their character. I would have thought that this nonsense was passé, until my wife and I had dinner with a Russian woman in St. Petersburg who kept scrapbooks filled with magazine photos of celebrities and was convinced she could divine your character by identifying which celebrity you most resembled. Clearly, you can sometimes interpret people's moods and emotions from their facial expressions and body language, but it is preposterous to assert that you can determine a man's character by measuring the width of his face (wider faces were once thought to signify aggression).

The best way to deduce a person's character is to examine how the person behaves. An individual's priorities, decisions, and values *in action* reveal much about what is in her heart and mind. Behavior is the best lens on character. But what, exactly, is character? There seem to be as many definitions as there are people to define it. As a starting point, however, I prefer this definition from Kevin Cashman, author of *Leadership from the Inside Out*. "When we are leading from our character," he writes, "we exude qualities of authenticity, purpose, openness, trust, courage, congruence, and compassion."[3] In his book, Cashman emphasizes the importance of authenticity and warns about the dangers of the "image persona," where you worry too much about how you present yourself in order to gain acceptance. If we agree that an authentic self is the core of strong character, then what else does character consist of? How do we know it when we see it? The most thorough taxonomy of character I have seen appears in Peterson and Seligman's *Character Strengths and Virtues,* which was a study done under the auspices of the American Psychological Association and is now owned and promoted by the Values in Action Institute on Character. As outlined here, this comprehensive study identified twenty-four character strengths in six areas, and these character strengths are considered to be universal.[4]

THE VALUES IN ACTION (VIA) CLASSIFICATION OF CHARACTER STRENGTHS

1. *Wisdom and Knowledge*—Cognitive strengths that entail the acquisition and use of knowledge
   a. *Creativity* [originality, ingenuity]: Thinking of novel and productive ways to conceptualize and do things; includes artistic achievement but is not limited to it.
   b. *Curiosity* [interest, novelty seeking, openness to experience]: Taking an interest in ongoing experience for its own sake; finding subjects and topics fascinating; exploring and discovering.
   c. *Judgment and Open-Mindedness* [critical thinking]: Thinking things through and examining them from all sides; not jumping to conclusions; being able to change one's mind in light of evidence; weighing all evidence fairly.
   d. *Love of Learning:* Mastering new skills, topics, and bodies of knowledge, whether on one's own or formally; obviously related to the strength of curiosity, but goes beyond it to describe the tendency to add systematically to what one knows.

    e. *Perspective* [wisdom]: Being able to provide wise counsel to others; having ways of looking at the world that make sense to oneself and to other people.

2. *Courage*—Emotional strengths that involve the exercise of will to accomplish goals in the face of opposition, external or internal
   a. *Bravery* [valor]: Not shrinking from threat, challenge, difficulty, or pain; speaking up for what is right even if there is opposition; acting on convictions even if unpopular; includes physical bravery but is not limited to it.
   b. *Perseverance* [persistence, industriousness]: Finishing what one starts; persisting in a course of action in spite of obstacles; "getting it out the door"; taking pleasure in completing tasks.
   c. *Honesty* [authenticity, integrity]: Speaking the truth, but more broadly presenting oneself in a genuine way and acting in a sincere way; being without pretense; taking responsibility for one's feelings and actions.
   d. *Zest* [vitality, enthusiasm, vigor, energy]: Approaching life with excitement and energy; not doing things halfway or halfheartedly; living life as an adventure; feeling alive and activated.

3. *Humanity*—Interpersonal strengths that involve tending and befriending others
   a. *Capacity to Love and Be Loved:* Valuing close relations with others, in particular those in which sharing and caring are reciprocated; being close to people.
   b. *Kindness* [generosity, nurturance, care, compassion, altruistic love, "niceness"]: Doing favors and good deeds for others; helping them; taking care of them.
   c. *Social Intelligence* [emotional intelligence, personal intelligence]: Being aware of the motives and feelings of other people and oneself; knowing what to do to fit into different social situations; knowing what makes other people tick.

4. *Justice*—Civic strengths that underlie healthy community life
   a. *Teamwork* [citizenship, social responsibility, loyalty]: Working well as a member of a group or team; being loyal to the group; doing one's share.
   b. *Fairness:* Treating all people the same according to notions of fairness and justice; not letting personal feelings bias decisions about others; giving everyone a fair chance.

    c. *Leadership:* Encouraging a group of which one is a member to get things done and at the same time maintain good relations within the group; organizing group activities and seeing that they happen.

5. *Temperance*—Strengths that protect against excess
    a. *Forgiveness and Mercy:* Forgiving those who have done wrong; accepting the shortcomings of others; giving people a second chance; not being vengeful.
    b. *Modesty and Humility:* Letting one's accomplishments speak for themselves; not regarding oneself as more special than one is.
    c. *Prudence:* Being careful about one's choices; not taking undue risks; not saying or doing things that might later be regretted.
    d. *Self-Regulation* [self-control]: Regulating what one feels and does; being disciplined; controlling one's appetites and emotions.

6. *Transcendence*—Strengths that forge connections to the larger universe and provide meaning
    a. *Appreciation of Beauty and Excellence* [awe, wonder, elevation]: Noticing and appreciating beauty, excellence, and/or skilled performance in various domains of life, from nature to art to mathematics to science to everyday experience.
    b. *Gratitude:* Being aware of and thankful for the good things that happen; taking time to express thanks.
    c. *Hope* [optimism, future-mindedness, future orientation]: Expecting the best in the future and working to achieve it; believing that a good future is something that can be brought about.
    d. *Humor* [playfulness]: Liking to laugh and tease; bringing smiles to other people; seeing the light side; making (not necessarily telling) jokes.
    e. *Religiousness and Spirituality* [faith, purpose]: Having coherent beliefs about the higher purpose and meaning of the universe; knowing where one fits within the larger scheme; having beliefs about the meaning of life that shape conduct and provide comfort.

The VIA Survey of Character is an instrument that measures an individual's character strengths along the dimensions outlined.[5] It is understood that everyone has a constellation of character strengths—some weaker and some stronger—and that a person's signature strengths are the ones he expresses most frequently. After surveying well over a million people, the Values in Action Institute on Character found that the top-ten character strengths, on average, are curiosity, love, fairness, judgment and open-mindedness, kindness, love of learning, creativity, appreciation of beauty and excellence, honesty, and humor. Conversely, the six least-common signature strengths are self-regulation, social intelligence, modesty and humility, zest, prudence, and perspective. These are the elements of character that are least likely to appear as signature strengths.

Can character be developed? If you don't naturally have strength in some elements of character as the VIA defines them, can you learn to improve those elements? Kim Ruyle and Evelyn Orr of Korn/Ferry International helped answer these questions by mapping the VIA's classification of character strengths with Korn/Ferry's Leadership Architect®, a framework that identifies sixty-seven leadership competencies along with the developmental difficulty of each one. By mapping the VIA model's six areas (referred to as factors I through VI) and twenty-four items of character strength with Korn/Ferry's Leadership Architect, Ruyle and Orr were able to estimate the developmental difficulty of the factors and items on the VIA classification. They discovered that the most difficult factors to develop were factors III (*Humanity*) and VI (*Transcendence*). Factors V (*Temperance*), I (*Wisdom and Knowledge*), and II (*Courage*) were significantly easier to develop, and the easiest was factor IV (*Justice*). At the item level, the four most difficult character strengths to develop were items 12 (*Social Intelligence*), 23 (*Humor*), 24 (*Religiousness and Spirituality*), and 5 (*Perspective*). The four easiest to develop were items 4 (*Love of Learning*), 7 (*Perseverance*), 17 (*Modesty and Humility*), and 9 (*Zest*).

Social intelligence is particularly noteworthy. As noted in the previous outline, the VIA defines this item as "being aware of the motives and feelings of other people and oneself; knowing what to do to fit into different social situations; knowing what makes other people tick." That this character strength would be the most difficult to develop supports Daniel Goleman's assertion that emotional intelligence is a critical skill that many people in business (and life) lack. In my research on power and influence, I also measured a range of interpersonal, interactive, reasoning, communication, and assertiveness skills, and I discovered a substantial difference between people who rated highest and lowest on such interpersonal skills as "having insight into what others value" and "being sensitive to others' feelings and needs." Those scoring highest in these skills were rated two to three times higher on leadership and influence effectiveness and nearly three times higher on character power. For this reason, developing your emotional/social intelligence is a powerful lever in making you a more effective leader or influencer. However, if you aren't naturally gifted with emotional/social intelligence, don't expect it to come easy. Developing this character strength is more difficult than it appears.[6]

► PROFILES *in* POWER

ELEANOR ROOSEVELT

Anna Eleanor Roosevelt was born in 1884 into a New York family of wealth and privilege. She was the niece of Theodore Roosevelt, twenty-sixth president of the United States, and would be the future wife of Franklin Delano Roosevelt, thirty-second U.S. president. As a child, she was shy and awkward. She felt unloved and unattractive, an appraisal echoed by her mother, who considered Eleanor "plain to the point of ugliness."[7] When she was just six, her mother said to her, "You have no looks, so see to it that you create manners."[8] She bore the burden of a disapproving mother and an alcoholic father through difficult childhood years but arrived at happier times when she attended the Allenswood Academy, a finishing school in England, where she became known for her compassion and helpfulness to others. When she returned to America, she began doing social work in the slums of New York City. From that point, she dedicated herself to improving the lives of the underprivileged, regardless of race, creed, or nationality.

She was first lady of the United States for more than twelve years and throughout her life was a tireless advocate for social causes. She was active in the Junior League, the League of Women Voters, the Women's Trade Union League, and the New York State Democratic Committee. She felt that women should be allowed to hold their own jobs, even if their husbands worked (which was an issue at that time). She lobbied for the creation of youth programs, opposed poll taxes (which restricted voting by minorities), championed civil rights, worked on federal housing programs, promoted the concept of a living wage (which led to the Fair Labor Standards Act of 1938), and successfully advocated for federal aid to the arts.

During World War II, she worked for the American Red Cross and did volunteer work at Navy hospitals. After her husband was stricken with polio, she traveled extensively around the country and became his eyes and ears with the public. After Franklin's death, President Harry Truman appointed her to the U.S. delegation to the United Nations General Assembly, where she served from 1945 to 1953. During that period, she was elected Chairperson of the UN Human Rights Commission and led the effort to draft the Universal Declaration of Human Rights, which the UN

General Assembly adopted on December 10, 1948. Finally, she was a noted speaker and a prolific author. In addition to nine books, she wrote a popular daily newspaper column called "My Day," which ran from December 1935 to her death in 1962. She also wrote monthly question-and-answer columns for *Ladies' Home Journal* and *McCall's* magazines.

Among her notable qualities was a fierce determination. Franklin Roosevelt sometimes bridled at her persistence and stubbornness, once complaining to her: "Your back has no bend!" Rexford Tugwell, a family friend, was witness to the way she influenced her husband. He said, "No one who ever saw Eleanor Roosevelt sit down facing her husband, and, holding his eye firmly, say to him, 'Franklin, I think you should . . .' or 'Franklin, surely you will not . . . ,' will ever forget the experience. . . . It would be impossible to say how often and to what extent American governmental processes have been turned in new directions because of her determination."[9]

Eleanor Roosevelt's power—and it was immense—stemmed from her multiple roles, knowledge, expressiveness, network, reputation, and history power (particularly with Franklin). But one of her greatest sources of power was character. She was wise, courageous, strong, humane, honest, kind, forgiving, compassionate, determined, and tireless in her efforts to improve not only the lives of the underprivileged, but humanity itself. She said late in her life that her greatest achievement was the Universal Declaration of Human Rights. Another great source of power for her was will power (for more on will power, see chapter 11). She accomplished more in her life than most people could manage in ten lifetimes. The content of her character made her immensely attractive to other people, though she would never have won a beauty contest. She became one of the most beloved, admired, and respected women of her era—and is considered by many to be one of the most influential first ladies in the history of the United States.

What We Can Learn from Eleanor Roosevelt

1. *The power of strong character.* "Your back has no bend," FDR told her. Eleanor's staunch character was one of her greatest sources of power. She became a formidable and widely respected leader through the moral force she projected. The lesson for business leaders? The vast majority of people demonstrate average character. If we were to plot a bell curve of character, we would probably see a huge average middle (the bell) and small wings on either end signifying those of lower-than-average character on the left and higher-than-average character on the right. To lead from a position of strong character, as Eleanor did, you need to be a leader of higher-than-average character. You need to reflect high character in everything you do and have the courage to make the right decisions even when you face widespread resistance. You need to exemplify the character traits Eleanor Roosevelt did, and this is especially important as you become a more senior leader in an organization.

2. *The capacity to lead through influence.* Throughout much of her life, she led without having the formal role power to do so. She was the first lady, not the president. She did not have the formal authority to issue commands or make executive decisions. For the most part, she had to exercise her leadership by influencing Franklin Roosevelt and others. The lesson for us? Leadership does not require executive authority. You can exercise substantial leadership by influencing others rather than commanding them. In fact, most leadership occurs through influence rather than authority.

3. *The value of courage and determination.* Eleanor Roosevelt had a phenomenal amount of drive, determination, and will power. And she had the courage to take on tough challenges. Much of her leadership effectiveness was the result of her clear vision about what was right and wrong and her determination to make a difference. The lesson? Power comes in part from fierce determination, from having the will power to persist, to overcome obstacles, and to forge ahead until you reach your goal.

CHARACTER AS A POWER DRAIN

Abraham Lincoln said that "nearly all men can stand adversity, but if you want to test a man's character, give him power." Power, especially great power, can distort the ego, judgment, and perspective of even the most educated and intelligent among us. John Thain, the last chairman of Merrill Lynch before it merged with Bank of America, is a prime example of the greed and irresponsibility that characterized the financial sector during the past decade. Before joining Merrill Lynch, he was CEO of the New York Stock Exchange, and before that, president, COO, and CFO of Goldman Sachs, where he reportedly received $300 million in Goldman Sachs stock. Upon joining Merrill Lynch, he was given a $15 million signing bonus and received more than $80 million in compensation in 2007. Yet after becoming Merrill Lynch's CEO, he reportedly spent $1.22 million in corporate funds to redecorate his office, a reception area, and two conference rooms, including $68,000 for a credenza, $131,000 for rugs, $87,000 for guest chairs, $35,000 for a commode, and $1,400 for a wastebasket. Then, while the financial meltdown of 2008 was occurring, he reportedly rushed billions of dollars in bonuses to Merrill Lynch employees while the brokerage firm was losing money. After the merger with Bank of America, it was revealed that Merrill Lynch had lost $15 billion in the fourth quarter of 2008 and more than $27 billion in all of 2008. Thain was forced to resign when all these transactions came to light.[10]

What is remarkable about this story is that it wasn't confined to one executive but typified the greed, excess, and gross lack of temperance across much of the financial industry—and all this occurred while millions of Americans lost their jobs, millions more saw their retirement savings slashed, and a countless number lost their homes. Thain later apologized for his colossal lack of judgment and repaid the money spent on the redecorating, but his actions had already revealed some fundamental character flaws brought on, one gathers, from the exalted positions he had attained and his exalted view of himself.[11] Although Thain's case was one of the most egregious examples of excessive excess on Wall Street, he was not alone in abusing the public's trust in its financial institutions. The actions of many companies and executives prior to and during the meltdown caused an industrywide character power drain in which legislators, the media, and the public lost confidence in financial institutions' collective ability to meet their moral, civic, and fiduciary responsibilities.

Unfortunately, there are numerous examples of character lapses in executive leadership. In one now-infamous example, in 1994 seven American tobacco company CEOs testified before a House subcommittee investigating whether the tobacco industry needed more regulation. William I. Campbell of Philip Morris, James Johnston of R. J. Reynolds, Joseph Taddeo of U.S. Tobacco, Andrew H. Tisch of Lorillard Tobacco Company, Edward A. Horrigan Jr. of the Liggett Group, Thomas E. Sandefur Jr. of Brown & Williamson Tobacco, and Donald Johnston of American Tobacco Company declared, one after another and under oath, that nicotine is not addictive, despite overwhelming scientific evidence to the contrary. Dubbed the Seven Dwarfs by the media, these CEOs exemplified what many people saw as a uniform and steadfast evasion of responsibility and conscience by the tobacco industry and its leaders.

Character becomes a power drain when auto company executives fly in private jets to Washington to ask for federal bailout money. It is a power drain when leaders act principally in their own interests rather than the interests of their organizations, employees, and shareholders. It is a power drain when a revered athlete like Tiger Woods is shown to have been cheating on his wife with multiple partners, or when record-breaking athletes like Marion Jones and Mark McGwire admit to using steroids. It is a power drain when a fire-and-brimstone evangelist preaches moral rectitude and then is discovered having an affair with a parishioner. It is a power drain whenever leaders say one thing and do another. And the role a person plays makes a difference. We have higher expectations of people whose positions in an organization carry fiduciary responsibilities, such as CEOs and CFOs. When those people reveal character flaws, we worry a great deal more. This holds true for people with moral responsibilities as well— teachers, guidance counselors, religious leaders, therapists, and others who act as caretakers. We hold them to a higher standard for character, so any flaws of importance are likely to be a substantial character power drain.

According to Kevin Cashman, "Character is the essence or core of the leader. Character is deeper and broader than action or achievement; it springs from the essential nature of the person."[12] This is a profound thought. It suggests that what drives people lies deep in their core. Although some aspects of character can be learned, other aspects are rooted so deeply in our psyche and so biased by what we fundamentally value and believe that they emerge either as the better angels of our nature or as the demons that haunt our humanity. But the truth about who we are may not come to light until we are either blessed or burdened with great power and make decisions that showcase our essential nature.

▶ PROFILES *in* POWER

ELIOT SPITZER

He was a reform-minded New York prosecutor and attorney general who vigorously attacked white-collar crime, price fixing, predatory lending practices, Internet fraud, securities fraud, labor racketeering, and organized crime. For his zealous pursuit of corporate criminals, he was dubbed the

 Sheriff of Wall Street. His tenacious investigation of Mafia control of Manhattan's garment and trucking industries brought down the Gambino crime family. In 2006, he ran for governor of New York on a reform platform, promising to change the ethics of state government. Bill Richardson, the governor of New Mexico and a candidate for the American presidency in 2008, said that Eliot Spitzer was the future of the Democratic Party, and many thought that his ascendency through political office would eventually lead to the White House.

His tenure as governor of New York was not without controversy. It became apparent after he took office that the tough talk and sharp elbows he'd relied on as New York attorney general were mainstays of his leader-

Photo by Timothy A. Clary/AFP/Getty Images.

ship style and that he had not made the transition from prosecutor to chief executive. Commenting on Spitzer's promise to make the state's government more functional, Nick Paumgarten wrote in the *New Yorker* that "Albany has in many ways become more dysfunctional than ever. The addition of an aggressive personality with an ambitious agenda has, perversely, gummed up the works. The acrimony between Spitzer and his enemies, born of scandal, policy disagreement, political desperation, tactical blundering, and personal animus, has all but stalled the workings of the government, or at least those which require the collaboration of the executive chamber and the Legislature."[13]

Spitzer referred to himself as a steamroller who would crush his opponents, and he was known to be irascible, difficult with his staff, and bitterly political with his opponents. Members of his administration were accused, for instance, of directing the New York State Police to spy on Joseph Bruno, a Republican and then the New York State Senate majority leader (a case dubbed "Troopergate"). Investigators later concluded that members of the governor's staff had ordered the state police to exceed their authority and then had lied about it. In response, Spitzer suspended his communications director and reiterated his pledge to make ethics and integrity central themes of his term as governor.

But that was not to be. In March 2008, the *New York Times* reported that Spitzer had been a client of a prostitution ring called the Emperors Club VIP. The preceding July, a New York bank had reported suspicious funds transfers by Spitzer, which prompted a federal investigation that led, months later, to Room 871 at the Mayflower Hotel in Washington, D.C., and twenty-two-year-old Ashley Alexandra Dupré, a call girl and aspiring pop singer with whom Spitzer had apparently had a number of assignations. Investigators estimate that over a period of several years, beginning when he was attorney general, Spitzer may have spent as much as $80,000 on Dupré and other hookers.

The fallout from the *Times* revelation was swift and devastating to Spitzer's family and supporters. Spitzer resigned in disgrace as governor, his political career as shattered as the look on his wife's face as he said, "The remorse I feel will always be with me. I look at my time as governor with a sense of what might have been."[14] For the vast majority of his public career, he had been known as a stalwart defender of individual investors, a crusader fighting the forces of corruption and mismanagement of the public trust. In short, he had built a power base on the strength of character. His meteoritic fall from grace is a classic tale of how character, which can be such a great source of power, can metamorphose into a power drain when a crusader falls on his sword.

What We Can Learn from Eliot Spitzer

1. *Hubris is dangerous.* Hubris means "exaggerated pride or self-confidence." Somehow, this very smart man, who held a public office with high visibility, convinced himself that he could get away with his trans-

gressions. How he came to believe that the rules didn't apply to him, that his actions would not inevitably be self-defeating, is one of the great mysteries of his sad saga. The lesson for business leaders? Engaging in morally questionable behavior is exceedingly risky. You aren't coated with Teflon. Your transgressions are likely to be discovered. You can't trust your most trusted aides to remain silent. Your character flaws are likely to be revealed, sooner or later, and you aren't so powerful that those flaws can't bring you down. Of course, transgressors do sometimes get away with it. But don't count on being among the lucky ones who can transgress and never be held accountable. In short, if you have character flaws that entice you to misbehave, don't assume you won't be caught—or punished when you are caught.

2. *The fall from grace can be remarkably swift and sudden.* Spitzer's fall from grace occurred virtually overnight. The road to hell is short and swift; the journey out of hell is long and uncertain. The lesson? If you misbehave, the end may come at any time, and you probably won't have time to backtrack, reverse the course of events, and somehow salvage your career or avoid the fall. It is likely to happen quickly and be totally beyond your control.

3. *Don't misbehave in the first place.* That, of course, is the greatest lesson to be learned. If you feel tempted, then reflect carefully on those impulses and keep them in check. Authentic leadership is all about character. If you lack character, you are not fit to lead.

WHAT THE RESEARCH TELLS US ABOUT CHARACTER POWER

Not surprisingly, high character power is a substantial lever in a person's capacity to lead and influence others. In my research, using a scale of 1 to 5, people who rated low on character power had an overall influence effectiveness rating of 2.23; those rated high on character power had a rating of 4.09. This substantial difference illustrates how much impact character has. People who rate high on character power are seen as role models and are expected to be exemplars of good conduct. In leading and influencing others, they typically prefer to offer logical reasons for their requests, engage and involve others by asking questions, and motivate others by being inspirational.

The halo effect operates with character power in much the same way it operates with attraction power. We tend to perceive the people closest to us as having high character and people we don't know or don't like as having lower character. People rated high in character are perceived to be more authentic and trustworthy, which we would expect, but they are also rated as being significantly more empathetic, sensitive, and insightful than people rated lower in character—and this finding is not surprising. It reflects the halo effect among character, attraction, and interpersonal skill or emotional intelligence.

Conversely, people rated low in character are perceived to be pushy and direct to the point of bluntness. They lead through command-and-control methods and rely on role, resource, and information power in leading and influencing others. They are far more likely to try to legitimize their requests by appealing to authority, and their greatest effectiveness occurs with people they already know. Once people question someone's character, that person is far less effective as a leader.

GLOBAL DIFFERENCES IN CHARACTER POWER

In my research, the gap in average character power ratings between the highest- and lowest-scoring cultures was just over 0.5, which is not statistically significant. Moreover, character had the highest average score of any of the ten power sources rated. More than 94 percent of 64,000 subjects gave themselves high character ratings (4 or 5 on a scale of 1 to 5); less than 0.25 percent rated themselves low (1 or 2) on character power. The other people rating them were not quite as generous. Still, more than 88 percent of these respondents gave the subjects a score of 4 or 5 on character and less than 2 percent gave ratings of 1 or 2. These results indicate that the people we studied (mostly white-collar professionals around the world) were generally perceived to be of high character.

The results show, however, that character is a more important power source in some cultures than in others. Character is an especially important power source in Latin countries, particularly in South America. Six of the seven countries with the highest average character power source ratings were in South America (plus Mexico). The lists are arranged alphabetically.

COUNTRIES WHERE AGGREGATE CHARACTER POWER IS HIGHER

Argentina, Australia, Brazil, Chile, Colombia, Ireland, Israel, Italy, Mexico, New Zealand, Peru, Portugal, South Africa, Spain, United States of America

COUNTRIES WHERE AGGREGATE CHARACTER POWER IS AVERAGE

Belgium, Canada, Czech Republic, Denmark, France, Hungary, India, Malaysia, Netherlands, Norway, Pakistan, Sweden, Switzerland, United Kingdom, Venezuela

COUNTRIES WHERE AGGREGATE CHARACTER POWER IS LOWER

Austria, China, Finland, Germany, Greece, Hong Kong, Indonesia, Japan, Poland, Russia, Singapore, South Korea, Taiwan, Thailand, Turkey

For more information on our global research on power and influence, and in-depth profiles of each of the forty-five countries studied, see www .kornferryinstitute.com, www.theelementsofpower.com, or www.terryr bacon.com.

KEY CONCEPTS

1. Character is a significant source of personal power. Being recognized as a person of character enhances your capacity to lead and influence others because they trust your intentions, are more confident in your leadership, and see you as a person worth emulating.

2. Character is the only source of power that can add or subtract from every other source. You can be very knowledgeable, eloquent, and attractive (in every respect), and have existing relationships with the people you are trying to influence, but if they perceive that your character is flawed, your power to lead and influence them will be greatly diminished.

3. The Values in Action classification is composed of six character strengths: wisdom and knowledge, courage, humanity, justice, temperance, and transcendence. Everyone has a constellation of character strengths—some weaker and some stronger.

4. Power, especially great power, can distort a leader's ego, judgment, and perspective. When that happens, character can become a power drain instead of a power source.

5. People who are perceived to be high in character are significantly more effective at leading and influencing others because of the trust and confidence they instill.

6. People rated high in character also tend to be highly effective at many interpersonal skills, including building rapport and trust, showing genuine interest in others, having insight into what others value, listening, and building close relationships.

CHALLENGES FOR READERS

1. I have offered a number of examples in this chapter of people who have high character power and some who have lost it. Think about the effect of character power in your own life and work. Who do you know who's had a reputation for strong character, exemplifying wisdom, courage, humanity, justice, temperance, or transcendence? How did having that character power enhance that person's capacity to lead and influence others?

2. How would people assess your character? What would they identify as your character strengths or weaknesses? Most people could probably strengthen others' perceptions of their character if they reflected on what they could do differently. What could you do differently to enhance others' perceptions of your character?

3. How would you score on the VIA Survey of Character? Review the twenty-four character strengths in the VIA classification cited in this chapter. Visit the VIA Institute on Character website (www.via strengths.org) and take the survey. What pleased you about your results? Surprised you? Disappointed you?

4. This chapter included several case studies of people for whom character became a power drain instead of a power source. Identify other cases where people with moral, civic, or fiduciary responsibility lost power because of behaviors that made others question their character. What did they do? What effect did it have on their capacity to lead and influence others? Were they able to recover from that lapse?

PART II

SOURCES OF ORGANIZATIONAL POWER

Role

Resources

Information

Network

Reputation

©iStockphoto.com/tstop123.

Where does power come from?

THE POWER TO LEAD AND INFLUENCE OTHERS WITHIN AN ORGANIZA-
TION DEPENDS ON THE STRENGTH OF YOUR PERSONAL POWER
SOURCES. YET, AS A MEMBER OF AN ORGANIZATION, YOU ALSO HAVE AD-
DITIONAL SOURCES OF POWER THAT ARE ROOTED IN THE ROLE YOU PLAY
IN THE ORGANIZATION, THE RESOURCES YOU CONTROL, YOUR ACCESS
TO AND USE OF INFORMATION, THE SIZE AND STRENGTH OF YOUR NET-
WORKS, AND HOW WELL OTHERS REGARD YOU. THESE FIVE ORGANIZA-
TIONAL POWER SOURCES (*ROLE, RESOURCES, INFORMATION, NETWORK,*
AND *REPUTATION*) ARE CRITICAL TO LEADERS IN BUSINESS AND EVERY
OTHER TYPE OF ORGANIZATION. THE STRENGTH OF THESE POWER
SOURCES DETERMINES WHETHER YOU CAN HAVE EXTRAORDINARY IM-
PACT AS A LEADER OR MINIMAL IMPACT. PART II OF THE BOOK EXPLORES
THE FIVE ORGANIZATIONAL POWER SOURCES AND WHAT THE RESEARCH
SAYS ABOUT THEM.

CHAPTER 6

HAIL TO THE CHIEF

The Power of Role and Resources

ONE OF THE WICKEDEST SATIRES OF BUSINESS AND THE MEDIA IS THE 1976 film *Network*. Television news anchor Howard Beale (played by Peter Finch) is given two weeks' notice because of sinking ratings, and he announces on the air that he is going to kill himself. The Union Broadcasting System (UBS) network immediately fires him, but he begs for one more broadcast so that he can make a dignified farewell speech. Reluctantly, they put him back on the air. Instead of a stately farewell, however, he rants about the inequities of life with an impassioned lunacy that raises the show's ratings so dramatically the network decides to give him his own show, *The Howard Beale Hour*. There, he enjoins the members of his audience to open their windows and scream, "I'm mad as hell and I'm not going to take it anymore!" All goes satirically well until Beale rants about an impending deal in which the Saudis plan to acquire his network. His diatribe puts the deal in jeopardy, and he is ordered to appear before the network's chairman, Arthur Jensen (played by Ned Beatty).

Beale steps into a darkened boardroom, the long conference table lit only by rows of muted blue lamps, which look like rows of candles leading to an altar. The chairman walks to the head of the table, clad in a three-piece suit, and launches into a sermon about how Beale has meddled with the primal forces of nature and must atone for his sins. Like a fiery evangelist, Arthur Jensen preaches the new religion to Beale: There are no ideologies and no nations. There is only business. A perfect world is coming where everyone will work in "one vast and ecumenical holding company" in which "all necessities are provided, all anxieties tranquilized, all boredom amused." Beale looks on, mesmerized, and then utters, "I have seen the face of God." In this scene, we witness the omnipotence of Arthur Jensen in his role as the chairman and Beale's power in his role as a television missionary who can spread Jensen's insane gospel to the masses. When Beale asks why he was chosen to deliver this message, the chairman replies, "Because you're on television, dummy. Sixty million people watch you every night of the week, Monday through Friday."

Although this film is a satire, it illustrates the often-remarkable influencing power embodied in the role a person plays in an organization. Arthur Jensen may have other sources of power, but it is his role as chairman of the network that gives him an almost godlike ability to lead and influence other people—principally inside UBS but also outside his network. Similarly, Howard Beale's role as a network news anchor and host of a television show that reaches millions of people gives him an extraordinary capacity to influence viewers. During the film, he tells his viewers to shout from their windows and thousands, if not millions, of people comply. This film distorts reality, but it also depicts some core truths about the power of the roles people play in organizations.

People gain the power to lead and influence others not only through their roles but also through the resources they control. I consider these as two separate but closely related organizational power sources because some people have role authority but little control of resources whereas others control resources but have relatively little role authority. Howard Beale has tremendous role power but little actual control of resources. Similarly, most chiefs of staff have great role authority but limited resource control. What they control is access to the boss and other key staff people as well as the flow of information between various staffs and functions. Conversely, wealthy individuals and people who own land or other natural resources can often exert tremendous power because of their control of resources but may have little role authority in an organization (they may not even belong to an organization). Supply officers in the military offer another example. They have limited role authority in the chain of command but often exert a significant amount of power because they control the flow and allocation of resources other officers need to do their jobs. This chapter explores role power and resource power and describes how they enhance a person's capacity to lead and influence others.

ROLE POWER

If you work for General Electric and Jeff Immelt asks you to meet with a customer and explain a GE product, you will be inclined to say yes because he is the CEO. You might also like him, or find him inspirational, or agree with what he wants. You might consider his request part of your job. But what is likely to be most influential with you is that he is the big boss in GE, and as the big boss he has the legitimate right to ask you to meet with this customer. Because of his role, Jeff Immelt has tremendous power at GE.

Role power exists because people live and work in social organizations, and for those organizations to function, the people in them have to play various roles (e.g., mother, father, teacher, principal, president, vice president, priest, rabbi, committee chairperson, fire chief, sergeant at arms, senior editor, electrical engineer, strategic account manager, human resources director, and so on). Implicit in those roles are expectations and agreements about the role's task responsibilities, span of control, decision authority, and relation to other roles. Sometimes, to ensure that everyone knows what he is supposed to do, those expectations and agreements are explicitly negotiated and codified. If the roles are formally defined, they represent the legitimate authority granted to the people playing those roles. Even when roles are not formally defined or when power is shared among group members, people act as though the roles various members are playing have legitimate authority.

Role power operates within a domain, and its power typically does not extend beyond that domain. A regional customer service manager for an appliance company, for instance, has role power within the scope of her responsibilities and her region, but she has little role power outside her region and no role power at home, at least not as a manager (although she may have power in her role as a partner, spouse, head of the household, or mother). Some roles, however, have a halo effect because of their significance. I am not a Buddhist or a Tibetan, but if I met the Dalai Lama I would show him deference (and probably allow myself to be influenced by him in ways acceptable to me) because of his character power, his reputation, and his role as one of the world's great religious leaders. On the other hand, if I met the managing director of a European company I don't work for, and he ordered me to open a branch office in Hong Kong, he would be trying to exercise influence well outside his role domain, and I would think he'd lost his mind.

Under most circumstances, role power is one of the strongest sources of power a person can have. Its strength comes from our tendency to conform to the social norms of the groups we belong to and therefore to accept a leader's legitimate right to tell, ask, lead, or influence us to do what he wants. We are inclined to comply if what the leader wants or demands is within the scope of his authority. If I am an assistant professor in a university, for instance, I understand that my department chair has certain powers by virtue of that position. The dean of the college I belong to has certain other powers (greater than my department chair's powers). The academic vice president of the college has even greater powers. And so on. Because I understand and implicitly accept the hierarchical system in which I am working, I expect the people in these roles to try to influence me in particular ways, and I will be inclined to go along with their leadership and influence attempts if I deem them legitimate.

Role power is one of the strongest sources of power. Its strength comes from our tendency to conform to social norms and accept a leader's legitimate right to influence us. We are inclined to comply if what the leader wants is within the scope of his authority.

However, human beings are not sheep, and most of us don't willingly submit to authority without feeling some tension between our urge to conform to the social norms of our culture and organization and our need for autonomy and freedom. Most Americans don't like to be told what to do (and I suspect this applies to most people in the world). Our impulse to express our autonomy begins in childhood as we develop an independent sense of ourselves and start to rebel against parental authority. As adults, most people come to accept the hierarchical structure that is part of nearly all organizations, so they grant people with role authority the right to make demands or requests of others. Still, because of the tension between the urge to conform and the need for autonomy, when role power is used to lead or influence people, the outcome is more likely to be compliance rather than commitment. In organizations, people may *accept* what someone with legitimate role power wants them to do, but they rarely *embrace* it, and this is particularly true in professional services firms.

As a group, professionals tend to be independent and self-directed. The leader of a group of professionals may have legitimate role power, but if he exercises it too forcefully he is likely to engender passive resistance or even open rebellion as many of the professionals he is leading react to his clumsy attempts to control them. Many professionals consider themselves equal to the person designated as the leader, and governance or oversight committees may circumscribe the leader's power and disperse some of that role power to others in the organization.

► PROFILES *in* POWER

INDRA NOOYI

Fortune named her the Most Powerful Business Woman in the World in 2006 and again in 2007. She was ranked third on the *Forbes* 2008 list of the World's 100 Most Powerful Women, the same year *U.S. News & World Report* called her one of America's Best Leaders. She is Indra Nooyi, chair-

person and CEO of PepsiCo, the world's fourth-largest food-and-beverage company.

She was born in southern India in 1955, and like many capable and ambitious people from her culture, she is driven and determined to succeed, both academically and profes-sionally. She received a bachelor's degree in chemistry from Madras Christian College in 1974 and an MBA from the Indian Institute of Management in Calcutta two years later. In 1978, she came to the United States and earned a mas-ter's degree in public and private management from Yale University. After graduation, she joined the Boston Consulting Group and later worked as a corporate strategist at Motorola and ABB. In 1994, she joined PepsiCo, was named president and CFO in 2001, and CEO in 2006.

She has the reputation of being a thoughtful and demanding leader—one who is single-minded and very focused on what she wants to accom-plish. Her mantra at PepsiCo has been "performance with purpose." To that end, she is driving the company toward healthier products and sustainabil-ity through the use of renewable sources of energy. Under her guidance, PepsiCo purchased more renewable energy certificates (which are similar to carbon credits) than any other corporation at that time and is now listed on both the Dow Jones Sustainability Index (DJSI) for North America and the DJSI World Index. Furthermore, to bring healthier products into the company's portfolio, she engineered PepsiCo's $3 billion acquisition of Tropicana and the $14 billion takeover of Quaker Oats, which includes the power drink Gatorade, and divested the company's fast-food holdings into Yum! Brands.

She comes across as calm, understanding, and soft-spoken, but there is no question who is in charge. A sharp strategic thinker with a mastery of PepsiCo's products and financials, she leads with a single-mindedness that is impressive but can be intimidating. She knows exactly where she wants to take the company, but can be so laser-focused that she doesn't entertain alternative points of view and may appear inflexible to those who work for her. Because of the enormous role power she has, however, there is very little deviation from the course she has set and little public dissent.

Beyond the role power she has as the CEO of a very large public com-pany with a strong brand and global reach, she has significant resource

Photo by Brian Ach/WireImage.

power, an excellent reputation inside and outside her industry, and a vast professional network (she is on a number of boards, including the Lincoln Center for the Performing Arts). Moreover, she can be charming in person and has a side that gives her strong attraction power, as Michael Useem noted in *U.S. News & World Report*: "She played lead guitar in an all-women rock band in her hometown of Madras, India. She was a cricket player in college. She sang karaoke at corporate gatherings. Today, Indra Nooyi presides over [198,000] employees in nearly 200 countries as the chief executive of PepsiCo. And she still performs onstage at company functions."[1] Her personal power sources may also be high, but make no mistake, it is her extraordinary role power that makes her one of the most powerful women in the world.

What We Can Learn from Indra Nooyi

1. *Role power grows with each success and diminishes with each failure.* Although Indra Nooyi's story doesn't reflect the failure part of this equation, it does reflect the success part. Role power in business depends on accomplishing what the role is expected to accomplish; it depends on getting results. The lesson for business leaders is obvious: In each successive role throughout your career, you need to achieve results. And yet I have seen (and you probably have as well) managers who are too focused on the mechanics of the role and not enough on getting results. Sooner or later, this strategy is a career derailer. I argue in this chapter that role power depends on the consent of the governed. Obviously, it also depends on the consent of those above you in the hierarchy.

2. *Role power is essential for command-and-control methods.* Indra Nooyi leaves no doubt about who is in charge, and although she is a modern leader, she is not averse to using command-and-control directness when she needs it. Without her substantial role power, command-and-control leadership methods would be less effective with most people. The lesson for business leaders? Your role power enables you to be directive when you need to be, so use that power when the situation calls for it. But remember that command-and-control methods can seem autocratic, and people today are more engaged by working environments that allow noncoercive power sharing, participation in decision making, and as much autonomy as the situation permits. It is best to be directive and commanding only when you need to be—but then to do so with self-confidence and the firmness of your positional authority behind you.

3. *Role power works best when it is complemented by other power sources.* Indra Nooyi's other strong power sources—including reputation, network, and attraction power—complement her role and resource power and give her greater respect and authority than she would have based on role power alone. The lesson for us? Build your role power but don't rely on it exclusively. It is not enough to be the

boss. You have to engender trust, confidence, and credibility in your leadership by developing other sources of power that make you a well-rounded leader.

In their study of the uses of social power, John French Jr. and Bertram Raven identified three sources that are relevant to organizational roles: *coercive* power, *reward* power, and *legitimate* power.[2] Coercive power is the power to punish—to create consequences for those who do not comply with what you want (i.e., conform to your demands or respond to your requests). The opposite is reward power—the ability to create favorable consequences (or remove negative ones) for those who do comply. Legitimate power is the perception that a person in a particular role has the right to prescribe behavior or make demands upon others who fall within the scope of that role's authority. A company president, for instance, can reward employees in the company by increasing their compensation, promoting them, awarding bonuses, giving them premier assignments, involving them in exclusive events, or recognizing them publicly. The president can punish them by firing them, withholding favors, reducing their responsibilities, shunning them (e.g., disinviting them to exclusive events), or chastising them publicly. The president's role gives her the legitimate power to issue orders, control activities and people in the company, and make demands and requests, which people are likely to comply with because they came from someone with the legitimate authority to make them and because that person has the power to reward or punish. French and Raven defined these as separate sources of power, but they are inherently part of any legitimate role in any organization, so I consider them all part of *role* power.

The capacity to reward or punish others in an organization (which could be a family, a business unit, a company, or a nation) makes *role* the strongest power source of them all. Consequently, role power is the source most likely to be abused. In the hands of an unscrupulous leader, role power has the capacity to inflict an extraordinary amount of damage. To understand how overwhelming role power can be, we have only to consider Hitler, Lenin, Stalin, Mao, Pol Pot, Idi Amin, Kim Il Sung, and Robert Mugabe—despots whose megalomaniacal rule proves that in the iron grasp of a dictator, backed by the coercive power of the police and the military, role power is stronger by many orders of magnitude than any other power source. History has repeatedly shown how difficult it is to effectively moderate that power once it has been granted unless a strong system of checks and balances is in place—and even then, determined autocrats have circumvented those checks and exercised power far beyond the legal authority they actually possess. Fortunately, in business, such abuses of power are the exception rather than the rule. In most organizations, checks and balances exist that either inhibit leaders from abusing their role power or prevent abuses from continuing for very long. The majority of business leaders follow their own moral compass in exercising their role power. The best of them do not use their role power heavy-handedly because they understand that the most effective way to motivate others and build a healthy organization is to inspire and delegate rather than to command and control people.

Badges of Authority and Situational Role Power

A role defines the rights, obligations, responsibilities, and authority of a position in an organization. For the person occupying the position, the job title is like a badge of authority, which is one reason people list their titles on their business cards. The title legitimizes their role power and facilitates their ability to influence others. Other badges of authority in the business world include three-piece suits and power ties, formal pantsuits and other executive women's wear, private offices with plush décor, chauffeured limousines, and other accoutrements of those who have greater and greater role power in their organizations. These signs of power are intended to communicate how powerful these people are and therefore how compliant others should be with their requests or demands. Badges of authority facilitate the influence process by offering proof that people have the legitimate right to influence others, which reduces resistance to their influence attempts.

Badges of authority are an expedient means of communicating role power, like the insignia military officers wear to indicate their rank. They are so expedient that con artists and hackers often adopt them to persuade people they are who they say they are. In the 2002 movie *Catch Me If You Can,* for instance, con artist Frank Abagnale Jr. (played by Leonardo DiCaprio) dons a uniform and wings to impersonate a Pan Am pilot and a white lab coat and medical insignia to impersonate a physician. Those badges of authority help persuade the victims of his con that he has the legitimate right to influence them, and they dutifully comply.

By definition, role power is transient. You have it only as long as you occupy the position. When you leave your position, the role power atten-

> A role defines the rights, obligations, responsibilities, and authorities of a position in an organization. For the person occupying the position, the job title is like a badge of authority.

dant to it now belongs to your successor. However, success in the role can build your reputation power (which I discuss in chapter 9). Jack Welch is no longer the CEO of General Electric, but he is widely regarded as having been a very capable CEO. Although he no longer has the role power associated with that position, he remains influential in business circles as well as in the public eye because of the reputation he developed while he led GE.

The most transient form of role power is situational role power. Situational role power is based on a temporary assignment or arrangement. A person named to chair a committee, for instance, is granted temporary power in that role, as are the people in a company who temporarily act as buyers for their company, perhaps as ad hoc members of a vendor selection team. If you have ever tried to sell your products or services to a company and have had to present your proposal to such a team, you know how much situational role power it possesses. Each of us has the same situational role power when we purchase a car or a house or any other major product or service. Because we are doing the buying, we have the power to say yes or no to the sale and its terms and conditions. That gives us a great deal of situational role power as long as we aren't too desperate. If we show that we are too eager to buy what the salesperson wants to sell us, then the power shifts to the seller. So the secret in negotiating a major purchase is to appear reticent to part with your money.

Let's say I ask Mark Smith, an employee, to coordinate the installation of a new customer service support system in our company. As soon as I announce to the other employees that I've asked Mark to do this job, they grant him the right to influence them as part of the normal course of this assignment. The scope of his influence is constrained, however, by the nature of the assignment. He doesn't have the right to influence them in other ways. He can't demand that they seek reassignment to another group or transfer to another office. But they will expect him to influence how they adopt the system, how they are trained on it, and how they use it. That's within the scope of his situational role power. When the system is installed, Mark goes back to his normal job and no longer has that situational role power.

The Consent of the Governed

Unbridled role power in a national leader can destroy countries and millions of lives (just think of Nazi Germany). In companies and other organizations, the scale of catastrophe may be smaller when leaders rule autocratically, but the damage to the organization and its stakeholders can nonetheless be severe. The poisoning of a nation occurs when a tyrant like Nicolae Ceausescu (president of Romania from 1967 to 1989) is protected by the secret police and the military, who silence those opposed to the leader's dictatorial rule. The poisoning of a corporation can occur when a powerful CEO is also the chairman of the board, and the other board members are merely rubber stamps for his decisions. Enron comes to mind. Had the board exercised appropriate oversight of Ken Lay, Jeff Skilling, and Andrew Fastow, Enron might not have failed so dismally. The poisoning of a religious organization can occur when bishops cover up the crimes of sexually abusive priests, as has happened in the Catholic Church, or when a cult leader's paranoia leads to a massacre, as happened with the Branch Davidians in Waco, Texas. Ultimately, tyrannical rulers and autocratic business leaders lose their power (and sometimes their lives) because role power depends on the consent of the governed, and when the governed become sufficiently aware of abuses and agitated enough to address them, the leader's role power will be curtailed as resistance mounts. I've seen this occur in businesses when an autocratic leader's abuses of power come to light through employee engagement surveys, higher-than-acceptable voluntary turnover, poor business results, or unfavorable exit interviews. One might argue that the direct reports of a tyrannical boss really aren't giving their consent, but in effect they are. They don't have to keep working for a tyrant or a jerk. They can vote with their feet, as often happens with bad bosses.

In his book *John P. Kotter on What Leaders Really Do*, John Kotter says, "Trying to control others solely by directing them and on the basis of the power associated with one's position simply will not work—first, because managers are always dependent on some people over whom they have no formal authority, and second, because virtually no one in modern organizations will passively accept and completely obey a constant stream of orders from someone just because he or she is the 'boss.'"[3] Leaders with formal role authority have power because the people in their domain consent to be led and influenced by them, but the range of outcomes is limited, as shown in figure 6-1.

Even with the best of managers, the typical successful outcome of a direct order is employee compliance. They'll do what the boss said to do. The outcome most leaders would rather achieve is commitment—where employees don't merely do what the leader wants but are inspired and deeply engaged in the process and the outcome. But leaders don't gain commitment by bossing people around; they gain commitment by engaging people, involving them in the solution, envisioning a desirable future, appealing to their core values, and inspiring them to commit to the cause. So if the average boss is successful in getting employees to do what she wants, the most probable outcome is compliance. She can gain their commitment, but this is likely only if she is revered, respected by virtue of her knowledge or character, and has already built a loyal following. When ordinary managers overplay their authority or are heavy-handed in bossing people around, their overbearing influence attempts may result in apathy, skepticism, or resistance. If they are so autocratic that employees can no longer tolerate their authoritative excesses, they may foment a rebellion. Then employees will try to undermine their manager's authority by malingering, gossiping, complaining upward, sabotaging work products, or leaving the company and encouraging others to do so.

A leader can also lose role power if he loses his moral authority and the respect of those in his domain. Before the 2008 presidential election, Barack Obama was an Illinois senator. Upon his election to the presidency, then Illinois governor Rod Blagojevich had the authority to appoint a successor to Obama's U.S. Senate seat. But in December 2008, Blagojevich was arrested by federal agents for conspiracy to commit mail and wire fraud and solicitation of bribery. They had been investigating him for some

Figure 6-1. Typical outcomes of a leader's direct order.

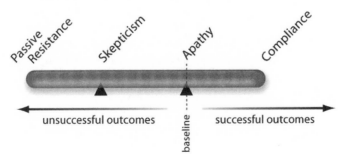

period, it turned out, and had evidence that he was trying to sell Obama's senate seat to the highest bidder. In early January 2009, the Illinois House of Representatives voted to impeach the governor on the grounds of corruption and misconduct in office. Later that month, he was convicted by the Illinois senate by a unanimous vote and was removed from office. This unsavory tale illustrates how a leader with considerable role power can lose that power when the governed no longer give their consent.

> A leader can lose role power if he loses his moral authority and the respect of those in his domain.

Ultimately, role power is a function of success. If the person occupying a role is considered successful, he will be accepted by the governed and will continue to have their support. The more successful he is perceived to be, the stronger his role power becomes and the more influence he is capable of exerting because greater success brings greater credibility and respect. However, if he is not perceived to be successful, his role power will diminish. As failures mount, people will lose confidence in him and he will eventually lose his role power altogether as his followers either wage a palace coup or jump ship.

WHAT THE RESEARCH TELLS US ABOUT ROLE POWER

A comparison of leadership effectiveness between people rated low on role power and people rated high on it shows that having high role power essentially doubles your capacity to lead or influence others—and while this is a substantial boost, it's not as large an increase as one gets from having high expressiveness, knowledge, reputation, attraction, or character power. Here's what this means: If all you have going for you is high role power, you will be moderately effective at getting others to comply with what you want. However, if you have high role power combined with strength in those other five power sources, you are likely to be compelling and masterful at leading others and getting what you want. Role power alone is not enough if you want to be an inspiring and compelling leader, so don't rely only on the strength of your position in your company to lead effectively.

Clearly, some business managers don't care about being inspiring or participative. Some are autocrats who either enjoy throwing their weight around or don't have the skill to lead and manage people any other way. Is role power sufficient for them? Can they get what they want simply by bossing people around? Yes, of course. But in the business world today, that is not a sustainable leadership style. Autocratic management will produce a *compliant* workforce (albeit with high voluntary turnover), but it won't produce a *committed* workforce. If you want to be a highly effective business leader in the twenty-first century you need to avoid using blunt force as much as possible and restrain your use of role power, even though you have it. Leading by influence rather than authority is far more likely to produce a workforce of engaged, committed, and loyal employees.

I found corroboration for this conclusion in my research. As part of the survey, I asked respondents to rate leaders on the extent to which they were threatening or intimidating. I found that leaders with high role power who were rated low for being threatening and intimidating had high reputation ratings. Conversely, leaders who were rated high on role power but also had a high rating for being threatening or intimidating had significantly lower reputation ratings. These findings suggest that command-and-control leaders who overuse their role authority are less well regarded by employees than participative leaders who restrain their use of role power. Of course, this is common sense. It's what we would expect, but it was interesting to find confirmation of it in the data. So even if you are in a position with considerable role authority, it is wise to use command-and-control methods sparingly.

People with high role power were also rated significantly higher on network power than people who were not in positions of authority, which confirms the commonsense belief that having a role in the hierarchy of an organization makes one an attractive member of other people's networks. The skills most closely correlated with high role power were principally *assertiveness skills*: behaving self-confidently, using a compelling tone of voice (having the voice of command), using authority without appearing heavy-handed, using assertive nonverbal cues, and behaving authoritatively. In each of these skills, people high in role power rated significantly higher than those who were low in role power. Clearly, the formal authority of their position boosts their self-confidence and willingness and skill at being assertive when they need to be. And, if they have the authority, it seems natural to others for them to use it.

It will come as no surprise that high-role-power people are perceived to be significantly more effective negotiators. Because they have the authority to say yes or no, their role gives them the power to negotiate from a position of command strength, the confidence to make decisions, and the responsibility for the outcome. Finally, people high in role power tend to be perceived as role models, coaches, and mentors. Their role in the hierarchy makes them attractive to others seeking guidance.

RESOURCE POWER

When I was eight years old, there was a kid in our neighborhood named Steven who had the world's best collection of marbles. At least we thought he did at the time. Going to his house to play marbles was like going to a candy factory. He had turtles, oxbloods, snakes, bumblebees, onionskins, and aggies, lots of aggies, and glazed jaspers, and multicolored alleys with corkscrews, spirals, and swirls. He had big, polished steelies that we tried to shoot hard enough to crack lesser marbles. And his collection of cat's eyes had cores of color we had never seen before. His father traveled on business, and he would find marbles for Steven in all the places he visited. It became an event in our neighborhood when Steven's dad brought back an especially exotic specimen. His mom would make lemonade, and we'd sit for hours marveling at the new treasure his dad had discovered. As you can imagine, Steven was a popular boy in our neighborhood. Besides being a good kid—and the best first baseman on our pickup baseball team—he had that incredible collection of marbles, which all of us envied.

What he also had was tremendous resource power. This is the power derived from owning or controlling resources other people need or want. It's one of the powers managers have by virtue of their management position. As John Kotter notes, "The manager identifies and secures (if necessary) resources that another person requires to perform the job, resources that he or she does not possess, and that are not readily available elsewhere."[4] Controlling scarce resources enables managers to help (or hinder) others by giving them the resources they need (or by withholding them). Scarcity is the key. Part of what gives people strong resource power is the relative scarcity of the resources they possess or control. If everyone has a car, then having a car gives you no power. If only you have a car, and everyone else wants a ride, then you have tremendous resource power as long as you occasionally drive others where they want to go. The secret to having resource power is that you have to use your resources now and then in ways that benefit other people.

However, you have to deploy your resources selectively. Consider Bill Gates, founder and chairman of Microsoft. His wealth gives him an extraordinary amount of resource power. If he hoarded that wealth, he would have less resource power because other people would know it's inaccessible. Conversely, if he gave away all his wealth, he would have no more resources. Instead, he and his wife created the Bill & Melinda Gates Foundation, a global philanthropic organization dedicated to health, education, and the fight against poverty. Through their foundation and its programs, grants, and scholarships, they are deploying their wealth in ways that increase their resource power because others know it is selectively accessible, and potential grant recipients have to compete for a share of it.

Resource power is the power of ownership, possession, and control. The farmer in a village who owns the prize bull has resource power. A collector of vintage cars has resource power. The woman who owns the local restaurant that sometimes donates food and wine to local charity events has resource power. In the business world, the people who control human resources, buildings, fleets, office space, equipment, supplies, services, and budgets have resource power, as do the people who control opportunities, assignments, and access. Budgets are particularly important, which is why the budgetary process is often fraught with power struggles, negotiations, and backroom deals as managers compete for their piece of the pie and why, toward the end of the fiscal year, they often rush to use everything in their budget so they can justify the same or a larger amount next year. Everyone understands that budgetary authority is (resource) power. As Jeffrey Pfeffer says in *Managing with Power,* "Because it is so important to control, and not merely to possess, resources in order to obtain power, there is often a great deal of hue and cry in organizations about the right to exercise discretion over resources."[5]

Finally, even when resources are scarce, they are not all equally desirable. When I was eight years old, marbles were important to me. They aren't now. So Steven's marble collection would no longer have power with me. The power from having or controlling resources derives not only from the scarcity of the resource but also from its importance to other people. If you want to influence me, it's important not only that you control resources I need or want, but that you control the resources I need or want *most*. So if your goal is to build resource power, then you need to amass or gain control of those resources that are most important to the people who need them.

▶ PROFILES *in* POWER

ALI AL-NAIMI

Sometimes, role and resource powers combine to give a person an extraordinary amount of power. Such a person is Ali al-Naimi, the Saudi Arabian minister of petroleum and mineral resources. Intelligent, thoughtful, and articulate, he is highly regarded for his knowledge of global energy resources, usage, and trading. Born in the Kingdom of Saudi Arabia, he joined Saudi Aramco in an entry-level position. The company sent him to the United States for his education, and he received a BS in geology from Lehigh University and an MS in geology from Stanford. Upon graduation, he returned to Saudi Arabia and worked for Aramco as a geologist in the exploration group. Later, he worked in the public relations department of a production division before becoming a production superintendent in 1969.

From there, he held a number of management positions of increasing responsibility—assistant director, then director, of production; vice president of production; and vice president of petroleum. In 1980, he was elected to the board of directors of Saudi Aramco and the next year was promoted to executive vice president of operations. In 1983, he became president and CEO of Saudi Aramco—the first Saudi to hold that position. He was named minister of petroleum and mineral resources in 1995.

In this capacity, he controls a substantial amount of the world's oil and wields considerable influence within the Organization of the Petroleum Exporting Countries (OPEC). Saudi Arabia is the world's largest producer of petroleum (about 10 million barrels/day) and has the largest petroleum reserves (estimated to be 267 billion barrels in 2008—in contrast, the United States had an estimated 21 billion barrels in reserve). Ali al-Naimi is well respected for his extensive experience in the petroleum industry, and he represents the most powerful member of OPEC. For that reason, he was named one of *Time* magazine's Most Influential People in the World in 2008.

His role in the Saudi government and his control of its oil production and reserves gives him an extraordinary amount of power. Furthermore, he is well networked around the globe and has a close relationship with members of the Saudi royal family, as well as with energy ministers, petroleum executives, and government leaders around the globe. As the Saudi minister of petroleum and mineral resources, Ali al-Naimi may not command a nation or a mighty military, but his resource power gives him the ability to impact the economies and industrial might of many other nations, and that makes him one of the most powerful people in the world.

Photo by Hassan Ammar/AFP/Getty Images.

What We Can Learn from Ali al-Naimi

1. *Resource and role powers combined can be an extraordinary platform for leadership.* Ali al-Naimi's positional authority, combined with his control of critical resources, makes him a formidable global leader. The lesson for business leaders? Aspire to positions where you not only have decision-making authority and responsibility for critical operations, but also control of important resources others need to do their jobs. That integration of role and resource powers can make you a formidable leader or influencer within your domain.

2. *Resource power depends on the scarcity and need of the resource—but also on its deployment.* Ali al-Naimi controls a large share of one of our planet's most precious resources at this point in history. The scarcity of the resource magnifies his resource power. But his power also depends on the Saudis selling some amount of oil every year. He influences how much oil is sold, and he influences other oil-producing nations in OPEC, which gives him considerable supply-side power. The lesson for business leaders? Careful deployment of the resources you control is crucial to how you use and build or sustain resource power. Increasing scarcity builds resource power, but controlling it too tightly and making the resource too scarce invites buyers to find substitutes, which in one way or another would curtail your resource power.

WHAT THE RESEARCH TELLS US ABOUT RESOURCE POWER

In terms of leadership and influence, resource power is the weakest of all the power sources. This is not to say that if you are a wealthy person or a manager who controls vast resources that you won't be a powerful leader. It is simply to say that extraordinary control of resources is rare. There are relatively few Ali al-Naimis or Bill Gateses or Warren Buffetts. For the average business leader, control of resources is likely to be a less important power source than all the others.

As we would expect, high resource power is strongly correlated with high role power. People in positions of authority in organizations typically have a commensurate amount of resource power. And, as with role power, people high in resource power tend to be more highly skilled in behaving self-confidently, persisting, and asserting themselves. High resource power also strongly correlates with high information power, which suggests both that people view information as a type of resource and that those with high resource power also control a great deal of information about those resources. (Interestingly, the reverse is not true: People rated high in information power are not necessarily rated high in resource power, so you can control a lot of information without necessarily controlling other types of resources.)

What is probably most interesting in the research on resource power is the correlation of high resource power with high and low skills ratings. Whereas people high in resource power rate highly in the assertiveness skills, they tend to rate very low in interpersonal skills: sensitivity to others' feelings and needs, building close relationships, having insight into what others value, and resolving conflicts and disagreements among others. In each of these areas, people high in resource power were rated significantly lower than people low in resource power. Moreover, people high in resource power tend to be rated significantly lower on attraction power. Simply put, having strong control of resources tends to make you unattractive or unlikeable to others.

Finally, we learned that people with high resource power are least effective at asking others for favors or otherwise appealing to an existing relationship with other people as a means of influencing them. This suggests that having strong resource control either isolates you from others or makes you less willing to put yourself in others' debt, probably because you fear they may ask you to reciprocate. In any case, high resource power comes with a price.

GLOBAL DIFFERENCES IN ROLE AND RESOURCE POWER

Role power tends to be highest in those countries that historically have been more hierarchical and where rank, title, and position are traditionally more important, including countries in Asia (China, Japan, and Indonesia) and South America (Argentina, Brazil, and Colombia). Role power is somewhat less important in the Anglo and Nordic cultures (Canada, United Kingdom, United States of America, Sweden, Finland, and Norway), which in the GLOBE study of cultural differences rank lower on power distance and are typically less hierarchical. The full list of country rankings (arranged alphabetically) follows.

COUNTRIES WHERE ROLE POWER IS HIGHER

Argentina, Brazil, Chile, China, Colombia, Hong Kong, Indonesia, Italy, Japan, Mexico, Poland, Portugal, Singapore, South Korea, Taiwan

COUNTRIES WHERE ROLE POWER IS AVERAGE

Australia, Austria, Czech Republic, Denmark, France, Greece, Hungary, Israel, Malaysia, Netherlands, Peru, Spain, Switzerland, Turkey, Venezuela

COUNTRIES WHERE ROLE POWER IS LOWER

Belgium, Canada, Finland, Germany, India, Ireland, New Zealand, Norway, Pakistan, Russia, South Africa, Sweden, Thailand, United Kingdom, United States of America

Resource power is also more important in most Asian countries (China, Indonesia, Japan, South Korea) but is somewhat less important in South America than role power. However, resource power is more important in the countries of central and southern Europe (Poland, Germany, Austria, Hungary, Switzerland, Italy, and Turkey). The rankings for resource power are indicated in the next list.

COUNTRIES WHERE RESOURCE POWER IS HIGHER

Austria, China, Germany, Hong Kong, Hungary, Indonesia, Italy, Japan, Malaysia, Poland, Singapore, South Korea, Switzerland, Taiwan, Turkey

COUNTRIES WHERE RESOURCE POWER IS AVERAGE

Argentina, Australia, Brazil, Chile, Colombia, Denmark, France, Greece, India, Mexico, Netherlands, Portugal, Spain, Thailand, Venezuela

COUNTRIES WHERE RESOURCE POWER IS LOWER

Belgium, Canada, Czech Republic, Finland, Ireland, Israel, New Zealand, Norway, Pakistan, Peru, Russia, South Africa, Sweden, United Kingdom, United States of America

For more information on our global research on power and influence, and in-depth profiles of each of the forty-five countries studied, see www .kornferryinstitute.com, www.theelementsofpower.com, or www.terryr bacon.com.

KEY CONCEPTS

1. People gain the power to influence others not only through the roles they play in organizations, but also through the resources they control.

2. Implicit in the roles people play in organizations are expectations and agreements about the roles' task responsibilities, span of control, decision authority, and relation to other roles.

3. Role power is one of the strongest sources of power anyone can have. Its strength comes from our tendency to conform to the social norms of the groups we belong to and therefore to accept a leader's legitimate right to influence us.

4. When role and resource powers are used to lead and influence others, the result is more likely to be compliance rather than commitment. And if role power is overused or heavy-handed, the result could be passive or active resistance.

5. Job titles, formal or business dress, private offices, and similar accoutrement are badges of authority that facilitate the influence process by offering proof that people have the legitimate right to lead or influence others. These badges of authority reduce resistance to their attempts to use role authority.

6. Leaders can lose role power if they lose their moral authority and the respect of those in their domain. Role power depends on the consent of the governed. If that power is abused and the governed become sufficiently aware of abuses and agitated enough to address them, the leader's role power will be curtailed as resistance mounts.

7. Resource power is the power of ownership, possession, and control. It derives from both the scarcity of the resource and its importance to other people.

8. Resource power is the weakest of all the power sources, probably because the extraordinary control of resources is rare.

CHALLENGES FOR READERS

1. What role do you play in your organization? What kind of role power does that give you? What is excluded?

2. Think about how you use your role power. Do you include your title on the signature block of letters and memos? In e-mails? Do you ever use the authority of your position to ensure compliance with an order

or request? If you are a manager, would people consider you authoritarian? Laissez-faire? People oriented? Driven? How would they characterize your management style, and what does that say about your use of role power?

3.   Think about the people you have worked for. How did they use their role power? If you consider one of them a model in the use of role power, identify what that person did (or did not do) to be an effective leader.

4.   Have you ever worked for or seen leaders who abused their role power? If so, how did they abuse it and what was the effect on you and others? On the organization?

5.   What resources do you control? Are they plentiful or relatively scarce? How do you use that resource power? Would others say that you use your resource power effectively? Or would they say you overuse it?

6.   Think about the people you've known who had great resource power. How did they use it? And what was the effect of their great resource power on others? How did it enable them to be more influential?

7.   What could you do to build your role or resource power?

CHAPTER 7

INFORMATION WANTS TO BE FREE

The Power of Information

IN THE 2005 SCIENCE FICTION FILM *SERENITY,* A SPACE WESTERN WITH A LARGE cult following, Captain Malcolm "Mal" Reynolds and his rogue crew on a cargo ship have picked up a mysterious passenger and are being pursued by operatives of the ominous Alliance, an interplanetary government intent on galactic domination. After a failed bank robbery, they land at a trading post where their passenger, River Tam, launches an unprovoked attack against the other patrons of a space bar. Startled by her behavior, and concerned that the Alliance will learn of this incident and locate them, they return to their ship and Mal gathers the crew to discuss their options. Hoban Washburne, the ship's pilot, says, "We're flying a lot blinder than usual here. We need to get our bearings. I think we need to talk to Mr. Universe."

Mr. Universe is a space geek manning a galactic listening post. Solitary, except for his robotic wife, he sits in his command post, surrounded by hundreds of video monitors, constantly scanning the universe for information. The crew of the *Serenity* asks if there is any news of the incident at the trading post, and Mr. Universe replies, "There is no news. There's the truth of the signal—what I see." He tells them he learned of the incident by hacking an Alliance security feed.

Mal says, "You can do that?"

"Can't stop the signal," Mr. Universe says. "Everything goes somewhere, and I go everywhere."

What Mr. Universe represents is the power of information. Having access to information, especially information others don't readily possess, can be a tremendous source of leadership and influence power. We are now living in the Age of Information. Globalization, rapid advances in information technology, a more techno-literate populace, the Internet, and the wiki phenomenon are combining to transform our access to and use of information in ways that will permanently alter how people use information to lead and influence others. In the good old days of just a few years ago, information was a scarcer commodity. Information power resided in the hands of librarians who collected reference books and other obscure sources and experts whose time devoted to their specialty enabled them to store, organize, and disseminate information that nonexperts could not readily access from other sources, which made the experts valuable. Today, a quick check on Google yields thousands of links to diverse sources of information on virtually any topic. While some of this information may have questionable accuracy and value, the fact is that more information is readily available to more people today than ever before. All it takes are a few mouse clicks.

One of the mantras of the information age is that "information wants to be free." The person who coined this aphorism was Stewart Brand, an eclectic author, editor, designer, photographer, technologist, scientist, organizer, and counterculturist who cofounded the *Whole Earth Catalog* (1968) and has written numerous books and articles on a variety of topics. At the Hackers' Conference in 1984, Brand said, "On the one hand information wants to be expensive, because it's so valuable. The right information in the right place just changes your life. On the other hand, information wants to be free, because the cost of getting it out is getting lower and lower all the time. So you have these two fighting against each other."[1] This idea has morphed, twenty-five years later, into Wikipedia, an online, user-created encyclopedia and a host of other Web-based information sources created, augmented, modified, and elaborated by millions of Internet users around the world. But wait, there's more. The Web is also host to hundreds of thousands of information sources from news media, academic journals, institutions, government agencies, corporations, and marketers, as well as millions of blogs, postings, reviews, rants, and tweets—flooding the Web with so many bits of information that no one, not even Mr. Universe, could absorb it all. And it's available to anyone with Internet access and the desire to go after it. Information wants to be free.

However, because some information is so valuable, governments and businesses go to extraordinary lengths to protect it. Many Internet sites are accessible only by subscription. Others are secured, accessible only by password, and some are encrypted. Many sites have firewalls and URLs so hidden that only those with privileged information would know how to find them. Hackers do their best to locate and penetrate these sites, sometimes for criminal reasons and sometimes just for the sake of curiosity. Such is the power of knowing what others don't know. That's why information wants to be expensive, too, because possessing it can give you tremendous power. One of the defining characteristics of nations ruled by autocratic regimes is that they restrict people's access to information. Keeping the populace uninformed is critically important to a ruling elite clinging to power. An informed populace is dangerous to dictators, especially if people can communicate with each other and organize resistance. So these regimes restrict information access and give people propaganda instead. In the former Soviet Union, for instance, there were two newspapers, *Pravda* (truth), the official newspaper of the Communist Party, and *Izvestia* (news), the official voice of the Soviet government. The joke at the time was that there was no truth in *Pravda* and no news in *Izvestia*.

RADIO: THE ELEMENTS OF INFORMATION POWER

No one would dispute that information, like knowledge, is power. When you work in an organization, what you know and can do (your knowledge power) is valuable, but since human capacity is limited (none of us can know and do everything), having access to important information can be even more valuable. Information extends your knowledge, and it can extend your knowledge almost without limit because you don't have to hold the information in your head; you just have to be able to retrieve it at the right time in the right way. Having *access* to the right information is a source of power, but it's not the only source of information power. Being able to *retrieve* information quickly and easily is also a source of power. So is *interpreting* that information, giving it meaning and context, and so is *organizing* the information in a way that makes it more usable and comprehensible. And, finally, so is *disseminating* the information to others in ways that help them gain insight and do their jobs.

These five capabilities—retrieval, access, dissemination, interpretation, and organization—constitute the elements of information power. Together and separately, they enable people to lead and influence others through the effective deployment of information. The first letters of these words form a mnemonic, RADIO, although in discussing these capabilities I will follow a more logical sequence, starting with access.

Accessing Information

Having access to information is obviously a prerequisite to gaining information power, but the amount of power that access gives you depends on

The five elements of information power form the mnemonic RADIO: retrieval, access, dissemination, interpretation, and organization. Together and separately, these capabilities enable people to lead and influence others through the effective deployment of information.

the importance of the information and the degree of difficulty involved in accessing it. If you work in a business and everyone in your department received the same report you received, then the fact that you have it gives you no power within your department. The report may be important, but it's easy for your colleagues to access. However, if you are the only person with access to the report and the information is valuable, then having access to it gives you some information power. On the other hand, if you alone received the report but it is of little use to anyone else, then its triviality diminishes the information power you might otherwise have had.

Of course, importance is in the eye of the beholder. What I consider important may depend on how *timely* the information is. Knowing that my competitors will have trouble filling orders in Southeast Asia may allow me to sell more of my products in that region—but only if I have that information before my competitors can resolve their production or shipping problems. Importance also depends on the *utility* the information has. If a consultant to my industry has access to test reports showing which mix of additives would make the paint I manufacture more durable, then I may be able to improve the quality of my products and gain a competitive advantage in the marketplace. The consultant's information therefore has great utility for me, and that would increase his information power. Finally, the importance of information generally increases with its *scarcity*. If I am the only person with information that others would consider timely and useful, then my information power increases. The more people who know it, the less power I have. This last point deserves more attention because scarcity is a function of how public or private the information is. We can segment information into four broad categories that illustrate how the increasing difficulty and cost of access to information increase the power of those people who do have access. These four categories are public, deep public, private, and deep private, as shown in figure 7-1.

Figure 7-1. The informational pyramid.

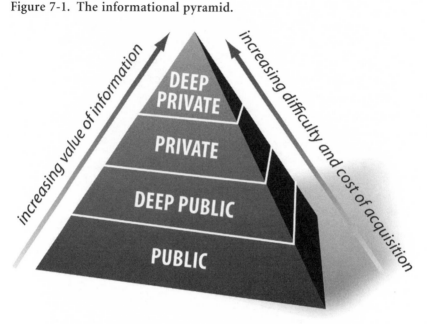

PUBLIC INFORMATION

Public information is the most accessible kind and is the least expensive to acquire; consequently, it has the least potential to build information power. It includes newspapers, magazines, books, encyclopedias, dictionaries, annual reports, catalogs, broadcast news reports, televised programs, government reports, easily accessible websites (e.g., CNN.com, MSNBC .com, and BBC.com), and anything else that most people can readily access if they wish to. Today, public information also includes anything accessible online through Google, Yahoo, and other Internet search engines, as well as information people have posted on sites like Facebook, MySpace, LinkedIn, and Plaxo. The amount of information accessible publicly today is many times what it was a decade ago, and it will likely be exponentially larger a decade from now.

The sheer volume of publicly available information means that, although anyone with reasonable facility *can* access this information, what they *do* access is but a small subset of everything available. There is simply too much information out there. Consequently, you can build information power with other people just by knowing how to access public information and having the time, energy, and interest to do it. As your colleagues discover your facility in information gathering, they may come to rely on your capabilities even though, if they developed the know-how and devoted the time to it, they would have access to the same information themselves. In effect, you become a convenience for them, and that gives you some information power.

Finally, access to publicly available information is limited by two important factors: geography and language. To some extent, the distribution of printed information is restricted to the region in which it is published. Even the largest libraries cannot collect all the printed materials published in the world every year. So if I live in London, I may not even be aware of most of the printed material published in France, even though much of it is publicly available. I may be able to find a copy of *Le Monde* at a newsstand in Victoria Station, but I probably wouldn't be able to find an informative guidebook on Place de la Bourse unless I travel to Bordeaux. Moreover, if I don't read French, I won't be able to understand French publications unless I can find a translation. The Internet overcomes some of the challenges of geographic access to information, but only a fraction of all printed information is online, and the language challenges remain.

DEEP PUBLIC INFORMATION

As I am defining it, public information is easily accessible and either free or available at low cost. *Deep public* information is public information that is more difficult to find or more expensive to access. In the business world, deep public information would include industry analyst reports available only by subscription. You can find *Fortune, Forbes, BusinessWeek,* the *Wall Street Journal,* the *Economist,* and other such publications on newsstands at relatively low cost, so they constitute public information, whereas *Value Line, Hoover's, S&P Industry Surveys,* and other sources like them are more costly and not available at newsstands, so they are deep public. Also falling into the deep public category are websites accessible only by subscription, special government publications that are more expensive because they are more costly to produce, and surveys or reports by industry associations or special interest groups that are typically available only to members or subscribers.

Deep public information is usually more comprehensive and insightful because developing it requires time, expertise, and a level of data analysis and interpretation that is beyond what purveyors of public information are capable of or interested in doing. For that reason, possessing deep public information usually gives you more information power than possessing public information, especially with people who have access only to the latter. Organizations with the buying power and staff to purchase and scrutinize deep public information therefore have an information advantage over organizations that don't make the investment, as well as ordinary people who lack the time or resources to do so.

PRIVATE INFORMATION

Private information is any information that is not published, broadcast, or posted on the Internet and is not intended to be publicly accessible. It includes private conversations, telephone calls, personal papers and letters, e-mail messages, internal company memos and reports, company proprietary information, and any other information that has limited, special distribution. Of course, in a large company with 200,000 or more global employees, the distribution of private company information could be fairly widespread within the company, but it is nonetheless private if it is not shared publicly or made available to people outside the organization. Private information has quite a range—from a private conversation between the CEO of a company and its head of marketing, for instance, to that company's employee directory, and from original research conducted in a pharmaceutical company to the research done by a university professor. These examples would obviously not have equal information power. The private conversation with the CEO would likely give the head of marketing considerably more information power than the global employee directory, which everyone else in the company presumably has access to.

Much of what happens in a company is private information, even in publicly traded companies, because of the need to prevent competitors from gathering intelligence that could weaken the company's competitive strengths in the marketplace. Private conversations between employees, internal problem-solving or product development meetings, task force discussions, and internal webcasts, podcasts, or e-mail announcements all serve to distribute private information on a limited basis, and the people who are privy to this information gain information power relative to those people who don't have such access. For this reason, the most powerful people in a company are often the ones who are best informed. In fact, if we could map all employees in a company and their relative access to private information distributed throughout the company—as well as their attendance at various meetings—we could develop a fairly accurate picture of the distribution of power within the organization.

The key to success in many professions, such as journalism, is developing and using private information to gain an exclusive advantage. In the 2009 film *State of Play,* for instance, investigative reporter Cal McAffrey

There are four levels of information access: public, deep public, private, and deep private. The deeper your level of access, the more information power you potentially have.

(played by Russell Crowe) uses a series of private sources to unravel a mystery involving a private security firm, a junior congressman, and the murder of his mistress. Ultimately, those private sources enable him and fellow reporter, Della Frye (played by Rachel McAdams), to break a front-page story no other newspaper has. Having access to private information can be a competitive differentiator—and a huge source of information power. Consequently, companies generally try to safeguard private information by compartmentalizing it (i.e., distributing it only to people who need to know it) or otherwise limiting its distribution, using patents or copyrights to protect it, and requiring confidentiality agreements from anyone who comes into contact with it.

Another form of private information is the proprietary research conducted by such firms as ACNielsen, J.D. Power and Associates, Gartner Group, Kantar Group, and a host of other market research firms. These firms commercialize private information by conducting research that yields insights on consumer interests, spending patterns, receptivity to advertisements, and other consumer behavior. They compile information using their own research processes and methods, and their clients gain access to it for a fee. However, anyone with the right skills and resources can conduct original research and create new knowledge and information, which remains private until it is published or sold and becomes more widely available and known.

DEEP PRIVATE INFORMATION

Deep private information is the most inaccessible kind. It consists of private information so hidden or protected that only people with special knowledge and access rights are able to see it. Deep private information is often so protected that most people don't know it exists. Government classified documents are an example. Classified documents contain information that is deliberately withheld from the public eye. Only people with security clearances are allowed to see it, and even they are only allowed to see information that is available at their clearance level (Confidential, Secret, or Top Secret) if they have a *need to know*. Some information is so sensitive that it is compartmentalized even further, which means that even with the appropriate clearance level, a person would have to be authorized to receive information in a particular compartment, and she would be excluded from seeing information in compartments for which she is not authorized.

Sometimes, a source of private information is so sensitive that even the name of the source is deep private information. During the *Washington Post*'s investigation of the Watergate cover-up, for example, Bob Woodward's deep private source was code-named, appropriately enough, "Deep Throat." For decades after that investigation, the source's real name was not revealed. Information from unnamed or confidential sources is often deep private. Communication intercepts from the U.S. government's National Security Agency fall into the category of deep private information, as is information gathered by spies for various intelligence agencies around the world. Access to deep private information typically gives someone tremendous insight but limited information power because the only people he can legally share it with are people with a similar level of access. Of course, people with access to deep private information sometimes do share it with unauthorized outsiders—and those guilty of breaches of confidentiality, including espionage, insider trading, or whistle-blowing, may suffer consequences—sometimes severe ones—for violating a trust.

In summary, access to information is a prerequisite to building information power. Except at the deep private level, where information may be highly restricted, the deeper your level of access, the greater your potential information power, particularly if you have access to important information others want or need to do their jobs. The most powerful information is timely, scarce, and has great utility—and the people with access to such information are likely to have tremendous information power.

Retrieving Information

Having access to information can give you some information power, but being able to retrieve the *right* information in the *right* form at the *right* time is another source of information power. Many people have access to information, especially public information, but there is an art and a science to information retrieval that not everyone has mastered. Those who have mastered it have more information power than those who haven't.

A Google search on virtually any topic is likely to return thousands, if not hundreds of thousands, of hits. This search engine tries to prioritize the hits by listing the most likely or compatible links first. Nonetheless, quickly finding the right information requires both knowledge about how search engines work and judgment about which links are most likely to bear fruit. Library searches are equally scientific (finding references, often in obscure places, and tracking them down) and artful (using instinct, experience, and judgment to focus on the most likely paths to follow, and recognizing the information when you see it). It's like the coast guard searching for a seaman who's gone overboard. Given an ocean of information sources available, it requires knowledge and skill (and sometimes luck) to locate the right information in a timely manner. People with the know-how to retrieve the right information in the right form at the right time are *resourceful,* in the sense of "full of resources," and this resourcefulness gives them information power because they are prized by those who lack that skill or don't have the patience to develop it.

People who are expert at reverse engineering develop information power through the art and science of information retrieval. An interesting example comes from two Tom Clancy novels. In *The Hunt for Red October,* the captain and officers of a Soviet Typhoon-class ballistic missile submarine try to defect with their ship, which has a revolutionary new magneto-hydrodynamic or "Caterpillar" drive, which makes it run so silently it is nearly impossible to detect by sonar. The Soviet captain recognizes that his ship could be used as a first-strike nuclear weapon and fears that it will upset the balance of power and lead to a nuclear war, so he chooses to defect. At the end of the novel, after much drama and suspense, the ship is secretly turned over to the American Navy. Then in Clancy's *The Cardinal of the Kremlin,* readers learn that the *Red October* submarine has been successfully reverse-engineered by American naval engineers.[2]

▶ PROFILES *in* POWER

PETER PRONOVOST, MD, PH.D.

He has the potential to become one of the most influential physicians of our time. His power derives from his knowledge (he has both a medical degree and a doctorate in clinical investigation), his expressiveness (he is a frequent speaker and prolific writer), his attraction (he has been called inspiring, enthusiastic, and engaging), and his character—but most of all, his power comes from his mastery of information. His studies on patient safety have already saved

Photo: Johns Hopkins University School of Medicine. Used with permission.

thousands of lives and millions of dollars. If his insights were adopted in hospitals throughout the world, the savings in lives and healthcare costs would be incalculable.

Dr. Peter Pronovost received an MD from the Johns Hopkins School of Medicine in Baltimore and a Ph.D. from the Johns Hopkins Bloomberg School of Public Health, where he studied intensive care units in Maryland and showed that having an intensive care specialist on the staff reduced death rates dramatically. Today, he is a practicing anesthesiologist and critical care physician at Johns Hopkins University, a professor at Johns Hopkins Medicine's Department of Anesthesiology and Critical Care Medicine and Department of Surgery, a professor at the Bloomberg School of Public Health, and medical director for the Center for Innovation in Quality Patient Care. In 2003, he established the university's Quality and Safety Research Group to study and promote patient safety, and he led a study of hospital-caused infections in intensive care units (ICUs) in Michigan.

During this study, Pronovost and his colleagues observed doctors as they put central venous catheters into patients. Although guidelines existed for this procedure, they discovered that doctors frequently skipped at least one safety step. So he created a simple, five-item checklist for reducing infections when doctors inserted these catheters. According to this checklist, doctors should:

1. Wash their hands with soap.
2. Clean the patient's skin with chlorhexidine antiseptic.
3. Put sterile drapes over the entire patient.
4. Wear a sterile mask, hat, gown, and gloves.
5. Put a sterile dressing over the catheter site.[3]

Although these steps were well known, they weren't being followed consistently, so Pronovost also convinced the ICUs in his study group to have nurses monitor doctors while performing this procedure and to stop them if they missed a step (ICU administrators agreed to back up the nurses if doctors were resistant). According to the *New Yorker,* "The results were so dramatic that they weren't sure whether to believe them: the ten-day line-infection rate went from 11 percent to zero. So they followed patients for fifteen more months. Only two line infections occurred during the entire period." By the Pronovost team's estimates, in this ICU alone, consistently following the checklist prevented forty-three infections and eight deaths, saving the hospital $2 million.[4] In the eighteen months after the checklist was introduced, the infection rate throughout all of Michigan's ICUs dropped by 66 percent, with estimated savings of 1,500 lives and $100 million. They sustained these results for nearly four years.

Pronovost is now an adviser to the World Health Organization's World Alliance for Patient Safety. In 2004, he won the John M. Eisenberg Patient Safety Award for research and was awarded a MacArthur Fellowship (called a "genius grant") in 2008. This accomplished researcher and physician has built a solid power base and become one of the most influential people in his field. He has a number of strong personal power sources, but information is the backbone of research. What distinguishes Peter Pronovost is the information power he has accumulated through research and then deployed in a way that has saved lives and lowered healthcare costs. We can only hope that his influence extends even further.

What We Can Learn from Dr. Peter Pronovost

1. *The extraordinary value of information gleaned from observation.* Pronovost and his team gained their insights on the key reasons for infections by observing doctors in the field and then used that information to make a profound difference. The lesson for business leaders? Ask yourself what you or your team can learn from observing your operations (e.g., purchasing, manufacturing, retailing, distribution, safety, HR, customer service). We often are so immersed in day-to-day operations and management that we neglect to step back and carefully and objectively observe what's going on: what's working and what isn't, what could be shortened or simplified or made more durable or better. Despite Six Sigma, quality improvement, and other initiatives you might have others conducting in your company, there is value in stepping back yourself and being a careful observer of what's happening.

2. *The impact information can have when it is applied in the field.* When the five-item checklist and improved monitoring procedure devised by Pronovost and his team was rigorously applied to Michigan ICUs, the result was so impressive that people found it difficult to believe the magnitude of the savings in lives and dollars. The lesson? Imagine if you could rigorously apply a simple procedural fix in one of your business operations and save your company $100 million in one year. Of course, the challenge is getting widespread buy-in and ensuring that the procedures are followed rigorously, but the results can be profound. This is not even a hidden opportunity; it's right out there in the open.

3. *The power of organizing and acting on information that is already readily available.* His study of doctors in ICUs did not result in startlingly new information. In fact, the items on his safety checklist were already well known. They just weren't being followed consistently. The lesson for us? The information that gives you power need not necessarily be groundbreaking or new. Organizing and acting on the information can build extraordinary power and achieve outstanding business results.

Interpreting Information

A lawyer working on a big case reviews thousands of pages of interviews, evidence, documents, and legal precedents and begins to draft a coherent story for the jury. A scientist in New Guinea, puzzled by the large incidence of a devastating disease in a particular tribe, studies how the tribe lives and begins to notice which people become ill with the disease and which don't. An investment analyst examines reams of economic and industry data and reports on the performance of many companies and identifies which companies he believes will outperform the market during the coming months. In each of these examples, someone develops power through the interpretation of information. It should be evident that interpreting information can be one of the greatest ways to build information power, partly because the interpreter may be the only person to develop those insights and partly because the interpretations themselves can have enormous impact.

Albert Einstein won a Nobel Prize and transformed our understanding of the universe by correctly interpreting information that many other physicists possessed but failed to comprehend as he had. D. Carleton Gajdusek shared the Nobel Prize in medicine for his discovery of how kuru, a fatal disease of the brain, was transmitted among the Fore people of Papua New Guinea. Warren Buffett made a fortune for himself and others invested in Berkshire Hathaway through his astute analysis of the stock market and ability to discern value. Legendary film critic Pauline Kael helped shape our understanding of the cinema through her thoughtful interpretation of films; and Herodotus, Sima Qian, Ibn Abd-el-Hakem, Jacques Barzun, Edward Gibbon, Johan Huizinga, and Isaiah Berlin have enlightened us with their insightful interpretations of history. It would be fair to say that much of human understanding derives from our accumulated interpretations of information.

What gives someone power is the ability to select the right information from the mass of what's accessible and then grasp it, analyze it, find patterns within it, summarize it, reframe it, and create meaning out of what would otherwise be noise. We all make meaning of our experience, so each of us has the potential to generate interpretive information power, but some people are obviously more expert at it, and they command our attention. They give information relevance, context, and meaning. They educate us, enlighten us, inspire us, and model how to make sense of the world— and this gives them tremendous information power.

Organizing Information

The volume of information available today has necessitated the invention of knowledge management systems, which are technology-based systems (hardware and software) for organizing information in ways that facilitate information organization, storage, retrieval, and dissemination. These systems are the high-tech equivalents of card catalogs, filing systems, Day-Timers, calendars, to-do lists, and other devices people have used in the past to organize information, and they are important enough in organizations to be an instrumental part of competitive strategy. Dictionaries, catalogs, and encyclopedias are some outcomes of people organizing information to make it not only easily accessible but more usable and memorable. Having technology to assist in organizing information is obviously advantageous, and whether you are taking a high-tech or low-tech approach, being able to organize information is a strong potential source of information power.

Interpreting information is the art of extracting meaning from raw information; organizing it is the art of *arranging* the information (including raw data and interpretations) in a form or structure that makes it more useful. For example, Korn/Ferry's Leadership Architect, which I introduced in chapter 5, is a competency model that is based on more than two decades of research on leadership effectiveness.[5] This model consists of a library of sixty-seven competencies and nineteen career stallers, organized into eight factors and twenty-six clusters. The competencies represent interpretations of research data, and the library structure is an organization of the information that makes a complex subject—leadership—more comprehensible.

Disseminating Information

Finally, people gain information power through the dissemination of information to other people who need it in a timely and accurate way. Consider an investment adviser. Her power comes from having access to the right investment data, from being able to retrieve it in the right form at the right time, from interpreting the information to give it meaning and context, and from organizing the information in a way that benefits her clients. But if she is unable to disseminate the information to clients in a timely and effective manner, then her power is essentially wasted. She must be able to keep her clients informed so that they can act at the right times. She does this by sending them monthly market reports, reviewing their investment strategies and portfolios with them periodically, and contacting them when she has urgent information they need.

Her plan for disseminating information to her clients is part of her client service strategy. If she executes it well, they feel informed and are able to make timely decisions about their investments. Because she has an effective plan for disseminating information, she gains information power. However, if she is lax in keeping her clients informed, if they feel like they don't know what's happening with their investments, or if they receive better and more frequent investment information from some other source, she is likely to lose information power, and it could cost her the accounts. When people trust that you will keep them informed by delivering timely and accurate information that is important to them, you gain information power. You lose it if you go silent.

I classify information as an organizational power source because the bandwidth and resources required to develop strong information power are normally available only to people working within organizations. The correlate in personal power would be knowledge. People working in organizations build their information power by increasing their access to information, developing their skills at information retrieval, organizing information so that its structure helps others access and understand it, and disseminating information in the right form to the right people at the right time. Lastly, and most importantly, they build information power by interpreting data and giving it context and meaning. People who create unique insights by interpreting information are invaluable to others and tend to be highly influential. This is the most effective way to maximize information power.

▶ PROFILES *in* POWER

FAREED ZAKARIA

Few people today have developed and used information power as much as Fareed Zakaria, who has thrust himself onto center stage as an author, editor, speaker, and political affairs host on television. Born in India, he was educated in Mumbai's Cathedral and John Connon School, a private school

recognized as one of the finest in the country. He later received a BA from Yale and a Ph.D. in political science from Harvard. At twenty-eight, he became the youngest managing editor of *Foreign Affairs* in the journal's history. Then, in October 2000, he was named editor of *Newsweek International,* which has a global readership of 25 million. He writes regular columns for *Newsweek* and the *Washington Post* and has had articles published in the *Wall Street Journal,* the *New York Times,* the *New Republic,* and the *New Yorker.* In addition to his columns, he has written or edited four

Photo by Joe Kohen/WireImage.

books: *The American Encounter: The United States and the Making of the Modern World* (1997, coeditor), *From Wealth to Power: The Unusual Origins of America's World Role* (1998), *The Future of Freedom* (2003), and *The Post-American World* (2008). The latter two were bestsellers and helped establish Zakaria as a provocative commentator on history, geopolitics, and changes in the global balance of social, economic, and political power. He got his start on television as host of a weekly news show for PBS called *Foreign Exchange with Fareed Zakaria*. For six years, he was also an analyst for *ABC News* and *This Week with George Stephanopoulos*. Most recently, he has become the host of a weekly political affairs program on CNN called *Fareed Zakaria GPS* (Global Public Square), where he regularly interviews national leaders, prominent cabinet officers, legislators, and experts in fields related to politics, economics, and history.

On the air, Zakaria demonstrates his intellect, eloquence, and deep knowledge of his subject matter. He is a thoughtful and engaging speaker with the manner of a kind but demanding professor whose mastery of the topic produces questions that invariably provoke answers more revealing than the interviewee may have intended them to be. The words to describe him have included shrewd, well connected, absorbing, articulate, intelligent, and penetrating. *Esquire* named him one of the most important people of the twenty-first century, and *Foreign Policy* and *Prospect* magazines listed him as one of the 100 leading public intellectuals in the world in 2007.

Zakaria has numerous power sources: knowledge, expressiveness, attraction, character, and (some) history because of the virtual history relationship he has with many readers and viewers. His positions as an editor and television show host also give him considerable role power. But two of his greatest sources of power are his network (he knows a great number of important people around the world) and information. He is like the roundabout on an information highway. With his connections and his roles, he has significantly greater access to information than most people. He is an expert at retrieving the right information, organizing it effectively, and disseminating it through print and broadcast media. However, one of his greatest strengths in the use of information is his ability to interpret what he sees and offer insightful commentaries on the worlds of politics, economics, and history. Not everyone agrees with Zakaria's analyses or conclusions, but there is no doubt that he is well informed—and highly influential because of it.

What We Can Learn from Fareed Zakaria

1. *Information power can substantiate your arguments and persuade others to accept your position.* Zakaria's access to and command of information makes him persuasive and compelling—and intimidating to any interviewee who is less prepared than he is. The lesson for business leaders? Information can give you the high ground in any meeting, discussion, or debate with your boss, peers, direct reports, and customers. Your persuasiveness increases to the extent that you provide

verifiable information that substantiates your arguments. Zakaria leads from a position of intellectual strength built on a deep foundation of information. So, be well informed, be prepared with information that will bolster your position, and use information appropriately to prove your points and inform others you wish to convince.

2. *Network and information power can be complementary.* Besides being well informed, Zakaria is well connected, and the two power sources feed on one another. People are attracted to his network because he is knowledgeable, and the people in his network bring additional valuable information to him. For Zakaria, network and information form a virtuous circle. The lesson for us? Make yourself so well informed that you can use information as one reason people are attracted to join your network, but also try to connect with people who can bring fresh insights and information to you. I have such a relationship with Ken DeMeuse, research director for Lominger, a Korn/Ferry Company. Besides being a pleasant companion, Ken is an intelligent, well-informed colleague who offers numerous insights into leadership and assessment (among other topics). Likewise, I bring some fresh insights and information to him. We enhance each other's network and information powers through a reciprocal collegial relationship.

INFORMATION AS A POWER DRAIN

I pointed out in chapter 1 that knowledge power can become a power drain if what you know is inaccurate, and this is true of information as well. If your information is wrong, if it is unreliable or biased, people will learn not to trust it, diminishing your information power, which is another way of saying that you will lose your credibility as a source. Ann Coulter (profiled in chapter 4) is an example. The "facts" she cites in making her arguments are often not factual at all, or reflect only one side of the story. While she's speaking, it can be difficult to distinguish between the truth and her polemical version of the truth, but when you examine her arguments in the cold light of reality, her distortions, misrepresentations, and omissions become painfully evident, and you learn not to trust the information she offers.[6] In fairness, Coulter is not the only public person who deserves this criticism. With virtually anyone who takes a strong political or philosophical stance and then tries to prove the point by offering factual evidence, you need to distrust the information until you can independently verify it. Ultimately, Coulter and others like her are propagandists. They mold information into a shape that fits their preconceived message. When accurate and conflicting information comes to light, and it's clear that some of the "facts" they use to support their arguments are distorted, misleading, or falsified, reasonable people learn not to trust them. A source of information is only as credible as the accuracy of the information she provides.

The old adage that you can't believe everything you read is perhaps truer today than ever before. At the start of this chapter, I mentioned the wiki phenomenon, which is the emergence and rapid growth of online, collaborative, information-sharing websites like Wikipedia, which is a free encyclopedia. As I write this, Wikipedia claims to have 12 million articles (nearly 3 million in English) written by volunteers around the world. Critics complain that Wikipedia's uncredentialed contributions have questionable reliability and accuracy and have identified instances where information on Wikipedia has been false, unverified, or biased. They note how easy it is for people with an agenda or a commercial interest to slant Wikipedia articles toward their interests and how Wikipedia's open access essentially undermines the trust users might have in the information the site provides. Nonetheless, Wikipedia and other online, collaborative sites like it are a fact of twenty-first-century life. We are likely to see them grow larger and stronger in the decades to come, so that when people try to influence you and cite Wikipedia or the equivalent as their source of information, you need to be thoughtful about their sources before accepting their arguments.

WHAT THE RESEARCH TELLS US ABOUT INFORMATION POWER

My research shows many parallels between resource and information power. Having high information power nearly doubles your capacity to lead and influence others, but of all the power sources it is the second-weakest in terms of its ability to boost your leadership power (the weakest overall is resource power). What does this mean? It likely reflects that information power is not particularly difficult to grow and having the greatest information power in an organization will not boost your overall leadership power as much as being rated high in most other power sources. Information just doesn't have the leverage that most other power sources do.

Interestingly, there is a strong correlation between high information power and high ratings on reputation and knowledge. In other words, being known as a source of information or an excellent interpreter of information tends to elevate what people in the organization think of you, and it convinces them that you are highly knowledgeable and skilled. However, the reverse is not true. High knowledge power is not strongly correlated with information power, so knowledge and information are not equivalent sources of power. You can be very knowledgeable without having great access to and control of information, but having great access to information does make you appear more knowledgeable.

People rated high in information power are significantly more effective at explaining their positions, using logic to offer rational arguments, and backing up their arguments with facts. People like Dr. Peter Pronovost and Fareed Zakaria, who have high information power, are also viewed as strong role models. Their mastery of information would appear to make them more effective and attractive teachers, mentors, and coaches. Furthermore, and as we would expect, their possession of so much information gives them the authority to legitimize their positions. When a person like Fareed Zakaria cites information to support his ideas, he is using the authority implicit in facts to influence his readers or listeners. They are more likely to accept what he is saying because he has the information to back it up. I should note that Ann Coulter does the same thing, but many of her "facts" are either bogus or slanted to support her political objectives. When you spout facts, it is important that they are verifiable and as unbiased as you can make them. Otherwise, you can quickly lose trust.

People rated high in information power also tend to be highly skilled at speaking conversationally, using a compelling tone of voice, asking insightful questions, building rapport and trust, building consensus, negotiating, and taking the initiative to show others how to do things. Their command of information appears to boost their self-confidence, arm them with the facts needed to be more persuasive in conversations and other kinds of interactions, and give them the insight to ask compelling questions. Conversely, people rated low in information are somewhat at a loss and have to rely on social methods of leadership and influence to get their way. Intriguingly, one of the highest-rated skills for people rated low in information power is their willingness to do favors for others (a skill that is typically rated low across the board). This suggests that they use favor granting as a way of ingratiating themselves with others. Typically, their strongest sources of power are character, attraction, and history, so their basic leadership strategy is to say, in effect, "I would like you to follow my lead because I'm honest, you know me, and like me." This may be an effective strategy sometimes, but it is limiting. Part of the power of having good access to and control of information is that it opens up many other possibilities in how you approach leadership and influence. Information power gives you a much bigger toolbox.

GLOBAL DIFFERENCES IN INFORMATION POWER

Information power is more important in some cultures than in others, but the distribution of average scores between the highest-rated country (South Korea, 4.49) and the lowest-rated (Finland, 3.83) is barely significant (0.66 on a scale of 1 to 5). This suggests that information as a power source has about equal importance in every culture around the world. Nonetheless, here are the distributions of average power source ratings by country. The lists are arranged alphabetically.

COUNTRIES WHERE INFORMATION POWER IS HIGHER

Australia, China, Colombia, Czech Republic, Germany, Hong Kong, India, Ireland, Italy, Netherlands, Singapore, South Korea, Switzerland, Taiwan, United States of America

COUNTRIES WHERE INFORMATION POWER IS AVERAGE

Austria, Belgium, Brazil, Canada, Denmark, France, Indonesia, Japan, Malaysia, New Zealand, Pakistan, Poland, Portugal, Turkey, United Kingdom

COUNTRIES WHERE INFORMATION POWER IS LOWER

Argentina, Chile, Finland, Greece, Hungary, Israel, Mexico, Norway, Peru, Russia, South Africa, Spain, Sweden, Thailand, Venezuela

For more information on our global research on power and influence, and in-depth profiles of each of the forty-five countries studied, see www .kornferryinstitute.com, www.theelementsofpower.com, or www.terryr bacon.com.

KEY CONCEPTS

1. In this Age of Information, having access to information others don't readily possess can be a tremendous source of leadership and influence power.

2. The five elements of information power form the mnemonic RADIO: retrieval, access, dissemination, interpretation, and organization. Together and separately, these capabilities enable people to lead and influence others through the effective deployment of information.

3. Having access to information is a prerequisite to gaining information power, but just how much power access gives you depends on the importance of the information and the degree of difficulty involved in accessing it.

4. There are four levels of information access: public, deep public, private, and deep private. The deeper your level of access, the more information power you potentially have.

5. People with the know-how to retrieve the right information in the right form at the right time are *resourceful,* in the sense of "full of resources." They are prized by those who lack that skill or don't have the patience to develop it.

6. Interpreting information can be one of the greatest ways to build information power, partly because the interpreter may be the only person to develop those insights and partly because the interpretations themselves can have enormous impact.

7. Sources of information are only as credible as the accuracy of the information they provide.

8. Information power is closely correlated with resource power. People who master information are considered to be authorities, which enhances their ability to be persuasive.

CHALLENGES FOR READERS

1. Information can be an extraordinary source of power. Think about how you have seen others gain power through their access to and control of information. What can you learn from them?

2. I use the mnemonic RADIO to help readers remember the five elements of information power: retrieval, access, dissemination, inter-pretation, and organization. How would you rate your information power in each of these five areas? How much *access* to valuable infor-mation do you have? How capable are you at *retrieving* the right infor-

mation, in the right form, at the right time? How effective are you at *interpreting* information? *Organizing* it? *Disseminating* it in a timely and focused manner?

3. What could you do in each of the five RADIO elements to increase your information power? (For help on this challenge, see chapter 12.)

4. There are four levels of access to information: public, deep public, private, and deep private. Which levels of access do you primarily have? What important sources, public or private, are you missing? If you could develop and exploit five more sources of information, at any level, which five would most help you build information power and become more influential?

5. Information masters are particularly effective at interpreting information. Reflect on some people you know (or know of) who are experts at interpreting information. How does it give them leadership and influence power? What's interesting about interpretation is that you don't have to have generated the information yourself. You simply need access to it. Are you missing an opportunity to examine some information you already have access to and provide an insightful interpretation of it for other people?

6. Information power can become a power drain if someone provides inaccurate information or offers a misleading or inaccurate interpretation. Have you ever known anyone who fit this description? What effect did it have on that person's ability to lead or influence others?

CHAPTER 8

IT'S WHO YOU KNOW

The Power of Networking

THE OLD ADAGE ABOUT SUCCESS IS THAT IT DEPENDS LESS ON *WHAT* YOU know than *who* you know. Being connected to other people, especially other people who are also well connected, is a strong source of leadership and influence power. Networks extend a person's reach. They facilitate the flow and range of information and influence. They enhance the social capital of active network members through reciprocal respect, admiration, favor granting, and collaboration. If you are a member of a large organization, no matter what role you play, your power will be limited unless you can develop and sustain a strong network of allies and supporters, including colleagues, superiors, direct reports, partners, and customers. No one knows this better than Ana D., an *über*-Connector who may be one of the best networked professionals in the country.

We are social creatures. Our world works because of the many ways we interact with and influence one another. We live and work in webs of human communities, large and small. These webs are our social networks. Some of them are formal, like the organizational structure of a company, which defines who relates to whom and how people are formally connected. But most of our networks are informal, based on the people we meet or work with most often, the people we like, enjoy being with, and feel the greatest satisfaction from knowing. The foundation of these informal networks is a mutual interest in staying in touch, and our informal networks grow as we meet more people outside of our immediate circle of contacts and develop new relationships. Within both kinds of networks, formal and informal, we have strong ties to some people—those we know best and interact with most frequently—and weak ties to others with whom we don't interact as often but still maintain contact.

People like Ana D. are facile at building and sustaining connections with other people. Genuinely interested in people, they are skilled at reaching out to others, building relationships, and sustaining many connections.

Their networks are usually large and dynamic because they interact with people continually. They are like the Grand Central Stations of their networks—the hubs where many other people connect. Unusually resourceful and well informed, they are the "go-to" people when someone seeks information, wants help getting something done, or needs access to someone else the well-connected person knows. Because they occupy such a central position in their social networks, and because they are so well connected with key people in other networks, they have an enhanced capacity to lead and influence others based on their network power.

Ana was born in Brazil, where family is the dominant social structure and building relationships is virtually an art form. She received an MBA from the Kellogg Graduate School of Management at Northwestern University, a master's degree in economics from Pontificia Universidade Catolica in Rio de Janeiro, and a juris doctor in international law from Universidade do Estado do Rio de Janeiro. She began her career as an attorney in Brazil and taught microeconomics, economic theory, and international finance in Brazil and the United States. For the past two decades, she has worked as a management consultant for five different firms (for privacy's sake identified only by letter) and has held a number of leadership roles. At this writing, she is an executive vice president of one of the world's largest talent management firms and CEO of its leadership and talent consulting business.

Ana lives in Chicago, is married and has three children, and considers herself part of seventeen social networks. Yes, you read that correctly, *seventeen*. They are (1) her family in Brazil, (2) childhood friends in Brazil, (3) colleagues and clients with whom she worked in Brazil as an attorney, (4) business and graduate school classmates, (5) firm A colleagues, (6) firm B colleagues, (7) firm C colleagues, (8) firm D colleagues, (9) firm E colleagues, (10) her management consulting clients for the past two decades, (11) members of two local boards she belongs to, (12) PTA members, (13) her husband's professional colleagues and their spouses, (14) her local tennis team, (15) members of her current global firm, (16) members of the business unit she currently leads, and (17) people she knows in the Chicago business community.[1]

As mentioned earlier, people have both strong and weak ties to others in their social networks. American sociologist Mark Granovetter elaborated upon this concept in a seminal 1973 paper entitled "The Strength of Weak Ties." He noted that strong ties exist between people who live, work, and play together. These are the people we know best and communicate with most often. Because we share ideas so frequently, over time we tend not only to think alike but to become similar in other ways. Weak ties exist with people we know but interact with less frequently. I would have strong ties with my parents, close friends, and some colleagues I work with every day and feel close to, but weak ties with cousins I talk to just once or twice a year, customers I see occasionally, and colleagues I know but may not interact with more than once a week.

According to Granovetter, the strength of our social networks lies principally in the number of weak ties we have. They are greater sources of new information and different perspectives. They keep us from being isolated and provincial, which could happen if we interacted only with people who are strongly tied to us. As he notes, "Individuals with few weak ties will be deprived of information from distant parts of the social system and will be confined to the provincial news and views of their close friends. This deprivation will not only insulate them from the latest ideas and fashions but may put them in a disadvantaged position in the labor market, where advancement can depend . . . on knowing about appropriate job openings at just the right time."[2]

The strength of our social networks lies principally in the number of weak ties we have. They are sources of new information and different perspectives, which keep us from being isolated and provincial.

Creativity and innovation are often fostered through weak ties. Information is spread more rapidly to more people through weak ties, which is why if I want to have greater influence, I must have weak ties to a broad number of people, many of whom also have many weak ties to people in other networks. Social networks with a considerable number of weak ties have low density, whereas networks with mostly strong ties among its members are high density. Information may flow rapidly within a high-density network, but it is confined mostly to that clique. What makes viral marketing a potent force are numerous low-density networks connected to each other by "bridge" members. People need both strong and weak ties in their social networks because each confers a different advantage. As Granovetter says, "Weak ties provide people with access to information and resources beyond those available in their own social circle; but strong ties have greater motivation to be of assistance and are typically more easily available."[3] With this in mind, I asked Ana D. to identify her networks, as well as the number of people in them, and indicate whether she had strong or weak ties to each of those people. A chart of her social networks is shown in figure 8-1.

Apart from the sheer number of people in her networks (more than 1,260), what's remarkable is the high percentage of weak ties (96 percent). By her own reckoning, Ana has strong ties with 54 people (more than half of whom are family members or people she is currently working with), but she has weak ties with approximately 1,200 people that span a long professional career with six firms, numerous client engagements, and many local business and social contacts. Her networks link her to many people who are themselves linked to other people, so she can reach across many organizations, locations, and functions when she wants to share an observation, get ideas from others, generate interest in a new initiative, get feedback on an approach to a problem, or get people excited about something she's doing. She can reach many influential people quickly, and they can reach her, knowing that she is a hub of knowledge, resources, information, and connection to the right people inside and outside her current organization. That's network power.

In *The Tipping Point*, Malcolm Gladwell writes about Connectors, people who seem to know everyone and are capable of making many connections. Connectors are "people whom all of us can reach in only a few steps because, for one reason or another, they manage to occupy many different worlds and subcultures and niches."[4] Connectors are powerful because when they become enthused about an idea, book, company, or product, they can convey their enthusiasm to many other people who occupy those different worlds, subcultures, and niches—and that enthusiasm can grow contagiously as some of the people the Connectors reached spread the word throughout their own networks. This viral communication flow through social networks linked to each other is precisely what happens when someone e-mails a joke, inspirational story, or interesting photograph to friends on the Internet, and those friends pass it along to their friends, and so on. Most people learned of the singing phenomenon Susan Boyle this way. She was the frumpy forty-seven-year-old Scottish woman who appeared on *Britain's Got Talent* and dazzled the judges and the audience with her powerful rendition of the song "I Dreamed a Dream." Within just five days of her appearance on the television program, the YouTube video of her performance had had more than 20 million viewings. (Within a year, there were more than 300 million viewings of this video.) Many people, like me, heard about Susan Boyle when a friend

Figure 8-1. Ana D.'s social networks.

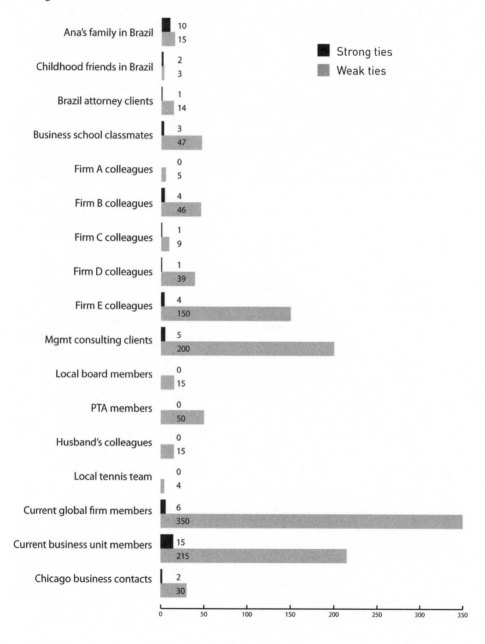

e-mailed the link to that YouTube video. That's the power of networking, too.

The challenge facing *über*-Connectors like Ana D. is maintaining all those weak ties over time. Clearly, if you neglect a weak tie for an extended period, the connection you had with that person will become less adhesive and will eventually dissolve. I asked Ana how she sustains 1,200 weak ties, and she said that, for her, every relationship is a personal one. She doesn't like to interact with people on a superficial level, so the quality of her interactions is more important to her than the frequency of them. She sustains ties with the people she enjoys by trying to have quality interactions with them as often as possible—and even if many of those personal interactions may be only once or twice a year, she tries to make every contact a rewarding one. Having quality interactions with the people you know is how you build your social networks, because when they enjoy interacting with you, they refer other people to you whom they believe will also benefit from knowing you.

> When Connectors become excited about an idea, book, com-
> pany, or product, they can convey their excitement to the
> people in their networks, who in turn pass it on throughout
> their networks, and so on. This is network power at work.

It helps that Ana D. is an off-the-charts extrovert with a passion for connecting with people. It also helps that her professional position requires many interactions with many people, that she loves the work, and that she has an extraordinary amount of energy. Even so, she admits that it is sometimes exhausting because she is continually contacting people. To maintain her network, she has to be deliberate about staying in touch with the people she wants to remain an active part of her world. Part of her network power comes from her capacity to proliferate ideas and to garner support from a broad number of people quickly, and part of it comes from other people's belief that being part of her network will enhance their ability to get results. As Gladwell notes, "It isn't just the case that the closer someone is to a Connector, the more powerful or the wealthier or the more opportunities he or she gets. It's also the case that the closer an idea or a product comes to a Connector, the more power and opportunity it has as well."[5]

▶   PROFILES *in* POWER

RAHM EMANUEL

When Congressman Marion Berry of Arkansas learned that Rahm Emanuel had been named as Barack Obama's chief of staff, he said, "Of all the people I've known in my life, he was born to be chief of staff to a great president. He's young and tough and smart, and can be mean when necessary.

He doesn't waste energy on foolish things."[6] It's been called the toughest job in Washington, so demanding that most chiefs of staff don't last an entire four-year term. The president may be at the center of power in the executive branch of the U.S. government, but the chief of staff manages that center.

Among his many duties, the chief of staff selects, organizes, and manages the White House staff; controls access to the president; manages the flow of information to the president; and manages the president's schedule. His principal role is to protect the president's interests, and in so doing he also confers with members of Congress and the judiciary, the military, special interest groups, foreign dignitaries, and officials throughout the president's cabinet and administration to advance the president's agenda. Because he controls access to the president, as well as the information the president receives, and because he works with people at the highest levels inside and outside the government who have business with the president, the chief of staff has enormous network power. He is the nexus of one of the most important and powerful networks in the world.

Anyone occupying this office is granted extraordinary role and information power. Strong network power emerges from both that power base and the chief of staff's role as gatekeeper to the president. But Rahm Emanuel had strong network power long before he was named chief of staff to President Obama. Emanuel was born in Chicago in 1959 and studied ballet as a boy. He was talented enough to earn a scholarship to the Joffrey Ballet but went instead to Sarah Lawrence College for a BA in liberal arts, and then to Northwestern University, where he earned a master's degree in speech and communication in 1985. Even before graduation, he began working in Illinois politics, first for Chicagoan David Robinson's congressional campaign and later for Paul Simon's 1984 campaign for the U.S. Senate. For his work in these campaigns, Emanuel began to develop a reputation as a tough, political street fighter and savvy fund-raiser. He was a senior adviser and chief fund-raiser for Richard M. Daley's campaign for mayor of Chicago in 1989 and raised more than $7 million—a phenomenal amount at that time.

Photo by Justin Sullivan/Getty Images.

Then, in 1992, he became the finance director for Bill Clinton's successful presidential primary campaign. Clinton later gave Emanuel substantial credit for the win: "He was then a little more brash and less polished than now, but he clearly had loads of ability and drive," Clinton said. "My first impression was, 'This guy is going to help us win.' And he did. I doubt we could have done it without him."[7] In 2002, he ran for office himself and won a seat in the U.S. House of Representatives from the Fifth Congressional District in Illinois. He was reelected twice when, in 2006, Emanuel was named chairman of the House Democratic Caucus, which made him the fourth-ranking House Democrat. During that year, he also chaired the Democratic Congressional Campaign Committee (DCCC) and is widely credited with the wins that gave the Democrats control of the House.

Emanuel is a close friend of David Axelrod, chief strategist for Obama's 2008 presidential campaign. Initially, Emanuel supported Hillary Clinton but did not endorse either candidate until Obama had won the primaries. Because of his connections in the Illinois Democratic Party machine (which Obama came from), his strong tie with Axelrod, his abundant talent as an organizer, and his web of connections throughout Washington, Emanuel was a natural choice as Obama's chief of staff. Few people in the federal government are as well networked as he is, and he uses his connections to lobby for support for the president's policies, to gain the allies needed to advance the president's agenda, and to ensure that the right people have the president's ear at the right time. He has been nicknamed "Rahmbo" (even his mother has called him that) for his profane, aggressive, take-no-prisoners style, although he is reportedly mellowing in a new role that requires finesse as well as connections. His key sources of power are role, knowledge, history, information, reputation, and a vast network that he manages with consummate skill.

What We Can Learn from Rahm Emanuel

1. *The importance of early and continuous network building.* Rahm Emanuel did not suddenly become a strong networker when he was named White House chief of staff. He's been a network builder from his earliest years. The lesson for business leaders? Building and tending your networks is a career-long activity. Your networks won't suddenly spring to life when you are promoted to a role that has many positional connections. You need to be building connections with people from your earliest adult years.

2. *The importance of position as a network attractor.* Rahm Emanuel has built powerful networks partly on the basis of his role as a presidential chief of staff. He would still be well networked if he'd remained in Congress, but the extraordinary network power he has today is unquestionably due to the nature of his current role. The lesson for the rest of us? In every role in business, the position itself will invite or demand certain connections. There will be some natural network connections—people and other functions whose work either feeds or depends

upon the work your function does—as well as formal connections within the hierarchy of any organization. Use all of these connections, but try to forge even stronger bonds with the people you are formally connected to. Make yourself an important person to know by sharing information and by demonstrating cooperation and collaboration, mutual support and respect, and business results.

SOCIAL NETWORKING ONLINE

Are social networking sites like Facebook, Twitter, LinkedIn, MySpace, and Plaxo useful in building and sustaining the kinds of social networks that enhance your network power? The answer is yes and no. Network power derives from the social capital we build as we develop relationships with other people. Social capital is a combination of attraction, need, and reciprocal obligation. I am able to build social capital with another person when we like or are attracted to one another (for whatever reason), when it serves both of our interests to maintain contact (when we have mutual need), and when we both reciprocate the other's gestures and favors. To maintain that social capital, we have to communicate from time to time and give something of ourselves that the other person values, such as sharing advice, opinions, favors, recipes, or jokes. Mutual trust is essential, as are respect, tolerance, responsiveness, judgment, and good listening.

It is challenging to build this kind of social capital without having some face-to-face contact, although some people have done it through letters, e-mails, blogs, and personal pages on sites like Facebook and MySpace. However, to build a robust social network like Ana D.'s—with some strong and many weak ties—and do it entirely online is probably impossible unless you have some other power source, such as a strong reputation, that attracts people to your network. (But, then, why would you want to sustain a tie with them in the first place unless they also have a strong reputation or some other power source that attracts you?) Once a relationship has been established, however, nurturing it through e-mail, tweets, blogs, and phone calls is not only possible but often necessary, given the physical distances that separate people in the kinds of social networks many people have today.

Online social networking sites are beneficial because they offer another channel for staying in touch with friends, former and current colleagues, customers, suppliers, partners, team members, and others. Sending letters, making phone calls, and seeing people in person are more costly and time-consuming than sending a quick text or Twitter message, although you trade the quality of the interaction for the expediency of the contact. Still, sometimes a short e-mail or text message is all you need to sustain the tie temporarily. For people within the same organization, online social networking also allows them to stay current with what's happening in the organization, rapidly disseminate information and news to a broad audience, and collaborate if they are unable to do it in person. Despite the criticisms of online social networking sites, I think it's clear that they do help people build and sustain their networks, but it's probably not possible to nurture a network entirely online, especially with people with whom you have strong ties. Strong social capital requires deeper and more sustained interactions than are feasible on Facebook.

NETWORK POWER AS AN EMERGENT PHENOMENON

An emergent phenomenon is an effect or behavior that emerges in complex systems from the interaction of simple entities operating as a collective. Consciousness, for instance, may be considered an effect that emerges from the electrochemical interactions among the millions of neurons in the complex system that constitutes the human brain. I am borrowing this concept from science to illustrate an important aspect of network power, namely, that it could not exist on its own. You could not be high in network power and have no other power sources. Network power originates only when you have developed a number of other power sources, such as information, knowledge, attraction, role, and resources. Those power sources attract others to you and help create the sticky bonds that keep people connected to you. That's how your network is built and sustained. Your network power emerges from the collective strength of your other power sources. Once your network is built, however, network power becomes a power source in and of itself.

Here's how it works. Imagine that Victor is hired by a company as a department head. He was well regarded in his previous company, has a good education, and knows his field. His position in the hierarchy of his new company gives him some role power—as well as a formal network consisting of his boss, colleagues, and direct reports. He may also have control of important resources that his direct reports and others outside his department need to do their jobs, so he also has some resource power.

People soon recognize that Victor is knowledgeable and has access to information they find useful, so he begins building knowledge and information power. In a short time, Victor meets and builds good working relationships with the other department heads, as well as customers, other employees of his company, and managers above him in his company. The people he's connected with soon learn that he can be trusted, that he knows what he's talking about, and that he's a solid performer and a good manager. His reputation grows, and people not only rely on him but start coming to him when they need information, assistance, or favors.

Network power originates only when you have developed a number of other power sources, such as information, knowledge, attraction, role, and resources. Those power sources attract others to you and help create the sticky bonds that keep people connected to you. That's how your network is built and sustained.

Victor's initial sources of power—role, resources, knowledge, and information—form a solid power base for leading and influencing others. But as people learn to trust and depend on him, he also gains character and reputation power. These power sources strengthen the connections he has with the people he works with, and they help attract others who learn about him by reputation or through a referral. In time, as his network grows, people come to see him as a well-connected manager. If he's well connected with some executives at the highest level in his company, his network power will increase even more because they are platinum members of his network, if you will. It's not only how many people you know, it's who you know (and who knows you). Platinum members of networks are those well-connected power brokers whose influence is substantial.

Victor becomes a valuable resource, a source of information, a hub of knowledge, a conduit for access to other key people (including those high-level executives), someone who can help when people aren't sure where else to go. The fact that Victor is so well networked becomes an additional source of influencing power for him, principally because he can reach out to so many people in the organization who know him, respect him, and feel some obligation to respond to him. When he offers an idea or makes a request, people are more likely to agree or consent in part because of the network and power base he's built. He knows a lot of people. He's well regarded. He has the ear of some senior executives. He's a main conduit of information and access. In the larger social network of this company, Victor is an important nexus. His network gives him power—and that power has emerged from the combined strength of his other power sources.

NETWORK POWER LOSSES AND DRAINS

Network power is self-sustaining under the following conditions: when your other sources of power remain strong and continue to attract people to your social networks, when you remain in your position in a hierarchy (the structure of the hierarchy reinforces your formal connections), and when you actively nurture your network and keep those bonds strong. However, by its nature, network power is transitory. It will begin to dissipate when you leave an organization and no longer have the formal connections in the hierarchy you once had—or the role and resource power that made you an important member of other people's networks. You may retain some of your connections informally, but even those tend to dissipate over time unless you work to replenish them. (How many of your high school or college friends or former colleagues do you still keep in touch with?) Network power also dissipates when you leave a professional association, team, club, or neighborhood. Of course, you start to rebuild network power when you join a new organization or move to a new neighborhood, but you will have relatively little power in these new domains until you have built trust, confidence, and credibility with the people in them and created the strong and weak ties that form your new social network.

Network power can also be lost, sometimes catastrophically, when someone does something so offensive or repellent that people no longer want to be associated with him. Bernie Ebbers, former CEO of WorldCom, was one of the high-flying chief executives at the turn of this century. At the peak of his power, he was a billionaire and considered one of the most powerful people in telecommunications networking. An ardent Baptist, he taught Sunday school and was highly regarded by the press and his community. Then in 2005, he was accused and convicted of fraud and conspiracy in the largest accounting scandal up to that time (it resulted in an $11 billion loss to investors). Proclaiming his innocence to the end, he drove himself to prison in his Mercedes and is now serving a twenty-five-year sentence. Subsequently he has been listed as one of the worst American CEOs of all time.[8] At the peak of his reign as CEO of the now-defunct WorldCom, Ebbers had a vast network of friends, colleagues, politicians, fellow executives, and other hangers-on who were attracted to his power, fortune, and celebrity. Needless to say, that network has shrunk considerably, most of his ties have been broken, and Bernie Ebbers can no longer reach out to those people and influence them as he once did.

> By its nature, network power is transitory. It dissipates when you leave an organization and no longer have the formal connections in the hierarchy you once had—or the role and resource power that made you an important member of other people's networks.

Social networks consist of hubs (people) and spokes (the ties between them). Those spokes exist because of some attractive force (family, friendship, trust, love, or caring—in the case of personal relationships—and admiration, respect, mutual need, collaboration, or interest—in the case of working relationships). If the leader behaves badly by abusing the trust, showing disrespect, or failing to reciprocate, then the attractive force can become repulsive and destroy the spokes that tie the network together. In some cases, this reversal of fortune is so dramatic and so public that the network can disintegrate virtually overnight.

▶ PROFILES *in* POWER

DICK CHENEY

For the past four decades, few people have been as well connected in Washington as Dick Cheney. In 1969, during the Nixon administration, he became an intern for Congressman William Steiger. Shortly thereafter, he went to work for Donald Rumsfeld, who was then director of the Office of Economic Opportunity. After a series of positions in the Nixon White House, he became assistant to the president under Gerald Ford when the Watergate scandal forced Nixon to resign. By that time, Rumsfeld was serving as the White

Photo by Alex Wong/Getty Images.

House chief of staff for President Ford. When Ford selected Rumsfeld as his secretary of defense, Cheney succeeded him as chief of staff and later became Ford's 1976 presidential campaign manager. In 1978, Cheney was elected to the U.S. House of Representatives from Wyoming and was reelected five times, becoming minority whip (the second-ranking House Republican) in 1988. He served in that role less than three months before being appointed secretary of defense by President George H. W. Bush. While he was in that role, Saddam Hussein's Iraqi army invaded Kuwait, and Cheney oversaw the first Iraq war, known as Operation Desert Storm, in 1991.

During the Clinton administration, Cheney left government service and became the CEO of the multinational company Halliburton, where he earned tens of millions of dollars in a relatively short period. In 1997, Cheney, Donald Rumsfeld, William Kristol, Lewis "Scooter" Libby, Paul Wolfowitz, Jeb Bush, and other neoconservatives were part of a think tank called the Project for the New American Century, whose fundamental proposition is "that American leadership is good both for America and for the world; and that such leadership requires military strength, diplomatic energy, and commitment to moral principle."[9] This philosophy of American dominance in the world was one of the red threads that linked a powerful network of neoconservatives that began forming in the Nixon-Ford years and reached maturity during the twelve years of rule by the Reagan and H. W. Bush administrations.

While Bill Clinton was in the White House, Cheney's network worked behind the scenes to engineer a neoconservative return to power, while a closely affiliated network (including Karen Hughes, Karl Rove, and Andrew Card) seized on Clinton's sex scandals and, promising a return to moral principles, planned for a presidential run by George W. Bush. In 2000, after Bush had won the Republican primaries, he chose Dick Cheney to lead the search for a vice presidential candidate, and Cheney emerged from that secretive process as Bush's running mate. After their election victory, it became increasingly clear that Cheney was not content to be a passive partner to the new president. As journalist Barton Gellman notes, Cheney demanded a strong role in running the country, and Bush consented: "[Cheney] was by any measure the dominant force in creating the Bush administration to be. He did not steal the role or sneak up on it. He asked for it openly, and Bush said yes."[10]

Dick Cheney had immense power in the Oval Office and was one of the most influential and controversial vice presidents in U.S. history. He was noted for his almost fanatical attention to detail, for inserting himself in processes and decisions vice presidents normally were not party to, and for his studied opacity. He was secretive, commanding, controlling, and frequently arrogant in his dismissal of all who disagreed with him or challenged his drive to increase the powers of the executive branch. For all the controversy, however, there was no question that Dick Cheney was a formidable power in Washington and that he, not Bush, was the nexus of neoconservative rule during that administration.

For a time, the old stalwarts of his network (Rumsfeld, Wolfowitz, and Libby) held powerful posts in the government and helped Cheney shape presidential decisions and policies. After 9/11, with the country solidly behind them, they pushed their agenda with willful confidence and launched the second Iraq war, this time with little international support, based on questionable assertions that Saddam Hussein had ties to Al Qaeda and either had or was building weapons of mass destruction. Then it began to fall apart: No weapons of mass destruction were found. The Iraqi invasion floundered when it became clear that the military had not thought through the occupation. Resistance and sectarian violence in Iraq grew and Al Qaeda took advantage of the chaos to foster anti-American resentment. Photos of prisoner abuse at the military's Abu Ghraib facility surfaced, and American public support for the war began to wane as more evidence of administration missteps became public. Rumsfeld resigned, Wolfowitz left the government, Libby was convicted of perjury and obstruction of justice, and Cheney was seen both as the mastermind behind the invasion and as the architect and defender of enhanced interrogation techniques, most notably waterboarding, as depicted in the Mike Peters cartoon below.

During the final year of the Bush administration, the approval ratings for Bush and Cheney plummeted. Cheney became the least-liked vice president in the history of polling[11] and such a controversial figure that he played virtually no public role during the 2008 presidential race. Even after

Comic: Mike Peters EDTCTN (New) © King Features Syndicate.

leaving the White House, Cheney has made the rounds of the talk shows, defending the decision to use waterboarding and, more broadly, the Bush administration and his role in it, but history is likely to be unkind in its judgment of him.[12]

As I noted earlier, network power emerges from the combined strength of one's other power sources, but it is also based on the formal connections that exist because of the role a person plays in an organization. At the height of his career, Cheney had extraordinary role power as vice president, as well as information, reputation, knowledge, and (to fellow neoconservatives) character as power sources—all of which gave him immense network power. That power diminished as his reputation waned and more people saw him as an incompetent president's malevolent shadow. At his peak, he had a profoundly powerful network, but network became a power drain for him when key members of his network, like Rumsfeld and Libby, fell out of favor and when Cheney himself became a pariah in a Republican Party, desperately trying (and failing) to retain power as the George W. Bush era ended. And he lost a significant amount of network power when he left office and no longer had access to the governmental functions the office of the vice president had granted him.

What We Can Learn from Dick Cheney

1. *The temporal and contextual nature of network power.* Cheney once had extraordinary network power based on the positions he held and the central role neoconservatives played in the government. As the context changed—as the second Iraq war lost support and outrage mounted over allegations of torture at military prisons—his network power diminished as he became a less attractive network member. Of course, his die-hard supporters remained loyal to him, but he increasingly became a lightning rod for dissatisfaction with the then-president's administration and anger over what many people saw as a weakening of America's moral stance in the world. The lesson for business leaders? Your network power depends in part on whether you and those associated with you are in favor at the moment. If your group fails to deliver results as expected, your "stock" within the organization may suffer, and you could become a less attractive person to be connected with. This occurs when a division of a company cannot meet its obligations or develops a negative reputation for some other reason. The leaders in that division can become tainted, and their network power may diminish. When business leaders transfer to different divisions or leave to join another company, their network power may also diminish, just as Cheney's network power abruptly fell when the Bush administration left office.
2. *The danger of being too polarizing.* Cheney was a bigger-than-life political figure with strong, controversial views and an arrogant pos-

ture toward those who disagreed with him. The lesson? Being bold and aggressive may serve you well while you are in power, but that posture may give your opponents considerable ammunition when you become vulnerable. This is as true in business as it is in politics.

WHAT THE RESEARCH TELLS US ABOUT NETWORK POWER

My research reveals that network power is one of the most important power sources you can have. Having high network power nearly triples your capacity to lead and influence others. Strong networkers are significantly more likely to be seen as role models and have more than three times the reputation power of people who are not well networked. They have substantially more information power and, according to the research findings, they are also able to inspire others more than twice as much as people with low network power. Clearly, the upside of being well networked is remarkable.

It seems intuitively obvious that people with very high network power like Ana D. would find it easy to build bridges with other people and use their network connections to form alliances. They have such reach, and their social skills are so well honed (the result, no doubt, of all the time they spend practicing those skills) that they are naturals at pulling people together in a concerted effort to lead and influence other people. They are like great terraformers causing many streams to flow together to create a mighty river. The rest of us see how powerful this gathering of the streams can be, so people like Ana become role models for us.

People with high network power must have excellent social and interactive skills, and the research bears this out. They were considered to be significantly more effective at building alliances (no surprise there), finding commonalities with others, and socializing. In fact, their skill ratings are quite high in many interpersonal, interactive, and communication areas: building consensus, negotiating, resolving conflicts, convincing people to help them influence others, building rapport and trust (which helps them build and maintain their networks), supporting and encouraging others, speaking conversationally, asking insightful questions, and taking the initiative to show others how to do things. Overall, people with high network power had average skill ratings in all these areas that were twice as high as those with low network power. People who are highly skilled are more likely to connect with other people and rise to positions where their network naturally expands, but the human interactions inherent in networking also help to improve people's skills, so networking is both an effect and a cause of higher skill ratings.

High network power is strongly correlated with high *role* and *resource* power, which indicates that people whose rank, position, or title gives them high role power tend to be well networked—and this is certainly true of Ana D. and Rahm Emanuel. Likewise, people who control significant resources (e.g., Bill Gates, Warren Buffett, Ted Turner, Richard Branson, Ali al-Naimi) also tend to be well networked. High network power also has strong correlations with high *knowledge, attraction,* and *character* power. The logical conclusion to draw from this research is that people with high network power are likely to be powerful in every other way. If you build your networking skills and devote the time to building and sustaining your professional and social networks, then others will likely perceive you as being more knowledgeable, attractive, and well informed, and to have higher character and a stronger reputation. If you aren't impressed by this finding, you should be. Skilled networking makes you significantly more influential.

GLOBAL DIFFERENCES IN NETWORK POWER

Social networks exist in every culture, so network power is an important power source around the world. However, in some countries, being well networked is somewhat more important than it is in others. Among the forty-five countries I studied, Germany ranked highest in network power (4.81 on a 7-point scale), and South Africa ranked lowest (4.17). The difference (0.64) is just barely significant, which indicates that network power is essentially of equivalent importance in every culture. Nonetheless, the variance between countries is used to create a ranking of countries, in alphabetical order, within three tiers.

COUNTRIES WHERE NETWORK POWER IS HIGHER

Australia, Austria, Brazil, Chile, China, Germany, Indonesia, Ireland, Israel, Italy, Malaysia, Pakistan, South Korea, Switzerland, Taiwan

COUNTRIES WHERE NETWORK POWER IS AVERAGE

Argentina, Belgium, Canada, Colombia, Denmark, France, Hong Kong, Hungary, India, Netherlands, Singapore, Spain, United Kingdom, United States of America, Venezuela

COUNTRIES WHERE NETWORK POWER IS LOWER

Czech Republic, Finland, Greece, Japan, Mexico, New Zealand, Norway, Peru, Poland, Portugal, Russia, South Africa, Sweden, Thailand, Turkey

For more information on our global research on power and influence, and in-depth profiles of each of the forty-five countries studied, see www.kornferryinstitute.com, www.theelementsofpower.com, or www.terryrbacon.com.

KEY CONCEPTS

1. Being connected to other people, especially other people who are also well connected, is a strong source of leadership and influence power. Networks extend a person's reach. They facilitate the flow and range of information and influence. They enhance the social capital of active network members through reciprocal respect, admiration, favor granting, and collaboration.

2. According to sociologist Mark Granovetter, the strength of our social networks lies principally in the number of weak ties we have. These ties foster innovation and creativity and speed the transmission of information from network to network, like a virus.

3. Connectors are people who seem to know everyone and have many network connections. They are powerful because when they become enthused about an idea, book, company, or product, they can convey their enthusiasm to many other people who occupy those different worlds, subcultures, and niches—and that enthusiasm can grow contagiously as some of the people the Connectors reach spread the word throughout their own networks.

4. Network power derives from the social capital you build as you develop relationships with other people. That social capital is a combination of attraction, need, and reciprocal obligation. Mutual trust is essential, as are respect, tolerance, responsiveness, judgment, and listening.

5. It's unlikely that someone could build a robust social network entirely online, but online social networking sites are useful channels for staying in touch and communicating ideas throughout the network.

6. Network power is an emergent phenomenon. It originates only when you have developed a number of other power sources, such as information, knowledge, attraction, role, and resources. Those power sources attract others to you and help create the sticky bonds that keep people connected to you. That's how a network is built and sustained.

7. Network power is one of the most important power sources you can have. Having high network power nearly triples your capacity to lead and influence others.

CHALLENGES FOR READERS

1. This chapter mapped (in figure 8-1) one person's social networks—seventeen of them! For each network, I asked the Connector to identify the number of people with whom she had strong and weak ties. Try that exercise yourself. Identify the number of social networks you belong to and then indicate the number of strong and weak ties in each network. What does that picture tell you? Are you well networked? Do you have mostly weak ties?

2. What role do you play in your social networks? Are you an active hub of energy, communication, information flow, and idea propagation? Or do you operate more on the periphery? What could you do to become more of a nexus of network activity?

3. How well connected are you to other people who are themselves well connected in their networks? In other words, are you networked with influential people in other networks? If so, who are they and what kind of extended access do they potentially give you? Do you make use of that access? If so, how? What more could you do to become better connected?

4. Network power emerges from the combined effect of your other power sources. What power sources do you have that attract people to your social networks and keep them there? What do you have to offer that other people find interesting or valuable?

5. Maintaining weak ties with people in your network is challenging because you don't see or communicate with them very often. What do you do to maintain your weak ties? What more could you do?

6. Do you belong to any social networking sites like Facebook, LinkedIn, or Plaxo? How would you describe the online connections you have made with people you didn't know? Strong? Weak? Genuine? Superficial? How much trust do you have with people you've met only online? Would you consider any of them key members of your overall social networks?

7. Reflect on the best-networked people you know. How does having an extensive number of contacts give them power? How do they use that power? Why are they so successful at building and sustaining relationships with many other people?

CHAPTER 9

THE TREE AND ITS SHADOW

The Power of Reputation

MANY PEOPLE WILL REMEMBER THE TAWDRY TALE OF JOHN EDWARDS, DEMO-cratic presidential contender in the 2008 U.S. presidential election. Edwards had been the vice presidential candidate in the 2004 election and was considered a serious possibility for the top slot in 2008. He garnered enough early support to launch a campaign and had raised nearly $44 million in contributions by the end of 2007; however, after repeated poor showings in the initial presidential primaries, he suspended his campaign on January 30, 2008. The following summer, the *National Enquirer* reported that Edwards had had an affair with a campaign worker, videographer Rielle Hunter, who subsequently gave birth to a daughter. Although initially denying the affair, Edwards later confessed that he'd had relations with Hunter since 2006, although he swore that her child was not his. (It wasn't until January 2010 that Edwards finally admitted that he is the child's father.) If Edwards had hoped for a political future or a key position in the Obama administration, his hope vanished as his reputation took a major dive. Infidelity aside, most damning to his former supporters was the realization that had he become the Democratic presidential nominee, when news of the affair surfaced, it would have doomed the prospects for a Democratic presidency. Edwards's infidelity, lack of judgment, and deceit irreparably damaged the electorate's view of his character, which substantially diminished his power base and, to the relief of many, doomed him as a national leader.

But this is not just a story about John Edwards. It's also a story about his once-noble wife, Elizabeth. She and John had previously lost their oldest son, and Elizabeth was diagnosed with an incurable form of cancer. Throughout much of their public life, she had been viewed as a stoic, accomplished woman who did not deserve what fate had given her. When the Rielle Hunter scandal surfaced, people were particularly outraged that John had cheated on a wife who'd lost a beloved son, was suffering from a deadly disease, and had stood at his side throughout the campaign. Public opinion of him sank as sympathy for her grew. Then she published *Resilience,* a sequel to her previous memoir, *Saving Graces: Finding Solace and Strength from Friends and Strangers.* Both memoirs address her battles with cancer, but in *Resilience* she also wrote about John's affair. After it was published, she hit the television talk show circuit, and in many people's eyes those appearances tarnished her reputation as well.

As Tina Brown wrote in a column on *The Daily Beast,* "If she had stuck with her health and her loss, Edwards might have held on to our sympathy. But her insistence on belittling to Oprah the dreaded 'other woman,' Rielle Hunter, who had 'spotted him in the hotel,' was so embarrassingly self-righteous it almost made me feel sorry for the Democratic twinkie John, who was always under the illusion that he was the next JFK. . . . Edwards kept painting Hunter as a fame seeker, eager to glom onto her husband's spotlight. Whereas it's Edwards who has written the book and dragged Hunter into the media glare. The evil perpetrator herself has not said a word."[1] Columnist Jenice Armstrong of the *Philadelphia Daily News* echoed the dismay Brown and other commentators felt: "Elizabeth wrote in her new memoir, *Resilience,* that when she learned about her husband's affair, she cried and threw up. Not to be crude but that giant gagging sound you hear is the sound of America retching. Democratic voters are choking at the thought of what would have happened if Edwards had somehow won the Democratic nomination, only to have lost the election once word leaked about his lover."[2]

Michael Goodwin, columnist for the *New York Daily News,* also castigated her for deceiving the public: "Elizabeth Edwards helped to perpetrate a fraud on voters, namely, that her husband was fit to be president. She knew better and now says she told him to drop out because of the affair. He didn't and she tried to get him elected, raising money and stumping with and for him. She excoriated the media for giving 'the Cliffs Notes' of the truth about candidates. If only we had known the truth she was hiding."[3] In this column, Goodwin quotes a reader who posted this comment on the *Daily News* website: "Her illness has put a halo over her head and it doesn't belong there. If she were not sick, there would be far more criticism of her for hiding this kind of news. . . . By participating in his charade, Elizabeth is mighty guilty herself."[4] However, the unkindest cut came from Kyle Smith in the *New York Post,* who wrote, "John and Elizabeth Edwards

Armstrong quote used with permission of *Philadelphia Daily News* Copyright © 2010. All rights reserved.

Goodwin quotes © *New York Daily News,* L. P. Used with permission.

have proven themselves the perfect match. On the one hand, you've got a lying, hypocritical, power-hungry narcissist. And then there's her husband." Noting the hypocrisy of Elizabeth Edwards's memoir and her appearances on the talk show circuit, he added, "Last year, she lashed out at 'sensationalism and profit without any regard for the human consequences.' In other words, she was blasting the *National Enquirer* for doing what she is now doing. Except the *Enquirer* was doing a public service that led directly to a federal investigation of the $100,000 in PAC [political action committee] payments to Hunter."[5]

The story of John and Elizabeth Edwards illustrates several important characteristics of reputation and the power it has to either enhance or diminish a person's capacity to lead and influence others. Reputation is an estimation of the overall quality of a person by others in a community (e.g., a team, company, or society) to which the person belongs. What's important about this definition is that a person's reputation reflects what the community thinks of him (or her). It amounts to a group consensus, a shared opinion of value or merit, and it will rise or fall depending on the person's words and actions. Moreover, opinion leaders within a group can shape a person's reputation by influencing others to perceive that person in a particular way. The previous chapter talked about how much influence well-networked people have. If someone at the nexus of a large network voices an opinion about a man, that opinion is likely to spread through the network—and quickly. If the opinion is positive, the man's reputation will be elevated; if not, his reputation will be diminished.

> Reputation is an estimation of the overall quality of a person by others in the community to which the person belongs.

When a chorus of commentators became critical of Elizabeth Edwards for her talk show performances, the widespread sympathy and esteem she had enjoyed in the public eye evaporated. Not everyone agreed with these assessments of her. Some people continued to support her, perhaps because she was a betrayed wife, or had lost a child, or suffered from cancer. However, the chorus of critics spoke loudly, and online postings show that a significant number of people, influenced by the criticism of various columnists, thought less of Elizabeth Edwards than they had previously. Columnists like Tina Brown, Jenice Armstrong, and Michael Goodwin are opinion leaders with an extensive public forum for airing their views. They influence the larger community's perceptions of people, positively or negatively, and the community's assessment of people strongly determines how effectively they can lead or how much influence they might wield. Within companies, opinion leaders throughout the organization play the same role—at their desks, in meetings, or at the watercooler—and their views help shape how people are thought of in the company.

In my research on power and influence, I discovered that people who rated higher in reputation are significantly more effective at leadership and influence than those rated lower in reputation. This may be a common-sense finding, but it is nonetheless profound when you grasp its significance. It means that no matter *how* they try to lead or influence others, no matter what approach they take, people whom the group holds in high esteem are substantially more impactful. Others in the organization will be more inclined to agree with them, consent to their requests, and do what these leaders want simply because of the group's estimation of their quality and character. Conversely, people with lesser—or merely average—reputations are significantly less effective at leading or influencing. People may comply with their requests because it's what should be done anyway, but they will be less inclined to take risks for those lesser-thought-of leaders, and they'll be less willing to join their bandwagons or hitch a ride on their coattails.

Because reputation power has such an extraordinary effect on the amount of influence people can wield, reputation is one of the most important assets any of us has. As the Bible says, "A good name is better than precious ointment" (Ecclesiastes 7:1). Shakespeare notes the importance of reputation in his tragedy of *Othello*, ironically from the lips of Iago, the Moor's artful nemesis and dark shadow:

> Good name in man and woman, dear my lord,
> Is the immediate jewel of their souls.
> Who steals my purse steals trash; 'tis something, nothing;
> 'Twas mine, 'tis his, and has been slave to thousands;
> But he that filches from me my good name
> Robs me of that which not enriches him,
> And makes me poor indeed.[6]

A good reputation is a precious asset, and it can take considerable time to build. People in your community—whether it's a team, business unit, congregation, club, tribe, neighborhood, or company—have to live or work with you long enough to know who you are and how you work. They need evidence of your quality and character and sufficient time for opinion to permeate the group and become a widely held view. However, your good reputation can be lost in an instant if something you do causes the community to reassess you. And, as research shows, it takes five positive impressions of you to overcome one negative impression—unless that negative runs egregiously counter to the community's social norms, in which case much of the positive capital you established will vanish.[7] As Warren Buffett says, "It takes twenty years to build a reputation and five minutes to ruin it. If you think about that, you'll do things differently."[8]

Because reputation power has such an extraordinary effect on the amount of influence people can wield, reputation is one of the most important assets any of us has.

YOUR REPUTATION IS YOUR BRAND

Tom Peters speaks widely about "the brand called You," and he's an expert on this topic, having done a yeoman's job of building his own brand. Peters notes that in organizations where there are many smart, well-educated, accomplished professionals, the smartest ones figure out how to distinguish themselves from every other smart, well-educated, accomplished professional. "Along the way," he writes, "if you're really smart, you figure out what it takes to create a distinctive role for yourself—you create a message and a strategy to promote the brand called You."[9] Although some people may find his notion of personal branding too blatantly self-promotional, Peters makes an important point about reputation: If you are indistinguishable from everyone else in your company, if you come across as one cog in a machine full of similar cogs, then your reputation will not be distinctive either. The most people will think about you is that you're average, a good soldier, a team player, nothing special. If they're asked, "What stands out about her?" they are likely to respond: "Nothing really. She does a good job. Like everyone else." You gain little reputation power from such an unremarkable assessment.

On the other hand, if you have built some distinctive qualities, skills, knowledge, or accomplishments, people may say, "He's an expert in X," or "She's done some outstanding work in Y," or "He's really good to work with—a great collaborator." Obviously, these evaluations contribute to the kind of reputation that enhances your capacity to lead and influence others. Reputation is an assessment of your value or merit. It affects others' regard for you, trust in you, desire to work with you, attraction toward you, willingness to follow your lead, and responsiveness to your influence attempts. And, as Tom Peters points out, these evaluations are always comparative. If someone asks me, "Is she an effective leader?" I invariably compare her to other leaders I've known and assess her merits on my personal scale of leadership quality. My comparison may be subconscious, but I really can't answer the question without seeing her leadership in the context of other leaders I've known, as well as my perhaps fuzzy notion of what leadership is.

To some extent, evaluation is culturally relative, too. A behavior that is seen as assertive in one culture (Britain, for instance) might be viewed as overly assertive in another (Japan) but unassertive in yet another (Greece). Business etiquette and cultural protocols for social interaction vary considerably around the world. How people evaluate you depends in part on whether you adhere to the social norms and conventions of the culture you are operating in and whether any deviations from those norms are perceived to be naïve, idiosyncratic, or blatantly disrespectful. So, the extent to which you behave in concert with the norms of your culture (or the culture in which you are working) will affect people's evaluation of you.

However, some evaluation appears to be based on more universal concepts of character. The classification of character strengths discussed in chapter 5 identifies a number of core virtues, such as courage. In their study of character strengths and virtues, Christopher Peterson and Martin Seligman note, for instance, that "French philosopher Comte-Sponville (2001), arguing for the universality of courage, reminded us that while fears and the acts to defeat them vary from society to society, the capacity to overcome fear 'is always more valued than cowardice or faintheartedness.'"[10] The authors believe that core virtues like courage are evolutionarily predisposed, so they appear in every culture: "These particular styles of behaving may have emerged, been selected for, and been sustained because each allows a crucial survival problem to be solved."[11]

Reputation power is extraordinary, then, because it represents a community's evaluation of a person within the context of some core virtues that define what it means to behave well (or badly) as a human being, as well as the social norms of that community that specify the behavioral expectations of anyone operating in that culture. Inasmuch as the brand of a product or company also signifies the community's assessment of quality or merit, then Tom Peters is correct. There is a brand called You, and your reputation is your brand.

▶   PROFILES *in* POWER

AUNG SAN SUU KYI

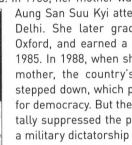

She is the daughter of a national hero, the man considered the father of modern Burma, the man who negotiated the country's independence from the United Kingdom in 1947. When she was just two years old, he was assassinated. In 1960, her mother was named ambassador to India, where Aung San Suu Kyi attended Lady Shri Ram College in New Delhi. She later graduated from St. Hugh's College in Oxford, and earned a Ph.D. at the University of London in 1985. In 1988, when she returned to Burma to care for her mother, the country's socialist leader, General Ne Win, stepped down, which paved the way, many Burmese hoped, for democracy. But the military junta that seized power brutally suppressed the people's demonstrations and imposed a military dictatorship that still survives.

In response to the oppression, Aung San Suu Kyi helped organize the National League for Democracy and was named its general secretary. Because she was the daughter of a national hero, the military junta could not do more than place her under house arrest, which they did in 1989. The following year, the junta called a general election. The National League for Democracy won by a landslide and intended to name Dr. Suu Kyi prime minister, but the junta refused to relinquish power, and she remained under house arrest.

While she was exiled, often in virtual solitary confinement, she was awarded the Sakharov Prize for Freedom of Thought and, in 1991, the Nobel Peace Prize, which her two children accepted on her behalf. In 1995, she was released from house arrest but told that if she left the country she would not be allowed to return. Her husband, who suffered from prostate cancer, left the country that year for medical treatment and was not allowed to return. She stayed in Burma to campaign for democracy and never saw her husband again (he died in 1999). In 2000, the junta placed her under house arrest again and has continually invented reasons to continue her house arrest, despite intense international pressure and a United Nations opinion that her detention is arbitrary and violates the Universal Declaration of Human Rights.

Aung San Suu Kyi is today the world's most visible martyr to the cause of freedom and democracy, having spent four of the last twenty years

Photo by Pornchai Kittiwongsakul/AFP/Getty Images.

in some form of detention for her advocacy of nonviolent protest in the service of peaceful social change. She has been the subject of many books and received numerous awards from governments and institutions around the world for her courage and persistence in the face of oppression, including the Jawaharlal Nehru Award, the Presidential Medal of Freedom, the Olof Palme Prize, and the Congressional Gold Medal. In 2006, the British magazine *New Statesman* voted her one of the "50 Heroes of Our Time."

Among her sources of power are knowledge, expressiveness (she is an eloquent speaker), attraction, and character—most notably, character. These are all personal sources of power. The junta has tried to limit her organizational power by denying her the role she legitimately owns, by restricting her network, by denying her the freedom to disseminate information, and by seizing her resources. But she remains an icon to millions of Burmese and an inspiration to hundreds of millions of people around the world who know of her selfless quest to bring freedom to her country (her plight was dramatized in the 1995 John Boorman film *Beyond Rangoon*). What the junta cannot curtail is her towering reputation, which is what prevents it from taking more drastic action against her. While she lives, she remains a beacon of hope to her people, and she keeps the junta on the defensive—isolated in the world as an illegitimate government, stigmatized by the international community, under continuous pressure to release her and reform itself. If she dies before the junta falls, her reputation is likely to gain power as she becomes a legend. The nameless generals who now rule the country will be lost in the obscurity of history, but Aung San Suu Kyi's name will live for centuries and inspire new generations of followers. That's the power of reputation.

What We Can Learn from Aung San Suu Kyi

1. *A powerful reputation can protect you.* The military junta in Burma (now officially the Union of Myanmar) would take harsher steps to silence Aung San Suu Kyi if it could, but the regard the Burmese have for her—and what she represents to them—limit the junta's options. The lesson for business leaders? Having a strong reputation in your company is like wearing a protective shield. Although not an absolute safeguard, it can protect you from political maneuvering and organizational changes that could affect you adversely. A strong reputation not only opens new doors and gives you greater power to exercise leadership, it acts as a buffer against forces that might otherwise limit your power or curtail your effectiveness.

2. *A strong reputation builds a legacy.* Aung San Suu Kyi has already earned herself a prominent place in history. Long after she's gone, her reputation, built on courage and moral certainty, will create a lasting legacy to inspire future Burmese to defy oppression as courageously as she has. The lesson for those of us in business? Your reputation is the raw material that forms your legacy in your company. Like Jack Welch at GE, Steve Jobs at Apple, Andy Grove at Intel, or Bill Gates at

Microsoft, your reputation is the basis of how you will be remembered. If your legacy is important to you, then having a strong, positive reputation is critical now.

HOW YOUR REPUTATION PRECEDES YOU

I recently received an e-mail from a distant colleague in my company, someone I hadn't met. In his opening paragraph he said, "Your reputation preceded you." His comment reminded me that one of the functions of reputation is to influence people's expectations of others. In effect, it conditions them to be more or less accepting of a person, more or less open to being led or influenced by that person. Imagine that I am about to meet a woman, a partner in a firm my company works with. My boss says, "You'll enjoy meeting Linda. She has a great reputation." That comment elevates my expectations of the person I'm about to meet. Because I expect more, I am conditioned to be more responsive to her if she tries to influence me in some way. If Linda advises me to take a particular course of action, I will be more inclined to agree with her because she is highly regarded. Of course, other factors matter, too. Her advice must make sense to me. It must be insightful and relevant. In other words, she has to live up to her reputation. But consider how differently I would have approached my meeting with Linda had my boss said, "I'm sorry. You need to meet her, but she doesn't have a very good reputation. I doubt you'll get much out of this."

Word of mouth is a key way reputation is communicated throughout a community. Along with referrals, recommendations, and formal or informal appraisals, gossip at the watercooler is an often-efficient way of communicating information about people that can impact how they are regarded by members of an organization. However, reputation may also be communicated through work products (I read a report he wrote and think it's outstanding), publications (I learn that she has had an article published in *Sloan Management Review*), affiliations (I learn that she was one of the original members of the Mars Rover team), and rewards or recognition (I find out he just received the President's Quality Award). When we interview people for a job, their résumé is a form of conditioning, as are their references. After I've interviewed the job candidate, my expectations will be validated or invalidated by my experience, and I may think, "He was much better than his résumé indicated," or "I wasn't as impressed as I thought I would be." When I pass my impressions on to the next person who will interview him, I am conditioning their expectations of the candidate, and I become part of the community's shared evaluation of the person.

An important caveat on word-of-mouth conditioning is that none of us believes everything we hear. If Juan tells me something about Viva, I assess both the source and the person he's talking about. If I trust Juan, I'll be more inclined to believe what he's telling me about Viva—if what he says is consistent with her reputation and my existing impression of her. If I don't trust Juan but do trust Viva, I'll be skeptical about what he says but may still have his assessment of her in mind when I see her again. After all, maybe she's changed? Maybe Juan knows something I don't? Or Juan could just be Juan—off base as usual. A person's reputation is a form of social currency, and it rises or falls in value as members of the community share information about that person and as the person's own words and actions affect other people's assessments. However we learn about people before we meet them, their reputation conditions our expectations and affects how responsive we will be to their attempts to lead or influence us.

THE STUFF REPUTATIONS ARE MADE OF

You may remember the stories of two captains: Chesley Sullenberger and Richard Phillips.

On January 15, 2009, Chesley "Sully" Sullenberger was the captain of US Airways Flight 1549, an Airbus A320 bound from New York's LaGuardia Airport to Charlotte, North Carolina. Shortly after takeoff, the plane hit a flock of birds, and both engines were disabled. He was flying above New York City at low altitude with 155 people on board, and suddenly he had no power. But with decades of training and experience under his belt, Sullenberger calmly brought the plane around and ditched in the Hudson River. After he and his crew evacuated the plane, and all were being rescued by boats that had witnessed the event and come to the rescue, he walked through the plane twice to ensure that everyone had gotten out safely. Only then did he leave the plane.

Richard Phillips was captain of the *Maersk Alabama,* a 17,000-ton cargo vessel carrying relief supplies to southern Africa, when his ship was attacked by Somali pirates on April 8, 2009. To save his crew, Phillips gave himself up as a hostage and was held captive for nearly a week in a small lifeboat as the pirates tried to negotiate a ransom for his return. When the U.S. Navy destroyer *Bainbridge* arrived at the scene, one of the pirates, who'd been stabbed in the hand during the attempt to seize the ship, went on board the *Bainbridge* for medical treatment and to act as their negotiator. Meanwhile, Navy Seal snipers took up positions on the fantail of the *Bainbridge*. When one of the pirates pointed an AK-47 at Captain Phillips, the Seals shot and killed the three pirates remaining on the lifeboat when they exposed their heads and shoulders. Afterward, Phillips was hailed as a hero, and his reputation soared. More recently, he's been criticized by some crew members for failing to take the pirates seriously and putting the ship and crew at risk. Whether or not these allegations have merit, Phillips exposed himself to mortal danger, and his fate was uncertain until the Seals brought the ordeal to an abrupt end. It's not clear how Phillips will eventually be regarded, but his story illustrates how a person's reputation power can rise or fall as the community continually reassesses him based on the latest information.

> *The way to gain a good reputation is to endeavor*
> *to be what you desire to appear.*
> —SOCRATES

Abraham Lincoln said, "Character is like a tree and reputation like its shadow. The shadow is what we think of it; the tree is the real thing." The courage, selflessness, and competence these two captains displayed is obviously the stuff reputations are made of, and of course their reputations stem from virtues endemic to their character. But reputation is built on more than character virtues like courage in the face of imminent disaster or threat of harm. In the workplace, people may develop reputations based on their work ethic, reliability, responsiveness, fidelity, respectfulness, collaborative spirit, willingness to work later/harder when necessary, foresight, commitment, personality, technical skills, knowledge, emotional intelligence, problem-solving skills, creativity, eloquence, ability to manage stress, willingness to share credit, and leadership. Among young teens, a boy may develop a reputation for his skill on a skateboard. On the basketball court, a player may earn a reputation for her finesse and skill at doing a pick-and-roll. A gang member may develop a name for himself because of his ruthlessness. Most people would not find this trait admirable, but reputation has meaning only within the community and social context in which people hold each other in greater or lesser regard.

Organizations and institutions have reputations, too, of course, and the people affiliated with them catch some of the aura of the institution's reputation. In the United Kingdom, Oxford and Cambridge are highly regarded institutions of higher learning; in France, the Sorbonne; in America, the Ivy League schools, MIT, Stanford, Caltech, and so on. Graduating from a prestigious institution enhances a person's reputation, as does receiving a prestigious award or distinction, accomplishing something recognizably difficult, or working for someone notable. These credentials are indicators of worth or merit, and they help build a person's reputation power. So if you represent a distinguished institution or firm, you "piggyback" on the institution's reputation when you present your business card. In effect, you borrow reputation power through your organizational affiliations.

▶   PROFILES *in* POWER

WARREN BUFFETT

If anyone was destined to become the world's greatest investor and self-made multibillionaire, it was Warren Edward Buffett. Born in Omaha, Nebraska, ten months after the Wall Street Crash of 1929, he grew up during the Great Depression that followed. Buffett was too young to remember

the waves of panic triggered by an unprecedented number of bank failures from 1930 to 1933, but throughout much of his boyhood the country struggled with economic hard times and then a world war. Buffett learned some powerful lessons during those years. First, he learned the rudiments of business, especially how to make money. As a boy, he bought six-packs of Coca-Cola for a quarter and sold individual bottles for a nickel, which gave him a profit of five cents on each pack. He also learned to work. In his early teens he had not one paper route, but five of them. He delivered more than 500 newspapers every day before school and made as much money as some working adults. While other boys his age were reading Western pulp magazines and Marvel Comics, Buffett was reading analysts reports and the *Wall Street Journal*.

Next, he learned to save money—as many people did who grew up during the Depression. He understood the value of amassing capital and

Photo by Nicholas Roberts/AFP/Getty Images.

investing it in undervalued assets. By his midteens, he had saved enough money to purchase farm property. He also bought a reconditioned pinball machine for $25 and talked a barber into letting him install the machine in the barbershop. Soon, he had made enough money on that machine to purchase six more pinball machines for other barbershops. He spent relatively little on himself back then and continues those frugal habits today. Frugality through his lifetime has allowed Buffett to build the capital he needs to indulge in his favorite pastime—buying companies.

Buffett's education in business and investing began with his father, who was modestly successful as a stockbroker and later became a congressman. But he learned the most about investing from a book published when he was a nineteen-year-old senior at the University of Nebraska: *The Intelligent Investor* by Benjamin Graham, a book Buffett later called "the best book on investing ever written." Graham distinguished between speculators, who gambled on swings in the market, and investors, who analyzed companies, looked for sound businesses, and invested in value growth over the long term. After graduating from Nebraska, Buffett went to New York to study business and investing at Columbia Business School, where Benjamin Graham was teaching. (Buffett had applied to and been rejected by Harvard Business School, a decision the school no doubt later regretted.)

In 1956, after completing his studies and working briefly with Graham, Buffett started an investment fund with $100 of his own money and just over $100,000 from seven other limited partners. Following the principles of value investing, he grew that initial investment into many millions of dollars and began attracting a following. More partnerships followed, making millions more. In 1962, he reorganized his partnerships into a single partnership, which he dissolved in 1969, having outperformed the Dow Jones average by more than 20 percent per year. He and some others reinvested their money in Buffett's new investment vehicle, Berkshire Hathaway, which became one of the most profitable and respected investment funds of all time. Today, Berkshire Hathaway owns (among other subsidiaries) GEICO, General Re, Borsheims, MidAmerican Energy, Dairy Queen, See's Candies, and has substantial stakes in Anheuser-Busch, Coca-Cola, and Wells Fargo. Buffett's personal fortune has fluctuated over the years, but for decades he has been counted among the country's and the world's wealthiest people. In 2009, *Forbes* listed him as the second-wealthiest person in the world (just behind Bill Gates), with assets of $37 billion.

Through his remarkable investment career, he has come to be known as the world's greatest investor. The Carson Group labeled him the top money manager of the twentieth century. His investing prowess is so well known that stocks sometimes experience the "Buffett effect"—a bump in price when it becomes known that he has invested in a company's stock. He is frequently consulted by presidents and business luminaries, and his annual meeting in Omaha for Berkshire Hathaway shareholders is referred to as "Woodstock for capitalists."

One of Buffett's primary power sources is knowledge. He may know more about investing than anyone in history, and he has extraordinary access to information (he spends much of his time reading). Obviously, he has a powerful role and commands vast resources as head of Berkshire Hathaway and owner of his own vast fortune, and he has an exceptional network. He's a capable speaker and has become a well-known philanthropist (having already given billions of dollars to the Bill & Melinda Gates Foundation and pledging even more of his fortune to charity). But one of his greatest sources of power is his reputation as the smartest and most successful investor of all time. Like anyone in the volatile field of investing, he doesn't have a perfect record, and his reputation has taken some hits from time to time, but in the end what matters most are results, and no investor has ever performed as well as Warren Buffett has. The extraordinary power he has attained through his reputation as an investment genius is best captured in the near-mythic label by which he's come to be known: the "Oracle of Omaha."

What We Can Learn from Warren Buffett

1. *The importance of results.* Warren Buffett's reputation is built on a solid foundation of long-term, superior results. The lesson for us? In business, nothing builds your reputation—or is as important to sustaining it—as achieving outstanding results. Whatever role you have, it is crucial that you lead your group with exceptional skill and meet or exceed your goals—month after month, year after year. Nothing is as important as results.

2. *The importance of focus and hard work.* Buffett does have other interests (he's an avid bridge player, for instance), but he has been singularly focused on value investing and growing wealth for much of his life. Moreover, he has been a tireless worker, frequently doing more and working harder than others around him. His success is well earned. The lesson? The kind of success that builds high reputation power depends less on luck and good fortune than on steadfast focus on a goal and the hard work necessary to achieve it.

3. *The value of steadfast adherence to basic principles.* Buffett was inspired to follow Benjamin Graham's value investing principles because they made good business sense. In the years he worked with Graham, he came to believe that Graham's criteria for sound investments were too stringent, and he found his own formula. Once that formula was set, Buffett did not deviate from it significantly—and that's been one of the foundations of his reputation. This is not to say that Buffett hasn't made mistakes and improved his business judgment through the years, but he hasn't been a mercurial investor, either. He avoided the dot-com craze and still won't invest in companies whose future profitability he can't predict. He's remained true to the principles he honed more than fifty years ago. The lesson for business leaders? Devote the time to discovering what works and then adhere to that

formula as long as you are achieving the results you set out to achieve. Beware of the trend du jour if it distracts you from the basic principles that make good business sense.

REPUTATION AS A POWER DRAIN

Jerry Yang was anointed one of the wunderkinder of Silicon Valley when in 1995, at age 26, he and fellow Stanford University electrical engineering student David Filo cofounded Yahoo, a Web portal that had previously been known as Jerry and David's Guide to the World Wide Web. One of the shooting stars of the dot-com craze, Yahoo grew exponentially and was trading at nearly $120 a share at its zenith. Yang became a billionaire with a similarly lofty reputation as a technical wizard and entrepreneur. Then, in June 2007, he was named chief executive of the company and, to drive a new era of growth, he had visions of transforming Yahoo to make it more competitive with the world's leading portal, Google. But that was not to be.

Yang's brief tenure (just a year and a half) as CEO was marked by tense shareholder relations; many executive departures; a marked decline in share price; and, most notably, a failed negotiation with Microsoft, which had sought to acquire Yahoo for more than $44 billion in cash and stock. The breakdown of the protracted negotiations with Microsoft, which some of Yahoo's board members (notably Carl Icahn) blamed on Yang, provoked the wrath of many shareholders. Shortly before Yang stepped down, Yahoo announced large layoffs, and the stock price plummeted to just over $10 a share. Although Yang was suited to leading a start-up venture, he seemed to lack the skills needed to lead a more mature enterprise. The announcement of his departure came before Yahoo's board had found a replacement—an unusual move in the corporate world—which signaled the board's desire to placate shareholders before the company declined further, and some shareholders expressed relief that the company's downward spiral might finally end.[12]

Some dot-com entrepreneurs were able to make the transformation from entrepreneur to mature business leader—examples are Bill Gates at Microsoft, Jeff Bezos at Amazon, and Steve Jobs at Apple—but many others, like Jerry Yang, weren't. They remind us that reputation hinges on success, and knowing what risks to take or what offers to accept is as important as knowing what risks to avoid and what offers to decline. As the old poker saying goes, "You have to know when to hold 'em and know when to fold 'em." Yang and the Yahoo board tried to spin his ouster in the most positive way, but it wasn't difficult to read between the lines, and his reputation invariably suffered because his brief tenure as CEO was largely unsuccessful. Reputation can be a fickle thing.

You can lose influencing power if your reputation is tarnished by moral failures, like John Edwards's was, or performance failures, like Jerry Yang's was, but it can also become a power drain if others in your organization perceive you as lazy, incompetent, careless, mistake prone, uncommitted, arrogant, stubborn, uncommunicative, untrustworthy, odd, or selfish. Reputation is an efficient mechanism for communicating and reinforcing social norms and socially desirable behaviors and attitudes. So any behavior that is out of sync with the behavioral norms of the community you belong to can lead people to lower their assessment of you. Reputation can be a significant source of power, and it can also be a significant power drain.

REBUILDING A DAMAGED REPUTATION

Is it possible to rebuild your reputation if it's been tarnished? The answer is a qualified yes. It depends on the nature and seriousness of the offense and the community's degree of forgiveness. Communities tend to be most unforgiving about ethical breaches. Egregious criminals like Bernie Ebbers and Bernard Madoff are unlikely to rebuild their reputations, but Michael Milken did. He was the junk bond king in the 1980s, and many people viewed Milken as the epitome of Wall Street greed. Indicted on ninety-eight counts of racketeering and securities fraud in 1989, he was sentenced to ten years but served less than two. Since then, he's dedicated his life to philanthropy, supporting education and medical research, and is now well esteemed.

The extent to which a person can rebuild a tarnished reputation depends, too, on whether he owns up to his failures (communities tend to dislike deniers), on whether he is contrite about his sins (communities disdain the arrogant and unrepentant), and on whether he does it again (whatever the abuse, it can't be repeated). Performance issues are often forgiven if the person self-consciously learns from her mistakes, accepts responsibility for them, and performs better in the future. However, this rebuilding process can take longer than building a good reputation does in the first place. In chapter 5, I told the story of Eliot Spitzer's fall from grace. He is working hard to reclaim his good name, and he's making some progress, although it is doubtful he will ever serve as a governor again. Jerry Yang is still a young man with considerable wealth, experience, and technical savvy. He may or may not serve as a CEO again, but he can certainly rebuild his reputation by finding the right venues and capitalizing on one success at a time.

WHAT THE RESEARCH TELLS US ABOUT REPUTATION POWER

To a certain extent, power is what other people grant a leader. Leaders can build their personal sources of power—knowledge, communication abilities (expressiveness), character, and the qualities that make them attractive (appearance, dress, manners, personality)—but the power they attain in an organization depends on the implicit consent of those who choose to follow them. Of course, management positions in a company confer a certain amount of formal authority upon leaders, but that formal authority goes only so far. True leadership power comes from people's admiration of and respect for leaders, from people's willingness to follow. So power is a relational concept; it exists mainly in relation to other people. This is why a leader's reputation in the organization is so important. When leaders are well thought of, people are more willing to follow them, more willing to consent, and more willing to grant them organizational power.

The bottom line is that your reputation is one of the most important power sources you can have, and my research bears this out. People of high repute in organizations are more than three times more likely to be viewed as role models, and they are more than three times as influential as people with lesser reputations. And they are significantly more likely to be viewed as inspirational leaders. They are more likely to succeed at building alliances with others, building consensus, and negotiating. They are substantially better at persuading others through logical reasoning, too. Why? Perhaps we are more apt to accept the logical arguments of people we regard highly because we trust that their arguments and reasoning are sound. Finally, and this is an intriguing finding, people with high reputation power are significantly more effective at *building rapport and trust* and *using authority without appearing heavy-handed*. Trust and authority are not always good bedfellows. So it's interesting that having a strong reputation enables you to use authority without causing distrust. This suggests that when someone has a strong reputation, we expect and accept the person's use of authority without becoming resentful or defensive about it, which is how we might otherwise react when someone we don't regard as highly tries to use authority to direct or control our thoughts or actions.

The power sources that are most strongly correlated with reputation power are *knowledge, information, expressiveness,* and *network.* This means that people with significantly higher reputations are also likely to be rated higher in these areas. Knowledge and information are about content, expressiveness is about communication, and network is about connections. Of these, by far the strongest correlation with reputation power is knowledge. This finding tells us that the best ways to build a strong reputation are to:

- Be highly knowledgeable or skilled in some area (develop some key content expertise)
- Demonstrate your skills and capabilities by achieving notable results
- Have access to or control information other people need
- Communicate forcefully and effectively (be highly expressive)
- Build a robust network of connections with other people

Interestingly, the power source least correlated with reputation is *resources,* which suggests that people who control key resources don't necessarily need a strong reputation to have influencing power. Their resource power is all they need.

What emerges from our research is that leaders who are highly regarded are considered to be more knowledgeable and skilled in every dimension. Reputation is like the rising tide that lifts all boats. It makes leaders appear better and more skilled in every way. In contrast, leaders with lesser reputations struggle. They primarily try to lead and influence others by stating directly what they want or by relying on existing relationships. Their strongest power source is *history,* which means their effectiveness is, to a large extent, limited to people they already know. Their highest-rated skills are persisting, asserting, and being willing to ask others for favors, which is typically a technique of last resort. If you can't convince people any other way, you ask them for a favor. So leaders pay a substantial penalty if they are not highly regarded by others in the company.

GLOBAL DIFFERENCES IN REPUTATION POWER

Reputation is an important source of leadership and influence power in every culture, but it is somewhat more important in central Europe (Germany, Austria, Switzerland, Czech Republic), the Mediterranean region (Greece, Italy, Spain, Portugal), and South America (Argentina, Brazil, Chile, Colombia). Reputation power is somewhat less important in countries where history power (the strength of existing relationships between people) matters more, including many Asian countries (China, Hong Kong, Indonesia, Japan, Taiwan, Thailand). The rankings are listed here, with countries arranged alphabetically.

COUNTRIES WHERE REPUTATION POWER IS HIGHER

Argentina, Austria, Brazil, Chile, Colombia, Czech Republic, Denmark, Germany, Greece, Italy, Norway, Portugal, South Korea, Spain, Switzerland

COUNTRIES WHERE REPUTATION POWER IS AVERAGE

Australia, Belgium, France, Hungary, India, Ireland, Israel, Malaysia, Mexico, Netherlands, New Zealand, Pakistan, Singapore, Sweden, United States of America

COUNTRIES WHERE REPUTATION POWER IS LOWER

Canada, China, Finland, Hong Kong, Indonesia, Japan, Peru, Poland, Russia, South Africa, Taiwan, Thailand, Turkey, United Kingdom, Venezuela

For more information on the global research on power and influence, and in-depth profiles of each of the forty-five countries studied, see www .kornferryinstitute.com, www.theelementsofpower.com, or www.terryr bacon.com.

KEY CONCEPTS

1. Reputation is an estimation of the overall quality of a person by others in a community (whether a team, organization, or society) to which the person belongs.

2. People who are rated higher in reputation are significantly more effective at leadership and influence than those rated lower in reputation. Because reputation power has such an extraordinary effect on

the amount of influence people can wield, reputation is one of the most important assets any of us has.

3.   Reputation is an assessment of someone's value or merit, and this evaluation is culturally relative because a behavior that appears overly assertive in one culture may appear unassertive in another. However, some evaluation of a person's merit is based on more universal concepts of character, like courage.

4.   Reputation conditions people by helping to set their expectations of people they are about to meet. What you hear about a person's reputation helps determine how responsive you will be to that person's leadership or influence attempts.

5.   Reputation is an efficient mechanism for communicating and reinforcing social norms and socially desirable behaviors and attitudes, so if people behave out of sync with the norms of their community, their reputation may suffer. Reputation is an extraordinary source of power, but it can also be a power drain.

CHALLENGES FOR READERS

1.   Identify three or four key people in your company. What are they known for? What are their reputations? How did they get those reputations? Try to trace their source.

2.   Think of several people you know whose reputations have suffered because of something they ostensibly said or did. What did they do? What effect did it have on how they were regarded? How did you learn of their actions, and what effect did it have on you?

3.   Among the people you have known, who had the best reputations? Why? What were their reputations based on? Did they appear to be more powerful or influential because of how they were regarded?

4.   What is your reputation? How are you regarded by those you live and work with? An interesting exercise is to list the top five things you think you are best known for. Then ask some colleagues to list the top five things they think you are best known for. Compare the lists. How accurate a picture do you have of your own reputation?

5.   Identify two or three colleagues whose reputations are not as good as they could be. If you were to advise them on how to enhance their

reputation, what would you advise? What would they need to do differently? How easy would it be to make those changes, and how long would it take for them to reverse any less-than-positive impressions people may have of them?

6. What could you do to build your reputation beyond what it is today?

CHAPTER 10

ORGANIZED RIVALRY IN
THE MONSTER'S DEN

Power in Organizations

SOMETIME IN THE 1940s, THEOLOGIAN REINHOLD NIEBUHR COMPOSED THE Serenity Prayer, which begins with these lines: "God, grant me the serenity to accept the things I cannot change; the courage to change the things I can; and the wisdom to know the difference."[1] This prayer became well known after Alcoholics Anonymous adopted it in the 1950s, and it evolved in the following decades into a piece of popular wisdom appearing, among other places, in needlepoint on the kitchen wall in my family's home. That prayer could be the mantra for this chapter because the amount of power you have in an organization depends not only on the strength of your personal and organizational power sources, but also on the authority structure and dynamics of the organization you belong to, as well as forces external to the organization that are beyond your control. You could have very strong personal and organizational power sources but still be relatively powerless in your company because you are in a division with a mediocre performance record or have a rival in a senior position who limits your opportunities or otherwise curtails your power. Or because market conditions change and the product you championed is rapidly losing market share, which may cast you as yesterday's news, a has-been who was once highly thought of but is now out of touch.

I proposed back in the introduction that we could think of power like a battery. The power sources I've discussed in this book are like the chemical cells in our individual batteries, so to speak. People with stronger sources of power are capable of exerting more leadership and influence over others because, metaphorically, their batteries contain higher voltage than people's with weaker sources of power. In organizations, the dynamics of power are complicated because people don't exercise power in a vacuum; they exercise power within the formal and informal structures of the organization in response to internal and external priorities and events, sometimes acting in concert with other people in the organization and sometimes acting in opposition to them. The power dynamics in organizations are like an electrical power grid, where all the components of the grid (i.e., the members of the organization) are interconnected in intricate ways, and power constantly fluctuates throughout the grid based on forces that either amplify particular power currents or resist them.

I like this metaphor because it illustrates the interconnectedness of power in organizations; however, electrical grids are rational and power in organizations often isn't. Unless some component fails or an accident or act of God occurs, electrical grids work the same way all the time. They are designed to be as stable and reliable as engineers can make them. In comparison, human organizations are often messy, ambiguous, and unpredictable. Aldous Huxley said, "One of the many reasons for the bewildering and tragic character of human existence is the fact that social organization is at once necessary and fatal. Men are forever creating such organizations for their own convenience and forever finding themselves the victims of their homemade monsters."[2] As I will show, you can gain or lose power in an organization for reasons you could not foresee and had nothing to do with. This doesn't mean that you have no control over your destiny; it simply means that despite your best efforts you cannot always plot your own course. To paraphrase Niebuhr, you need to accept what you cannot control, manage what you can, and be wise enough to know the difference.

THE DYNAMICS OF POWER IN ORGANIZATIONS

There are five forces that modulate the distribution and use of power in organizations—and consequently how much power any member of the organization has relative to other members of the organization. Those five forces are (1) the formal authority structure of the organization; (2) the prevailing leadership paradigm; (3) the environment in which the organization operates; (4) the informal working processes or neural nets of the organization; and (5) the ambitions and allegiances of individual members of the organization, particularly as they complement or clash with the ambitions and allegiances of other members.

Formal Authority Structure

The most easily recognizable force affecting the distribution of power and authority in organizations is the formal organizational structure. The division of an organization into logical parts, the functional purpose of those parts (as well as the relationships among them), the hierarchy of management roles and responsibilities, the identification and description of jobs or roles, the allocation of decision-making authority, the formal channels of communication and work flow—all these elements dictate how power is designed to be distributed among the various parts of the organization and the people who play roles in each function at each level. It is important to recognize that the organization chart—which amounts to a power distribution and functional relationship map—represents the distribution of power *in theory.*

The organization chart shows how the organization is meant to work, how its designers (whoever they might be) believed the organization would operate most efficiently and effectively. In other words, the formal authority structure of an organization represents the most rational distribution of power, assuming that the people occupying various positions use the power and authority vested in them ideally, that rational relationships exist among the divisions of the organization, and that environmental forces have no distorting effect on the organization. If the people who put together the organizational charts were conducting a scientific experiment, they would say, "Under controlled laboratory conditions, this is how the organization will operate at optimal efficiency."

> Five forces modulate the distribution of power in organizations: the formal authority structure of the organization, the prevailing leadership paradigm, the environment in which the organization operates, the informal working processes of the organization, and the ambitions and allegiances of individual members.

One of the decisions organizational designers must make is how centralized or decentralized the organization will be. In centralized organizations, many decisions are reserved for centralized functions (e.g., HR, R&D, finance) rather than operating units or regional divisions. So if you occupy a management position in the centralized organization, you are likely to have more decision-making authority and power than a manager in one of the operating units. In decentralized organizations, which may have a very small central organization, more power is distributed to the operating units or regions, so managers in those units typically have greater decision-making authority or power. The differences in decision-making authority may revolve around budgetary authority but could also include workforce management, the selection of partners and suppliers, regional marketing strategy, choice of IT systems, and so on. I wouldn't argue that one type of organization is always superior to the other, but the distribution of authority is clearly affected by how centralized or decentralized the organization is.

Another impact on the distribution of power in an organization is the organization's position in its life cycle. Like living things, organizations can be thought of as having an organic life cycle proceeding from birth through childhood and adolescence, to adulthood or maturity, and then aging and decline, leading in many cases to death as the organization dissolves. Ichak Adizes published one of the most complete descriptions of this metaphor in his book *Corporate Lifecycles*. Adizes proposed that organizations have nine predictable stages in their life cycle: courtship, infancy, go-go, adolescence, prime, stability, aristocracy, early bureaucracy, and bureaucracy/death.[3] When an organization is formed, power resides principally with the founder, who may or may not relinquish some power as the organization grows. Founders who are reluctant to delegate a meaningful amount of power to their management team often stifle growth by disenfranchising the leaders whose energy and creativity they need to grow the organization beyond the limits of the founders' capacity to effectively make decisions at increasingly more granular levels. Wiser founders find people capable of assuming responsibility for managing parts of the organization's operations and invest them with the power and authority to make appropriate decisions at their level. These founders also find ways to attract and reward the innovators who can invent new products, solutions, markets, and approaches that help the company survive and mature.

In the early entrepreneurial stages of an organization, the people who typically gain power are those the founder most depends upon: (1) partners or early joiners who first believed in the founder's dream and helped get it off the ground; (2) later joiners who adopted the founder's vision, values, and work ethic and whose performance demonstrably contributed either to new product creation or major successes with customers; and (3) the people whose skills, drive, energy, and creativity accelerated the organization's growth and differentiation toward the adolescent and prime stages. The people who can lose power as the organization grows include (1) early joiners who try to usurp more power than the founder is willing to relinquish, (2) people who become misaligned with the founder's vision or operating style (thus becoming a distraction), and (3) people whose performance becomes subpar. Typically, the subpar performers were once good performers when the organization was young, but their performance growth fails to keep pace with the evolving needs of the organization. They just can't keep up.

As organizations mature and reach the prime stage, many things have to change. People can no longer fly by the seat of their pants. Decisions must be more studied and less ad hoc. Processes and systems must be established to help manage an organization that would be unwieldy without them. Managers have to become more professional, and performance has to be measured more systematically. Many companies go public when they reach maturity, and everyone is under more performance and regulatory scrutiny, including the founders (if they are still around). In these increasingly mature organizations, more power accrues to (1) the people who occupy key positions in the hierarchy, (2) professional managers and problem solvers who can institute and manage systems and deliver results consistently, and (3) the key performers whose measurable success makes them role models for the new organizational citizens. The people who lose power typically include old-timers who long for the good old days when the organization was more like a family and who abhor the rigidity and rules of this new place.

In the latter stages of the organizational life cycle, bureaucracy reigns. Systems, processes, rules, and procedures have become ossified. People are highly protective of their turf and change is suspect. People are in denial about the warning signs of decay and assume that markets and customers should conform to the way the organization does business (rather than the other way around). In organizations at this stage of their life cycle, power goes to the systems managers and bureaucrats, to the maintainers of the status quo, and to those in denial who reassure worriers by proclaiming that all is well and devote more energy toward protecting the status quo and politicking to preserve their power base than adapting to the changing demands of the environment and innovating to keep the organization current. The people who lose power typically include those who valiantly try to reawaken the organization by introducing change and are squashed by more powerful change resistors, and those who give up and disappear within the folds of the bureaucracy.

For examples of organizations in different parts of the organizational life cycle, think of Facebook (still very much a go-go company), Amazon (now at its prime), and Wang (dead and gone). Of course, companies that enter the bureaucratic stages of the life cycle are not necessarily doomed. Before an organization becomes moribund, a vigilant board may fire the caretaker CEO and find a new chief executive who can transform the lumbering giant before it collapses. IBM has reinvented itself several times, most notably under Lou Gerstner. In recent years, Ford Motor Company has transformed itself and become viable again (General Motors, on the other hand, remains a bureaucratic behemoth and may not survive, at least in its current form). Organizational structures evolve as organizations respond to the changing environmental conditions in which they operate. Periodic reorganizations are done to realign the organization with its current environment or align it with a new prevailing leadership paradigm (more about this later), but the redesigned structure still represents a best guess on the part of the designers about how the organization will operate most effectively.

In conclusion, the amount of power you can have in an organization depends not only on the strength of your personal and organizational sources of power (particularly *role* power, which stems from your position in the formal authority structure of the organization), but also on how aligned you are with the organization's design and life-cycle stage. Another very important factor is how aligned you are with the prevailing leadership paradigm governing the organization.

► PROFILES *in* POWER

MARK ZUCKERBERG AND FACEBOOK

Like Bill Gates, Mark Zuckerberg is a Harvard dropout who cofounded a software company and became a billionaire in his early twenties. Zuckerberg was a smart, geeky kid who grew up in a well-to-do family and had an early fascination with computers. By middle school, he was developing computer programs, which later included a communications program for his father's office and a music player called Synapse that learned users' music preferences. He attended an exclusive private school, Phillips Exeter Academy, where he excelled in the classics, and then enrolled in Harvard University, where he intended to

Photo by Suzanne Plunkett/Bloomberg via Getty Images.

study psychology. But in his first year at Harvard, he got sidetracked by a sophomoric prank that became an Internet phenomenon.

Harvard did not have a centralized public face book—a student directory with photos that listed names, class years, and majors—although individual houses or dormitories had that information. So Zuckerberg accessed protected areas of Harvard's computer system and downloaded students' photos and information from the houses he could hack into. With this information, he created "Harvard Face Mash," a version of the website Hot or Not, where visitors can rate how attractive people are based on their photos. In Face Mash, Zuckerberg randomly paired student photos and invited users to rate which one of each pair was hottest. Not amused, the university promptly revoked his computer privileges and put him on probation. It also insisted that he apologize to his fellow students.

But Zuckerberg had seen the future, and the future was the appeal of social networking and people's willingness to share private information on the Web. Unfazed by the university's public rebuke, Zuckerberg and friends launched thefacebook.com at Harvard on February 4, 2004. This site lacked the "hot or not" feature but allowed users to indicate their relationship status and what they were looking for in a companion, an appealing feature for hormonal college students. Within three weeks of the site's launch, it had more than 6,000 subscribers. After Harvard, they created face books for other Ivy League schools and universities, then high schools, and then . . . the world. Their fledgling venture took off rapidly, and in his sophomore year Zuckerberg and his friends left Harvard, moved to Palo Alto, and built the foundations of the Facebook that exists today.

One of the fastest-growing websites in history, Facebook, as of this writing, has more than 500 million users globally. By some accounts, more than 10 percent of the total time people now spend online is on Facebook. That's an astonishing statistic for a company barely six years old, but it speaks to how appealing online social networking is to so many people in the developed world. That appeal has catapulted Facebook up the corporate life-cycle curve like a clumsy infant guzzling growth hormone. Facebook now has more than 1,200 employees—too many for the company to remain an enfant terrible, thumbing its nose at corporate elders like Microsoft who've grown to maturity. But much of the youthful zeal remains. Facebook's offices look like dorm rooms. Amid the clutter are scores of twenty-somethings in mazes of desks focused on the screens in front of them, some listening to iPods while they write code, all intent on changing the world as we know it.

Zuckerberg has been and remains the majority owner of Facebook. He can't be fired, can't be shoved aside (as Steve Jobs once was at Apple by an inept board in the mid-1980s). Zuckerberg's role and resource power in the organization are obviously immense. Who else has power at Facebook? His cofounders—Adam D'Angelo and Dustin Moskovitz—did at one time but are now departed. Considerable role power now goes to some of the newer kids on the block, many, interestingly enough, from Google. Googler Sheryl Sandberg was hired as the COO, and David Fischer (a renowned Google advertising executive) was brought in as VP of advertising and global operations. Other ex-Googlers include Elliot Schrage, who became VP of global communications, marketing, and public policy; Don Faul, who directs global online operations; Ethan Beard, who directs the Facebook developer network; and Grady Burnett, who directs online and inside sales. Most recently, Joanna Shields (former Bebo CEO) was hired to run sales and business development in Europe, the Middle East, and Africa (EMEA).

If this sounds like a mainstream corporation, it is. Facebook is well into its organizational adolescence and won't reach maturity unless it formalizes its operations and treats itself as a serious business, which is clearly what Zuckerberg is doing by hiring experienced executives and building a formal organizational infrastructure. But this doesn't mean the company has become stodgy. In March 2010, *Fast Company* ranked Facebook as the world's most innovative company (ahead of Amazon, Apple, and Google).[4] The company is still driven by a CEO who used to end meetings "by pumping his fist in the air and leading employees in a chant of 'domination.'"[5] And in this environment of astronomical growth combined with Edisonian experimentation, power will always accrue to the young geniuses in T-shirts and jeans who can get more done in less time than is reasonable and who get the product right. They are the ones Zuckerberg values most, and he rewards them, not by patting them on the back (he is not known as a warm and fuzzy leader), but by inviting them to tackle the next set of challenges. In this kind of organization, with this kind of leader, people build power by consistently achieving results.

What We Can Learn from Mark Zuckerberg and Facebook

1. *The importance of fit between your style and strengths and the organization's need.* Power in organizations is shaped by the formal organizational structure and the company's position in its life cycle. Highly creative, rapidly evolving organizations like Facebook have different leadership needs than mature organizations in their prime (e.g., Amazon) or aging organizations that have become bureaucratic (e.g., General Motors). Your ability to gain and exercise power will depend on how well your style and strengths as a leader are aligned with the organization's needs.

2. *The importance of fit between your and senior leadership's philosophy and practices.* This is especially important in go-go organizations like Facebook, which has an entrepreneurial, seat-of-the-pants, learn-as-you-go leader like Mark Zuckerberg. To build power in an organization run by this type of leader, you must have a high degree of learning agility as well as the perspicacity to anticipate the evolving leadership needs of the organization and develop yourself accordingly.

3. *The importance of getting results faster than seems reasonable.*

Power in high-growth, entrepreneurial organizations is built on a foundation of sustained high performance in a pressure-cooker environment.

Prevailing Leadership Paradigm

The prevailing leadership paradigm in an organization is the set of cultural beliefs about the kind of leadership practiced in the organization. It reflects the attitudes, operating styles, and behaviors of the organization's dominant leaders and may be so deeply embedded in the organization's culture that leaders who come in from the outside and behave differently are rejected by the culture. The prevailing leadership paradigm may be anchored in long tradition (e.g., the Catholic Church, General Motors, Sears, Wal-Mart) or may reflect the seat-of-the-pants practices of a young entrepreneur who occasionally sleeps under a desk because he works such long hours (e.g., Bill Gates in Microsoft's early years). In organizations with a dominant chief executive or managing director, the prevailing leadership paradigm usually reflects the alpha leader's operating style, beliefs about leadership, and personality—and over time that evolves into a cultural imperative about how all leaders in the organization should practice leadership.

What new leaders bring to an organization—besides their personality and operating style—are their beliefs about and approaches to leadership that reflect what they've learned about leadership, experienced as leaders, or observed in working with other leaders. The sum of their beliefs and experiences forms the leadership paradigm they bring to the position. A leader may have a strong need for power and control, for instance, and practice strong-handed, authoritative leadership. This style may have worked well for him in the past and may be one reason the board hired him as the chief executive (e.g., "Chainsaw" Al Dunlap, whose turnaround at Scott Paper and reputation as a downsizer led to him being hired as the CEO of Sunbeam—with disastrous results). Or the leader may believe in shared leadership, a strong employee-oriented culture, and his role as inspirer and chief cheerleader (e.g., Herb Kelleher at Southwest Airlines). The alpha leader may have invented the organization's breakthrough product and be an innovative leader (e.g., Steve Jobs at Apple) or be a collaborative, people-oriented leader (e.g., Robert Greenleaf's notion of servant leadership). There are bullish leaders like George S. Patton and balanced leaders like Dwight D. Eisenhower. There are crown prince leaders like

Calvin Klein and Richard Branson and patriarchal/matriarchal leaders like Walt Disney and Mary Kay Ash. As long as they lead their organizations successfully, alpha leaders put their stamp on the organization and subordinate leaders tend to emulate the alpha's style and approach.

As noted in chapter 4, people like other people who are similar to them, who think like they do. Wise CEOs may ensure that their senior teams include contrarians who challenge their assumptions and bring fresh perspectives to the ongoing management dialogue, but the reality is that most CEOs, like other leaders at all levels, tend to surround themselves with subordinate leaders who think and behave like they do. It creates less friction and conflict and has the self-confirming benefit of reinforcing their beliefs about how the organization should be led, as well as validating their own leadership style. Moreover, many alpha leaders participate in their organization's leadership development programs, and what they teach naturally reflects what they believe about the right way to lead in their organization (e.g., as Jack Welch at GE, Andy Grove at Intel, and Roger Enrico at PepsiCo did during their CEO tenures).

The prevailing leadership paradigm affects the distribution of power by creating a process of "natural selection," whereby people who adhere to the paradigm are more likely to be identified as high potentials and given more educational opportunities, choice assignments, and promotions, whereas the opposite is true for the contrarians, who are likely to be viewed as cultural misfits. You gain power by thinking and behaving in ways that are culturally sanctioned. You pay a penalty for behaving differently, even if you're right. As John Kenneth Galbraith once observed, "In any great organization it is far, far safer to be wrong with the majority than to be right alone."[6]

The prevailing leadership paradigm is often reflected in the hiring and promotional decisions of newly hired senior leaders. The new senior vice president and manager of Division X, for example, may have been a management consultant earlier in his career and may believe that being a management consultant is the best training for a general management position. Furthermore, he may have the greatest confidence in other consultants he knew in his former firm. After he takes over Division X, he hires a new second in command from that firm, a person he knows and trusts. This person shares his philosophy and can draw from a common set of management practices. As the division expands, he hires other consultants from his former firm into key leadership positions. Before long, members of Division X realize that unless they have the pedigree the senior vice president trusts, their chance of promotion into leadership positions is unlikely.

In this example, which is not as far-fetched as it may seem, the distribution of power in the organization is obviously skewed toward people who share the executive's background, especially those who are and have been employed in his previous firm.

The prevailing leadership paradigm can have a profound effect on the distribution of power in an organization or a negligible effect, depending on the strength of the culture and the relative dominance of the top leaders. Obviously, in stronger cultures or organizations with dominant senior leaders, people brought in from outside the organization are less likely to succeed if they are hired into positions of organizational authority. SAS, the North Carolina–based business software firm that routinely ranks among *Fortune*'s best companies to work for, has a strong employee-centric culture. Reflecting on the company culture, Jim Goodnight, the CEO of SAS, said, "Our culture is a lot like the human immune system. If you bring a stranger into a leadership position, it attacks."[7] Consequently, one of the biggest challenges facing newly hired executives from outside an organization is understanding and becoming simpatico with the organization's culture and prevailing leadership paradigm before they try to institute changes. If they successfully get on board, they can sustain the role power granted to them and eventually build other sources of power in the organization. If they fail, they will lose power and eventually wash out.

The prevailing leadership paradigm affects the distribution of power by creating a process of natural selection in which people who adhere to the paradigm are more likely to be identified as high potentials and given more educational opportunities, choice assignments, and promotions, whereas the opposite is true for contrarians, who are likely to be viewed as cultural misfits.

Environment in Which the Organization Operates

The distribution of power in an organization is also influenced by the need for stability versus the need for adaptability. In organizations of any kind, managers strive for stability because stability promotes efficiency and predictability. Doing the same things the same way enables managers to increase the efficiency of their operations. With capable management, a highly stable organization can become a well-oiled machine. Stability is a premium for fast-food companies, fire departments, restaurants, railroads, airlines, assembly-line manufacturers, power plants, banks, and ships, for instance. These organizations emphasize processes, procedures, training, and accountability—and power goes to the managers who can keep their operations running smoothly and resolve problems quickly.

The degree of stability organizations can attain is a function of the environment in which they operate. If their environment is stable and predictable, then organizations will invariably strive for highly efficient operations, and the most powerful people in those organizations will be those who meet their performance goals on time, every time. However, if their environment is changing, especially if it's *rapidly* changing, then organizations must be highly adaptable. Think of advertising firms, television networks, management consultancies, software developers, computer manufacturers, pharmaceutical companies, clothing manufacturers, sports teams, and other types of organizations where consumer preferences and market conditions continually evolve or where competition drives innovation so quickly that no organization can afford to be stable for very long. When what's true today is not true tomorrow, stability means decline, and more power accrues to those people in the organization who are innovative, flexible, and quick to adapt their outlooks, approaches, and practices to the new environmental conditions.

The environmental forces most likely to affect an organization are its markets (or the constituencies it serves) and competitors (or the alternatives for its constituencies). Changing customer needs or preferences or hot new products/advertising from competitors will destabilize an organization sooner or later and cause it to adapt or risk declining. Other environmental influences may include governments, capital markets/banks, lobbyists or special-interest groups, the media, emerging technologies, and other changes in the marketplace—such as changes in distribution channels or supply chain partners or in the availability of raw materials, legal decisions, accidents or weather-related problems, and so on. Although organizations may try to manage some of these forces (by lobbying against laws that could impact their business, for example), by and large these environmental forces are beyond an organization's effective control.

How do environmental forces affect the distribution of power in organizations? Like Darwin's survival of the fittest, when environmental conditions force an organization to adapt, the balance of power in the organization typically shifts toward the successful adapters and problem solvers and away from those managers or leaders who either stubbornly cling to the former status quo or are too slow to adapt. Korn/Ferry's research on learning agility shows conclusively that the highest performers in organizations, especially over the long term, are those who are agile in the face of changing environmental and business conditions.[8]

Informal Working Processes or Neural Nets of the Organization

I said earlier in this chapter that the formal authority structure of an organization—as represented by an organization chart—is the distribution of power *in theory*. The informal working processes or neural nets of the organization reflect the distribution of power *in practice*. I am using neural nets as a metaphor because what happens in organizations is very similar to what happens in the human brain as people interact with their environment, solve problems, and learn. The human brain has a defined structure (its organization chart, so to speak), but what happens at the neuron level is very fluid. Connections between neurons are strengthened when one neuron fires and sends an electrochemical impulse to a connected neuron, which in turn may fire and excite other neurons. And when we learn, the neurons in our brains form new connections. So while the overall structure of the brain may not change, at the microscopic level our brains are constantly changing as some neural connections are reinforced, new connections are formed, and underused connections weaken. The human brain's neural networks do the real work—making sense of stimuli, forming connections, processing information, and creating a mental map of the world as we know it.

A similar process occurs in organizations. The formal authority structure of the organization is a roadmap for how power is meant to be distributed—and how work is meant to be done. But as people do the organization's work, they develop connections with other people, some of whom may be in different functions, departments, or regions of the organization. They learn who does what and which people are more knowledgeable, informative, or helpful. They discover who the best problem solvers are, who knows the products or customers best, who is most reliable, who is best informed, and who is most forthcoming. They build relationships with the people they like and trust. And they discover who the power players are, who has the boss's ear, and who is best connected with other key people throughout the organization. They also learn where to expect obstacles and how to work around the people or areas of the organization where those obstacles occur. If we could map each person's connections and interdependencies throughout the organization, we would have what amounts to the organization's complex neural nets—the informal but more accurate view of how power is distributed throughout the organization.

> The formal authority structure of an organization is the distribution of power *in theory*. The informal working processes or neural nets of the organization reflect the distribution of power *in practice*.

This neural net would reveal that some people are at the hubs of informal networks that stretch throughout the organization. They know more people, communicate more, have more information, know how to get things done, and are essential to the organization's effective functioning. We would discover that many of these well-connected people are not part of the management hierarchy. Some of them would be trusted individual contributors. Some would be executive assistants. Some would, in effect, have their second desk at the watercooler. They would know all the gossip. Some of them would have a better understanding than management about how the organization is working and what people are feeling because they are good listeners and people talk candidly to them. Some would be powerful because they know how the systems and processes are supposed to work—and know how to bypass the bureaucratic roadblocks and get things done. Clearly, some people in an organization are powerful because of their positions, but whereas a management role may be a sufficient condition for power, it is not a necessary one.

In the organization's neural net, many people who are not managers will be influential, to one degree or another, because they have strong sources of organizational and personal power. They may be well connected to others throughout the organization (network power), better informed than others (information power), and highly regarded and trusted (reputation power). Yes, they may be powerful because they are well placed in the organization (e.g., the executive assistant to the CEO or another senior leader), but it is also likely that their informal power is based on what they know (knowledge power), how communicative they are (expressiveness power), how likeable they are (attraction power), and how trustworthy and discreet they are (character power). The informal working relationships of an organization—the self-organizing neural nets I've been describing—

may mirror the formal organization chart to some degree, but it will always be a fuzzy reflection.

In *Power and Influence: Beyond Formal Authority,* Harvard's John Kotter observes that one of the dynamics of power in organizations is diversity versus interdependence. He defines diversity as "differences among people with respect to goals, values, stakes, assumptions, and perceptions."[9] Interdependence occurs when two or more people depend on each other and thus have some power over each other. This dynamic creates the potential for productive collaboration but also for conflict, bureaucratic stagnation, divisive politicking, and worse. As Kotter notes, "When a high degree of interdependence exists in the workplace, unilateral action is rarely possible. For all decisions of any significance, many people will be in a position to retard, block, or sabotage action, because they have some power over the situation. This power might be based on the formal authority of their positions, on financial or human resources they control, on their special expertise or knowledge, on legislation or legal contracts, or on any number of other things."[10] In pathological organizations, power struggles can become so intense that they create poisonous factions that damage or destroy the organization. In healthy organizations, these struggles can stimulate creative problem solving; a clarification of assumptions, goals, and priorities; and a realignment of people toward a common purpose.

In formal, hierarchical organizations like the military and the church, the distribution of power is likely to adhere to the formal organizational structure, so power mirrors the divisions and levels in the hierarchy. This doesn't negate the organization's neural nets; it simply means that the formal power structure has considerable bearing on who in the organization has what kind of power. In looser organizations, particularly those with a matrix structure, the distribution of power is more likely to reflect the organization's neural nets, and this is especially true if the top leaders' leadership paradigm is more collaborative and consensual. When people are granted the latitude to develop the relationships and channels that best facilitate accomplishing their work and goals, they start to self-organize in ways that may appear chaotic but in fact are highly efficient. When this happens, power is distributed organically, as it were, along lines that reflect the strength of each individual's personal and organizational power sources.

▶ PROFILES *in* POWER

JEFF BEZOS AND AMAZON

He has an explosive laugh, a curious and nimble mind, and unerring business instincts. Since 1994, he has pioneered the field of e-commerce, built one of the most recognizable brands on the planet, been named *Time*'s Person of the Year and one of America's best leaders by *U.S. News & World*

Report, and made himself and his parents billionaires. The boy who would be an Internet mogul was born in Albuquerque and raised in Houston by his mother, Jackie, and adoptive father, Miguel (Mike) Bezos, a Cuban émigré. When he was three, he wanted a normal bed instead of a crib, but his mother said no. She later found him taking the crib apart with a screwdriver. Throughout his youth, he tinkered, experimented, and built science projects, like trying to convert an old Hoover vacuum cleaner into a hovercraft (Jackie complained that as he got older the projects got larger but their garage didn't). He spent summers on the farm of his maternal grandfather, Preston Gise, west of San Antonio. Gise had been a manager for the Atomic Energy Commission, so he was a perfect mentor for his grandson, encouraging his scientific interests and teaching him many practical mechanical skills, such as how to weld, lay pipe, and repair machinery. Jackie later said that one of the greatest lessons Jeff learned from Pop Gise is that no problem is unsolvable. Every obstacle presents an opportunity.

Valedictorian of his high school class, Bezos went to Princeton to study theoretical physics but switched to computer science and graduated summa cum laude in 1986. In his initial jobs after graduation, he used computers to solve problems or present information in ways that are commonplace now but were groundbreaking back then. In 1990, he was hired by D. E. Shaw & Co. in New York City to create a computer program for determining the optimal time to make stock transactions. During this period, Bezos became increasingly aware of the World Wide Web and was fascinated to learn that it was growing at an exponential 2,300 percent annually. When David Shaw asked him to explore new business opportunities on the Internet, Bezos studied the problem thoughtfully and told him that selling books was the best opportunity. To his surprise, Shaw said no, and so Bezos and his wife, MacKenzie, decided to do it themselves.

Their little company was initially called Cadabra (as in "abracadabra"), but when someone mispronounced it "cadaver," Bezos changed the name to Amazon, after Earth's largest river, with its numerous branches and tributaries—a fitting metaphor for the e-commerce business he envisioned. Amazon began in the garage of their rented house in Seattle. With a door as a desk and a patchwork of computers, power cords, cables, and phones

Photo by Toru Yamanaka/AFP by Getty Images.

as their infrastructure, Bezos, MacKenzie, and their small team of programmers invented the tools and processes for conducting e-commerce on the Internet. They had 300 friends test the site and then launched it on July 16, 1995. In the first week, they had more than $12,000 in orders. In the first month, they sold books to customers in all fifty states and forty-five other countries. At the heart of their growing success was the customer experience they created online, an experience they have continually reinvented and refined since.

It is difficult now to remember a time when the e-shopping experience Amazon created did not exist. Bezos's genius was to envision what the Web made possible and to persevere when so many naysayers said it couldn't be done. Among Amazon's many innovations was listing millions of book titles online, including rare books, far more than traditional booksellers could stock; enabling customers to write and post reviews of books and share book lists; showing customers interested in a book what books other buyers had also purchased; establishing an associates program that allowed other merchants to sell their products through Amazon; building a search engine that allowed customers to search the Web for any product; creating the "sample page" and "look inside" features that allow online shoppers to search inside a book before buying; inventing "one-click shopping" that makes buying easier for repeat customers; and, most recently, developing the Kindle e-book reader.

In the sixteen years since it was founded, Amazon has grown at an even faster rate than the Web itself. The world's largest online retailer now offers more than 12 million products, including music, videos, toys, electronics, clothing, kitchen appliances, computers, furniture, beauty products, solar panels, sports equipment, and power tools. It is the modern, global, electronic equivalent of the Sears & Roebuck catalog of the twentieth century. The journey hasn't always been smooth. The company didn't make money until late 2001, and at various times analysts predicted its demise, but Bezos remained confident through it all. As a leader, he's been both visionary and obsessively focused on details, intuitive and analytical, intense and relaxed. His motto: "Work hard. Play hard. Make history." And the people he sought to hire had to be "intense, hardworking, smart people."[11] Amazon is fully an organization in its prime, and power in Amazon goes to those intense, hardworking, smart people who reflect Jeff Bezos's combination of playfulness and intensity, focus on the customer experience, and transformational business thinking.

In 1994, Bezos told his initial investors that they would probably lose their entire investment. The Internet was new, and nothing like Amazon had ever been attempted. Nevertheless, his parents contributed $300,000, which was much of their retirement savings. "We weren't betting on the Internet," his mother later said. "We were betting on Jeff."[12]

What We Can Learn from Jeff Bezos and Amazon

1. *In mature organizations, power goes to systems architects and innovators.* Leaders like Jeff Bezos need (1) people who can build and manage

systems that deliver consistent superior performance and (2) innovators who are envisioning and inventing what the organization needs to
continually improve the customer experience while outpacing competitors' ability to catch up. If you are in an organization like Amazon, know
which of these profiles best fits you and then perform exceptionally
well.

2. *Playfulness is as important as intensity.* Words to describe Jeff Bezos
would include hardworking, driven, and intense, but as he and Amazon
have matured, Bezos has not lost the playfulness and curiosity he had
as a kid. What sustained him and his enterprise through some tough
times was his youthful conviction that Amazon would succeed as well
as the joy he felt in continual exploration. You would never use the word
satisfice to describe Jeff Bezos or anything he leads. If you want to
build power in an organization like Amazon, that word can't describe
you either.

Ambitions and Allegiances of Individual Members

The final force affecting the distribution of power in organizations consists
of the ambitions and allegiances of its individual members. American sociologist Charles Horton Cooley (1864–1929) said, "The general fact is that
the most effective way of utilizing human energy is through an organized
rivalry, which by specialization and social control is, at the same time,
organized cooperation."[13] Cooley was best known for his concept of the
"looking glass self," by which he meant that the concept of the individual
is meaningless except as it relates to society; in other words, we perceive
ourselves by looking through the mirror of the society we belong to. I have
argued similarly that power is a relational concept. People don't have
power except in relation to other people. So when we consider how power
is distributed in organizations, it is important to include the effect of everyone's ambitions (as they relate to and potentially conflict with everyone
else's ambitions) and the allegiances people form with various other people
in the organization.

If organizations are, as Aldous Huxley claimed, "homemade monsters," then what occurs within them is organized rivalry in the monster's
den. That rivalry stems from the simple fact that organizations are meritocracies. Some people advance faster than others. Some people become managers whereas others remain individual contributors. Some receive higher
pay raises or bonuses, and some are recognized and rewarded for superior
contributions whereas others aren't. Some people become favored by their
superiors, for any number of reasons, and have more opportunities come

their way than those who are not favored. It is human nature, as well as the nature of organizations, for competition to arise in groups. That competition may be subtle. In the spirit of altruism and brotherhood or sisterhood, people may want to deny rivalry, but it still exists because all people are motivated in part by self-interest. The best people apply themselves to whatever they're doing for the sake of the organization and its customers, but they also look out for themselves.

Most people strive, to a greater or lesser degree depending on how ambitious they are, to further their own interests inside and outside their organization. Many of them join social, charitable, political, or professional groups outside their organization to meet like-minded people, network with others in their industry, or advance their careers. No matter how loyal they may be to their employer, people know that there are no guarantees of employment, and many are upwardly mobile and eager to advance in their careers, so they do what they can to make themselves highly employable. Some pursue educational opportunities and other experiences to build their résumés. Some are very mobile and move from one company to another every few years seeking positions of greater responsibility (and compensation). Everyone knows that organizations are pyramid shaped, so the higher you go in the organization the fewer promotional slots there are above your current level. So at every level you are in effect competing with others at your level (and perhaps qualified external candidates) for the next promotional opportunity.

> If organizations are, as Aldous Huxley claimed, "homemade monsters," then what occurs within them is organized rivalry in the monster's den. That rivalry stems from the simple fact that organizations are meritocracies.

That rivalry may be casual at lower levels in the organization, but at senior levels it can be intense and even vicious. Most rivals at the senior level avoid open confrontation, but a number of senior leaders are masters of covert conflict. I once coached a senior vice president in a company whose challenge was collaboration with his peers. It was an issue for him because he perceived that they were all competing for a small set of positions at the next level. He saw it as a game of musical chairs, and when the music stopped, someone was going to wind up in a disadvantageous position. Whether or not this outlook is healthy, it was his perspective, and the issue it raised for him was how much he and his peers cooperated with each other and how much they worked against each other. He saw both happening and felt he was the victim of covert sabotage involving backroom politicking with the CEO.

When the ambitions of individual members of an organization clash, their overt or covert rivalry can militate against cooperation, and this affects the distribution of power in several ways. The winners of these Machiavellian struggles can gain power at the expense of their defeated rivals (unless a superior recognizes what is happening and negates it). A fine example was Jeffrey Skilling's rivalry at Enron with executive Rebecca Mark. In the mid-1990s, Skilling headed Enron Finance and Mark led Enron International. Both were favorites of CEO Ken Lay and were deemed superstars in the Enron galaxy. Both aspired to become president and chief operating officer of Enron and were bitter rivals for that position, but Skilling proved to be more masterful at manipulating Lay. When the position became available, Skilling threatened to quit if he did not get the job, reportedly saying to a colleague, "I'll tell you one thing. If that bitch gets it, I'm outta here."[14] Skilling galvanized his allies, who made sure Lay got the message that Skilling would leave and Enron would suffer if Mark became president. Lay was terrified of losing Skilling because the traders he led were earning astronomical profits and were reportedly fiercely loyal to Skilling, so Lay buckled and named Skilling the president. Mark subsequently resigned as head of Enron International and left the company barely a year before it collapsed.

As happened at Enron, the distribution of power can be affected by the coalitions that form within organizations when disagreements and conflicts emerge. Rebecca Mark and Jeffrey Skilling had allies whose support fell on either side of the philosophical divide the two antagonists represented: whether Enron should be an asset-light business (Skilling) or an asset-rich business (Mark). When Mark's nemesis gained the throne, she and those allied with her lost power. And so it may be in organizations where the diversity of perspectives creates factions centered on products, ideas, or leaders whose rise or fall may dictate where and how power shifts within the organization.

NAVIGATING THE FIVE FORCES

Let's recap. Power in organizations is shaped by organizational structure, which defines the formal power and authority relationships; by the neural net of informal working relationships and channels that develop as people work together and discover the best pathways for solving problems and getting work done; by the prevailing leadership paradigm in the organization; by external forces, most notably the markets the organization serves; and by the ambitions and allegiances of individuals in the organization as they strive to further their self-interests, which may complement or collide with others' self-interests. As these five forces act on the organization, the distribution of power continually changes. Most of the time, these changes are slow and subtle until a tipping point is reached and a quantum shift occurs. Sometimes, the changes are swift and jarring—when a new senior leader comes on board who has a substantially different leadership paradigm, for instance; or when the organization experiences the tidal effects of a huge environmental change (e.g., a coup in a country the organization serves abruptly alters government policy); or when the organization experiences a substantial reorganization, merger, acquisition, or divestiture.

As I said at the outset, many of these forces are beyond your control, so no matter how much power you have in your organization, your power may grow or diminish based on the effects of these five forces. Even CEOs are not immune from their effects. However, this doesn't mean that you are completely at the mercy of these forces. You can build your sources of power and protect and grow your power base—if not always in your current organization, then perhaps in the next one you join. Here are some tips on how to successfully navigate the five forces:

► *Expand your power sources.* The power sources you build before joining an organization are the price of admission. They are what you bring to the table. If you want to be powerful in any organization, you need to continually develop the power sources I've described in this book, particularly your personal sources (knowledge, expressiveness, history, attraction, and character). To build on my metaphor of human power being like a battery, when you apply for a job, your résumé is like a voltmeter. It measures the amount of power you can bring to the organization—how much you know, how skilled you are, what experiences you've had, and what previous roles you've played. The job interview gives potential employers another view of your power sources—how articulate you are, how appealing or likeable, how forthright and candid.

Your organizational power sources are also important, particularly reputation and network. The reputation power you've gained primarily reflects your previous work performance. Your references can speak directly to how well regarded you were in the previous organizations you belonged to, and job interviewers can infer a great deal about how you are likely to perform in their organization based on the reputation you built elsewhere. The breadth and quality of your network is also a key measurement of the power you can bring to an organization. Sales and public relations professionals, marketers, and consultants, for instance, are often hired based on the size and quality of their networks and the contacts they can bring to the new organization.

If your goal is to advance in your organization, industry, or profession, then building and maintaining these sources of power is crucial because it increases your value in the organizations you belong to or join. In short, it protects you in your current job and makes you more employable if you leave.

▶ *Assess your fit with the organization.* The power you have in an organization depends to a great extent on how well you fit the organization. First, you must be aligned with the mission and purpose of the organization. That is obviously paramount. When I was the CEO of Lore International Institute, I told employees, "This is who we are and what we do. If that's who you are and what you enjoy doing, then this is the right place for you. But if not, you should go somewhere else where you'll be happier and more fulfilled." It's more than about job satisfaction. You will lose power in an organization you don't believe in because your heart will not be in it.

Also critically important is cultural fit. You can otherwise have strong sources of power, but if your attitudes, values, or operating style are misaligned with the cultural norms of the organization, you are likely to lose power as the culture rejects you (recall the earlier discussion of SAS in this chapter). It's also important to be aligned with the prevailing leadership paradigm in the organization, especially if you are in a management or leadership role. I'm not arguing that people have to conform completely to "organization think," but the reality is that serious misfits grate on the organization's nerves and are eventually isolated and rejected. To gain power in an organization, you must be aligned with what works well and is held dear, or you must obtain cultural acceptance for changing what doesn't work well.

A number of people who have held power in an organization lose a significant amount of that power when the organization is acquired by or merged with another organization and the culture or prevailing leadership paradigm undergoes a substantial transmutation that leaves them on the losing side of the new power curve. When a paradigm shift occurs, some people typically discover that they no longer fit the new organization. Whether or not a significant shift occurs, people and organizations evolve over time, and some people may eventually conclude that they no longer fit the organization as it now exists. It's best for them to reassess whether they can adapt to the new mission, purpose, culture, or leadership paradigm, because without that alignment they will certainly lose power and may be dissatisfied.

► *Maintain visibility in the organization.* No matter how powerful you might be otherwise, you won't build power in an organization if you aren't visible to other members of the organization, particularly the leadership. You must have visibility—not only with your peers and immediate superior, but also with the level of leadership above them. Visibility is an essential ingredient in building network, history, and reputation power throughout the organization.

You build visibility—first and foremost—with exceptional performance. I once heard a partner in a McKinsey & Company office speaking to a group of associates, and someone asked what associates needed to do to succeed in the firm. The partner gave one of the best responses I've ever heard to such a question. He said, "You have to create demand for yourself, and you do that by doing great work." Exceptional performers get noticed. They are offered more of the choice opportunities. Managers want them on their teams. They get stellar performance reviews, and when it's time for promotions, they are at the top of the list. They build substantial reputation power through the results they achieve, particularly if they are also likeable and collaborative—and this increases their visibility with their peers and the organization's leaders.

You also gain visibility by networking outside your immediate group, office, and function. Take advantage of opportunities to work with people from other parts of the organization, serve on multifunctional project teams or task forces, and participate in training programs with attendees from other parts of the organization. Power is a function of visibility, and when you meet and work with leaders of the organization, you also begin building history power with them.

► *Demonstrate your value and potential.* Power in organizations is also partly a function of the amount of value you bring to the organization and others' assessment of your potential. The organization may consider some positions more valuable than others, especially those requiring more knowledge and expertise or a more critical customer interface. Clearly, if you occupy a highly valued position and are performing well, you are going to have more power in the organization because management won't want to lose you. Related to the concept of value is the availability of substitutes. You will have more power, often considerably more, if you are considered irreplaceable or difficult to replace. You'll also have more power if you are considered a high potential—that is, if management believes you have the capacity to grow, to assume more responsibility or perform at an even higher level. Potential is an assessment of future value, and you will have more power if you are deemed important or essential for the organization's future.

► *Seek mobility.* People in technical positions or positions requiring special expertise may be valuable to an organization, but they may not be very mobile. They may be needed critically where they are and have little mobility. If you are such a person and are content to perform your function expertly, your power will be limited to the value you offer in that position and the scarcity of substitutes (internal or external) who could do that job. But experts who offer more (e.g., leadership, management skill, mentoring or coaching of others, innovation) are more mobile and typically have more power because of their potential to contribute to other parts of the organization or add value in other important ways.

► *Establish important functional affiliations.* Finally, the amount of power you have in an organization—and your potential to gain more power—may depend on the functions you belong to or are affiliated with. Just as some positions may be considered more valuable to an organization, some functions may have higher value as well. Typically, the frontline, customer-facing functions are more important to most companies. That's where business is won or lost, where customers are either delighted or disappointed with products or services. In organizations where outstanding customer service is critical to the organization's success, the services functions are more important. In finance-driven companies, the finance groups are more important. Generally speaking, of course, you will have more power if you have a visible, high-performing role in your organization's most prominent functions—the ones led by the organization's most highly regarded leaders, the ones closest to the action. If you are a jockey, you want to ride the fastest horse, and the metaphor applies here.

Sometimes it's a matter of finding your sweet spot. Roger Enrico is the former CEO of PepsiCo. After college, he began his career in the human resources department of an office of General Mills but found that he did not like the work. He left business for a stint in the military during the Vietnam War. When he returned, General Mills rehired him in one of its brand management groups, and he found his groove. After moving to Frito-Lay, a division of PepsiCo, he quickly rose through the ranks in brand management and marketing, where he excelled and had very high visibility, and that experience propelled him into senior leadership positions at PepsiCo. As his example illustrates, power comes from finding your sweet spot and performing well in a functional area that is essential to the organization and gives you high visibility among the senior leaders who recognize your value and potential and promote you to increasingly more powerful roles.

One of the key lessons of this chapter is that power in organizations is complicated, and the larger the organization, the more complicated it becomes. In an organization, you are one member of the power grid. What you bring to the table are your personal and organizational sources of power. The formal structure of the organization and the role you play in it are key factors in determining how much power you can exercise. But power is also a function of the informal working relationships that develop as people work together—in other words, the neural nets of the organization. And the distribution of power may also be affected by external forces that are essentially beyond anyone's control.

In organizations, power is relational and dynamic. It fluctuates continually as people work with or against each other, as changes in leadership affect the prevailing leadership paradigm, and as the ambitions and allegiances of the many individuals in the organization foster alliances or rivalries. The amount of power you can develop depends on the value you bring to the organization (the strength of your personal and organizational power sources) as well as your fit with the organization. It also depends on how highly you are regarded, how much potential you are deemed to have, how mobile you are, and whether you have high visibility in one of the organization's most important functional areas.

Your ability to gain and exercise power in an organization is conditional, and you cannot control many of those conditions. However, you can build your personal and organizational sources of power (see chapter 12). You can try to find your sweet spot and apply yourself so that you create demand for yourself by doing great work. You can build your network and visibility. You can either ensure that you are a good fit for the organization or, if not, find another organization where you are a better fit. Most of all, you can gain power by knowing what you want and having the energy and determination to make that dream a reality. It turns out that the greatest source of power is your will, and that is the subject of the next chapter.

One closing thought is important. I argued in the introduction that power is morally neutral, that it may be the instrument of evil but not the agent. I also said that power can distort power holders, especially when their power is absolute and unchecked. However, I believe that with authentic leadership and ethical influence, power and character go hand in hand. Authentic leaders wish to become more powerful, not for the sake of having power, but because it gives them the capacity to lead others in a worthwhile pursuit and accomplish things great and small. Whether they are inventing a platform for social networking online or reinventing the way retailers bring products to market, authentic leaders exercise power not at the expense of others but in service to them, and not for self-aggrandizement but for the good of the organizations they lead and the constituencies they serve. If your pursuit of power is all about you, then you are treading on a slippery slope, because power without a worthwhile purpose is a pathway to abuse. Authentic leadership is never about you; it's always about other people.

KEY CONCEPTS

1. In organizations, the dynamics of power are complicated because people don't exercise power in a vacuum; they exercise power within the formal and informal structures of their organization in response to internal and external priorities and events, sometimes acting in concert with other people in the organization and sometimes acting in opposition to them.

2. Five forces modulate the distribution and use of power in organizations: (1) the formal authority structure of the organization; (2) the prevailing leadership paradigm; (3) the environment in which the organization operates; (4) the informal working processes or neural nets of the organization; and (5) the ambitions and allegiances of individual members of the organization, particularly as they complement or clash with the ambitions and allegiances of other members.

3. The amount of power you can have in an organization depends not only on the strength of your personal and organizational sources of

power (particularly role power), but also on how aligned you are with the organization's design and stage in its life cycle.

4. The prevailing leadership paradigm affects the distribution of power by creating a process of "natural selection," whereby people who adhere to the paradigm are more likely to be identified as high potentials and given more educational opportunities, choice assignments, and promotions, whereas the opposite is true for the contrarians, who are likely to be viewed as cultural misfits.

5. The formal authority structure of an organization is the distribution of power *in theory*. The informal working processes or neural nets of the organization reflect the distribution of power *in practice*.

6. If organizations are, as Aldous Huxley claimed, "homemade monsters," then what occurs within them is organized rivalry in the monster's den. That rivalry stems from the simple fact that organizations are meritocracies.

7. The power sources you build before joining an organization are the price of admission. They are what you bring to the table. So, if you want to be powerful in any organization, you need to continually develop your power sources.

8. Serious misfits grate on an organization's nerves and are eventually isolated and rejected. To gain power in an organization, you must be aligned with what works well and is held dear, or you must have cultural acceptance for changing what doesn't work well.

9. In organizations, power is relational and dynamic. It fluctuates continually as people work with or against each other, as changes in leadership affect the prevailing leadership paradigm, and as the ambitions and allegiances of the many individuals in the organization foster alliances or rivalries.

10. The amount of power you can develop depends on the value you bring to an organization (i.e., the strength of your personal and organizational power sources) as well as your fit with the organization. It also depends on how highly you are regarded, how much potential you are deemed to have, how mobile you are, and whether you have high visibility in one of the organization's most important functional areas.

CHALLENGES FOR READERS

1. Here's a challenging but insightful exercise: Look at the organization chart for your organization or the part of your organization you know best. It reflects how power and authority are distributed *in theory*. How does power actually work in your organization? What is the distribution of power *in practice*? Which people are more or less powerful than their positions suggest? Where are there friendships and allegiances among people or groups that affect communication, problem solving, decision making, and work flow? Where are the "hidden" sources of power among the people and groups that make up your organization?

2. Where is your organization in its life cycle? Early? Prime? Late? Are you in an entrepreneurial organization? A mature organization? A bureaucratic organization? How does your organization's position in its life cycle affect who has power, who gains power, and who loses power?

3. What is the prevailing leadership paradigm in your organization? What does your top leader think about how organizations should be run? Which beliefs and behaviors are rewarded by your leaders and managers, and which aren't? If you are a leader/manager, what must you do to succeed (i.e., to build or sustain power)? What would cause you to lose power?

4. How do environmental forces affect the distribution of power in your organization? Which forces are most impactful and why?

5. Reflect on the informal working processes or neural nets in your organization or your part of the organization. What do these neural nets look like? How do things actually work? Identify some nonmanagers who have more power than their roles would indicate. Why do they have that power? What can they do with it?

6. Are there any pathological processes at work in your organization? Political struggles? Is there any bureaucratic infighting? Backstabbing? If so, how do these dynamics affect the distribution of power in the organization?

7. Do you observe any rivalry among peers in your organization? Are people overtly or covertly competing for those next-level opportu-

nities? Can you identify any situations in the past where there was a clear "winner" and "loser" in these rivalries?

8. How well do you fit your current organization? Are you a good fit with the culture? Why or why not?

9. How visible are you in your organization? To your superiors? Peers? Customers? What could you do to increase your visibility?

10. Review again the section "Navigating the Five Forces." Considering these factors and the tips I offered, how would you assess your power in your organization? Are you gaining, holding steady, or losing power? What is contributing to your gaining or losing power? Does it matter to you? If so, what can you do about it?

PART III
THE WILL TO POWER

Where does power come from?

ANDREW CARNEGIE SAID, "IMMENSE POWER IS ACQUIRED BY ASSURING YOURSELF IN YOUR SECRET REVERIES THAT YOU WERE BORN TO CONTROL AFFAIRS." ULTIMATELY, YOUR ABILITY TO CREATE IMPACT AS A LEADER AND TO INFLUENCE PEOPLE AND EVENTS DEPENDS ON YOUR DESIRE TO BE POWERFUL. IT DEPENDS ON THE STRENGTH OF YOUR DETERMINATION TO INFLUENCE OTHERS, CREATE NEW THINGS, AND MAKE A DIFFERENCE. IT DEPENDS ON YOUR WILL. YOUR ABILITY TO TURN PLANS INTO ACTION AND MAKE DREAMS A REALITY—THROUGH THE FORCE OF DETERMINATION AND IN DEFIANCE OF OBSTACLES—IS THE MOST IMPORTANT SOURCE OF POWER YOU CAN HAVE. THIS PART OF THE BOOK EXPLORES THE WILL TO BE POWERFUL AND IDENTIFIES THE MANY WAYS YOU CAN BUILD ALL THE SOURCES OF POWER DESCRIBED IN THIS BOOK.

CHAPTER 11

FIRST STEPS DOWN NEW ROADS

The Power of Will

WHAT DO RAY KROC, GERT BOYLE, AND TOM MONAGHAN HAVE IN COMMON?
They all started with little, faced many setbacks, and were told they would
fail, but they persevered through hard times and created McDonald's,
Columbia Sportswear, and Domino's Pizza. Virtually anyone who's ever
founded a successful company knows that the most important ingredient
is determination—the will to stick with it no matter how great the obstacles. The secret sauce, the magic formula, the one thing that can give you
more power than all the other power sources I've described in this book is
the power of will. The amount of power you have depends to a great extent
on your desire to be more powerful and your courage to act on that desire.
As Ayn Rand said, "Throughout the centuries there were men [and
women] who took first steps, down new roads, armed with nothing but
their own vision."[1] Power goes not to the people who have the biggest
dreams but to the people who act on their dreams, not to the people who
have a vision but to the people willing to take those first steps down new
roads.

If you want to be more influential or have more impact as a leader,
nothing matters quite as much as your desire to be more powerful coupled
with the courage to act. Some people instinctively understand this and
work hard to build their skills, acquire the knowledge, gain control of the
information, build the connections, seek the right positions, amass the
resources, and so on, until they've become powerful. Not content to sit on
the sidelines, they do what it takes to build their bases of power. They are
the power seekers, the Dick Cheneys and Jack Welches of the world who
do what it takes to put themselves in the right place with the right people
at the right time. They learn how the system works, and they march with
dogged determination toward their goal. They are pragmatists. Others are
idealists, like Albert Schweitzer, Mohandas Gandhi, and Aung San Suu Kyi,
who don't strive as much for power as they strive to make a difference, to

right a wrong, to perform a great service. Depending on your point of view, one approach may be more preferable than the other, but power follows no compass. It simply is. Both of these approaches to power are evident in Barack Obama, an idealist who wants to make a difference who is also a pragmatist who skillfully built a power base.

If power has no compass, it claims no birthright, either. You don't have to have been born with power or privilege to become powerful. Obama came from modest beginnings, as did Jack Welch and most other people who have risen to great heights and done great things. César Chávez was born in 1927 to a modest Mexican-American family near Yuma, Arizona. After working as a farmworker and serving in the U.S. Navy during World War II, he became one of the most recognized, respected, and powerful labor activists in the United States. He cofounded and led the National Farm Workers Association (NFWA), which later became the United Farm Workers (UFW). Throughout his life, he organized marches, strikes, protests, and boycotts that resulted not only in essential improvements in the lives of farmworkers, but also significant advances in workers' rights. He and fellow activists like Dolores Huerta (cofounder of the NFWA) gained power because they were committed to change, and they chose to act. As Margaret Mead noted, "Never doubt that a small group of thoughtful, committed citizens can change the world. Indeed, it's the only thing that ever has."[2]

> *Mediocrity is self-inflicted. Genius is self-bestowed.*
> —WALTER RUSSELL

I noted in the book's introduction that the power of will comes from within and can magnify every other source of power. I consider it a *mega-*source of power because it is uniquely individual, is not culturally determined or biased, and is available to anyone with the courage and determination to seize it. Will power depends entirely on a person's decision to act; it requires passion and commitment but also energy and action. It is different from ambition, which is laudable but may be nothing more than a dream. It is different from desire and longing. It comes not from the impulse to act but from acting on the impulse. Any number of people look at a situation and say something should be done; only a handful go and do it—and they become more powerful and have greater capacity to influence others because of the power of their will. It's the difference between dreamers and doers.

Sister Mary Scullion of the Sisters of Mercy in Philadelphia is one such person. For more than thirty years, she has been an advocate for the homeless and mentally ill. In 1985, she cofounded a permanent residency with support services for mentally ill women, and in 1988, the Outreach Coordination Center, a program for outreach and case management for people living on the streets. Then, in 1989, along with Joan McConnon, she founded Project H.O.M.E. (Housing, Opportunities for Employment, Medical Care, Education). This nationally recognized nonprofit started with one emergency winter shelter and has grown to nearly 500 units of housing and three businesses that offer employment to previously homeless persons. Its facilities include a learning center and technology lab for occupational training. Since its inception, Project H.O.M.E. has leveraged more than $50 million in equity toward housing development.[3]

For her lifetime of work to eliminate homelessness in the city, Sister Mary has been called the Mother Teresa of Philadelphia. Humble and self-effacing, she is nonetheless tireless, persistent, passionate, and quietly determined in the pursuit of her mission. *Time* magazine selected her as one of the "World's 100 Most Influential People in 2009." Commenting on her selection for this honor, Nan Roman, president of the National Alliance to End Homelessness, said, "Sister Mary is a formidable leader. She's been a driving force in reducing homelessness in Philadelphia, and an example for communities all over the country. Her blend of deep compassion and hardheaded practicality make her an invaluable ally and teacher."[4] Modest as usual, Sister Mary's response to the honor was to say, "All of us have influence. Now more than ever, we need to use that influence—that energy, that power—to build a society where all citizens can flourish and contribute. Let's work to make that vision a reality."[5]

> *Strength does not come from physical capacity. It comes*
> *from an indomitable will.*
> —MOHANDAS GANDHI

Walt Whitman called the power of will "personal force." He said that character and personal force are the only investments worth making. Personal force is the will to do something when others merely dream about it or talk about it. When you combine this personal force with character, with the commitment to do what's right, you can make mighty things happen. An otherwise unremarkable man named Jeremy Gilley made something mighty happen—and continues to do so. An English actor and filmmaker of modest success, he became disturbed by televised images of violence and inhumanity and wondered whether humankind was funda-

Sister Mary Scullion. Photo by Jeff Fusco/Getty Images.

mentally evil and whether it might be possible to bring an end to the violence—even for just one day. So, in 1999, he founded the Peace One Day project, whose vision states: "If we are to move from a culture of war to a culture of peace then we will have to unite around the most fundamental issue that humanity faces—the protection of each other and our environment. 21 September is the starting point. Individuals can make a difference. By working together there will be Peace One Day."[6]

Starting with very little support, recognition, or money, Gilley launched a global campaign to urge an end to violence around the world every September 21. Among his initial successes was persuading the United Nations General Assembly to adopt a resolution declaring that day to be the International Day of Peace, a day of global ceasefire and nonviolence. It has been an epic struggle since then, but with the help of celebrities, corporate sponsors, governments, and a growing global network of supporters, Gilley has transformed his vision into a global movement. On Peace Day 2007, Ahmad Fawzi, director of the news and media division of the United Nations, estimated that more than 100 million people in 100 countries were marking the day in some fashion, including with vaccination campaigns, peace walks, peace-related discussions and debates, poetry readings, peace prayer ceremonies, art exhibitions, and memorial services.[7]

Peace One Day has its skeptics. There are those who believe that gestures like an international day of peace won't change human nature; such efforts may be decent but fruitless. But there is no triumph without trying. As Theodore Roosevelt said:

> It is not the critic who counts; not the man who points out how the strong man stumbles, or where the doer of deeds could have done them better. The credit belongs to the man who is actually in the arena, whose face is marred by dust and sweat and blood, who strives valiantly; who errs and comes short again and again; because there is not effort without error and shortcomings; but who does actually strive to do the deed; who knows the great enthusiasm, the great devotion, who spends himself in a worthy cause, who at the best knows in the end the triumph of high achievement and who at the worst, if he fails, at least he fails while daring greatly. So that his place shall never be with those cold and timid souls who know neither victory nor defeat.[8]

What makes people like Ray Kroc, Gert Boyle, Tom Monaghan, César Chávez, Sister Mary Scullion, and Jeremy Gilley remarkable is that they are unremarkable except for the strength of their will. Their passion and commitment to action give them an extraordinary amount of power, and they use that power to lead and influence many others—sometimes millions of others—to see the world differently, adopt a course of action or support a program, assume a different attitude toward other people, or

Peace One Day's Jeremy Gilley. Photo by Astrid Stawiarz/Getty Images.

become inspired by a loftier vision of humanity. The power of will comes from authentic leadership, and nothing great was ever created except from this source of individual power.

KEY CONCEPTS

1. If you want to be more influential and have a greater impact as a leader, nothing matters quite as much as your desire to be powerful.

2. The power of will comes from within and can magnify every other source of power. It depends entirely on a person's decision to act—on passion and commitment but also on energy and action.

3. Will power is different from desire and longing. It comes not from the impulse to act but from acting on the impulse.

4. The power of will comes from authentic leadership, and nothing great was ever created except from this source of individual power.

CHALLENGES FOR READERS

1. Think about the people you have known who have strong will power—people who acted and made a difference. Where did their will come from? What sources of strength, courage, or determination did they draw upon to take action?

2. Study the lives of successful entrepreneurs. Most of them have faced numerous obstacles and prevailed because they were too stubborn not to, or because the dream was so vivid in their minds they couldn't imagine a world without their creation, or because they refused to allow their naysayers to be right. Choose a successful entrepreneur and then learn as much as you can about how that person prevailed through the force of will. How is this person the same as or different from you?

3. Have you ever known anyone who started an initiative with great dreams and plans—and then the initiative failed or the dream died? What happened? What was missing? Did the person encounter some insurmountable obstacles? How did the person react to the failure?

4. How would you assess your own power of will? If you have had the impulse to act but have not acted, reflect on why you didn't act. What prevented you from just doing it?

5. Ultimately, despite all your other power sources, what will give you the greatest capacity to be influential is the power of your will. What are you doing now to strengthen your determination to make things happen?

CHAPTER 12

INCREASING YOUR VOLTAGE

How to Become More Powerful

IN THE INTRODUCTION, I OBSERVED THAT INFLUENCING POWER IS LIKE A BAT-
tery. The more voltage a battery has, the more electrical power it can
deliver, and the greater its potential to do work. Likewise, the more power
you have, the greater your capacity to lead or influence others. Each of us
has five personal sources of power—knowledge, expressiveness, history,
attraction, and character—and five organizational sources—role, resources,
information, network, and reputation. In addition, we have one mega-
source of power: the power of our will. You can become a more powerful
leader and more influential in general, whether or not you are leading
others, by increasing any of these sources of power.

There is one important difference, however, between batteries and
people. Unless a battery is recharged, it begins its useful life with a maxi-
mum voltage rating and its power is depleted as the battery is used. With
people it is the opposite. We start life with relatively little power but have
the ability to increase our "voltage" throughout our lives. In this chapter,
I describe ways you can increase your sources of power, as well as some of
the ways those power sources can be diminished. At the end of the chapter,
I include a Power Sources Self-Assessment to help you measure the relative
strength of your power sources.

If your goal is to become a more powerful leader, this is an important
chapter for you. You may want to focus on building a particular power
source, or you may be looking for the best ways to build your power base
across all the sources. One suggestion I'd make is to pick the "low-hanging
fruit" by finding the three or four areas where you can make the greatest
gains in the shortest amount of time. Some of my suggestions will be easier
for you to accomplish, and some will be more difficult. Some take more
time; others can be done fairly quickly. Some require a huge investment of
time and effort; some require relatively little.

For each of the power sources, I first identify what diminishes the power source. You may be doing something or may lack something that is diminishing that source of power for you. If so, it is important to understand why that's happening and whether you can change it. Then I identify ways you can build the power source. Sometimes, building the power source means not doing something that diminishes it, but other times it means building a new skill or doing something that others have found to be a best practice.

I would wish you good luck, but becoming more powerful is not about luck. It's about awareness, discipline, and hard work. More power to you.

KNOWLEDGE POWER

WHAT DIMINISHES THIS POWER SOURCE?

1. Not having distinctive knowledge, skills, or capabilities. This is why education is one of the most important investments you can make in yourself. Knowledge is power, and people who devote time and energy to developing their knowledge and skills are substantially more influential than those who don't.

2. Being wrong. You can lose hard-earned credibility when knowledge you purport to have is later shown to be wrong. On the other hand, we all make mistakes, and the best of us learn from those mistakes. What is damaging is being obstinate about something that is not true; what's even more damaging is being arrogant about it. Hence, some people would describe former U.S. Vice President Dick Cheney as arrogant, as someone who was frequently wrong but never in doubt.

3. Faking knowledge and being found out. Don't fake it. If you don't know, say so.

4. Having a know-it-all attitude. Nobody knows it all. When you pretend you do, wiser people see you as the fool you are.

5. Being unable to prove an assertion. If you make a claim, it is best to be able to back it up with proof. Otherwise, you look like a braggart (and an ignorant one at that).

6. Not crediting the real source of knowledge. If you claim to have invented something and it's later shown that someone else invented it, you will lose credibility and trust quickly.

7. Bragging about a skill and then not performing. This is like a baseball player claiming he's going to knock the ball out of the park and then striking out every time he gets at bat. It's better to be modest and exceed people's expectations than to be cocky and fail to deliver.

8. Not being knowledgeable about what the group you are managing does. Managers of technical groups don't necessarily need to be experts in all the technology, but they must know enough to ask intelligent questions and make competent statements about the group's work.

HOW TO BUILD KNOWLEDGE POWER:

1. Most importantly, if you haven't done so already, build an area of distinctive knowledge, enhance your capabilities, and sharpen your skills. Recognize that people with exceptional knowledge power work hard at it and continually seek improvement. Truly exceptional people are lifelong learners and never believe they have learned or developed enough.

2. Apply your knowledge or skills in ways that achieve demonstrable results or improve the organization.

3. Join teams, clubs, task forces, committees, or other groups where your knowledge power will be most useful.

4. Communicate your knowledge in a way that enables others to recognize what you know. Beware, however, of becoming too self-promotional. The "tall poppy syndrome" operates in many cultures. Standing out too much, especially if you are the one drawing attention to yourself, can diminish your power even if your knowledge or skills are real and exceptional. Let others promote you instead.

5. Publish what you know. Write or contribute to blogs, articles, white papers, books, and other tangible works that allow you to share your knowledge.

6. Find opportunities to speak about what you know.

7. Seek opportunities to represent your group or organization to outsiders.

8. Become a coach, mentor, teacher, consultant, or adviser where you can use your knowledge to help others develop.

9.   Take advantage of higher education and continuing education opportunities. Go to college if you haven't. Get an advanced degree if you haven't already done so.

10.   Take advantage of your company's training and education programs. If you are a senior leader, become a facilitator or faculty member in such programs.

11.   Join user groups that focus on areas of interest to you. Become a contributor. Engage.

12.   Read. Study on your own. Learn all you can. If you want to build knowledge power, there are no real substitutes for continuous learning. Similarly, if you want to develop a skill, practice it as often as you can. Find a coach to help you. Study the greats. And practice, practice, practice.

EXPRESSIVENESS POWER

WHAT DIMINISHES THIS POWER SOURCE?

1.   Being inarticulate. Not knowing your language well enough to speak it correctly diminishes your credibility. Making grammatical errors may make you sound folksy but uneducated.

2.   Having a limited vocabulary or using repetitive verbal tics. Verbal tics, such as "like," and "uh, I'm like, you know," are annoying and detract from your message. Eliminate them.

3.   Being inexpressive or uncommunicative; not contributing enough. People who are quiet may have other power sources, but to have high expressiveness power, you have to engage.

4.   Dominating the conversation; speaking too much (while saying nothing); not listening. Being expressive doesn't mean dominating every conversation. It means being eloquent and impactful, saying the right things at the right time in the right way.

5.   Being unclear or confusing. Using logical fallacies while you are trying to prove a point indicates muddled thinking. When someone like former Vice President Dan Quayle uses non sequiturs or hasty generalizations when he speaks, he appears laughable at best and ignorant at worst.

HOW TO BUILD EXPRESSIVENESS POWER:

1. Most importantly, learn the language well enough to speak articu-
   lately. If you need help, find a coach, take a class, or find a good self-
   help grammar text.

2. Find opportunities to speak. Join Toastmasters or a similar public
   speaking organization, or take a class on public speaking. Then
   prepare carefully. Know what you want to say. Rehearse and practice
   delivering speeches until yours are focused and effective.

3. If you tend to be quiet, develop a point of view on topics before you
   go into a meeting and then force yourself to speak up. Don't wait for
   others to make the points you'd like to make. Don't sit back. Don't
   hesitate. Highly expressive people are more assertive; they take more
   airtime (but don't dominate the conversation) and are more influential partly because they know how to express their ideas simply and
   powerfully.

4. Find ways to amplify your voice—by writing papers, articles, or books
   that are widely distributed; by delivering powerful speeches or presentations that many people hear; by making audio or video recordings;
   or by using blogs, websites, YouTube postings, and other means to
   reach across the Internet.

5. Develop your writing skills. Write more than you do now. Keep a
   journal. Set aside time to write down your thoughts. Select the key
   points; support them with facts, stories, or illustrations; and write
   them in a form that can be sent to others. Express your key points as
   simply and elegantly as possible.

6. Read the famous speeches of great people. Listen to great speakers like
   Martin Luther King Jr. and Winston Churchill (audio recordings are
   available at various online archives or through the Library of Congress
   or public libraries). Note how they use the rhythm and music of
   language to express their thoughts powerfully and how they use
   images and stories to bring their thoughts to life. True eloquence may
   be as much a gift as a skill that can be developed, but you can become
   more eloquent with study.

7. If you are a senior leader, ensure that you devote enough time to
   communicating throughout the groups you manage. Hold town hall
   meetings, send out podcasts, and take every opportunity to speak to

people about the company, your vision, and what's new and what's coming next. Overcommunicate rather than undercommunicate.

HISTORY POWER

WHAT DIMINISHES THIS POWER SOURCE?

1. Failing to develop or sustain close relationships.

2. Failing to reciprocate. History power depends to a large extent on loyalty, similarity, and reciprocation. If friends do favors for you but you don't return the favor when asked, they will come to believe that you are a taker but not a giver, which will damage the relationship.

3. Betraying a trust with someone who has trusted you.

4. Being inauthentic; being a user of people rather than a genuine friend, colleague, boss, or leader.

5. Asking something of a close friend or colleague that the other person would consider inappropriate, unethical, or excessive.

HOW TO BUILD HISTORY POWER:

1. Cultivate close relationships or relationships with people with whom you share some important similarities. Stay in touch. Be friendly and collaborative. Reciprocate.

2. Be authentic in your relationships. Let the people closest to you know who you are. Allow yourself to be vulnerable and disclose things about yourself that few other people know. Authentic disclosure, done at the right time in a developing relationship, builds empathy, compassion, trust, and caring.

3. Affiliate with people who share your interests. If you enjoy chess, join a chess club. If you are a bird-watcher, find fellow bird-watchers and go on excursions together. People form bonds based on shared experiences, values, and interests. Whatever your passion may be, find others who share that passion. Get to know them and let them get to know you.

4. Extend yourself to newcomers and try to be more open and friendly toward people you don't know. You are likely to develop history power with some of them.

5. Use social networking sites like MySpace, Facebook, LinkedIn, and Plaxo to stay in touch with people you feel close to, but who are physically distant from where you live. Use these sites to stay in touch and maintain close connections. However, don't rely on them alone. By and large, face-to-face interactions are necessary for building close relationships.

6. Ensure that your development of close relationships is culturally appropriate. In some cultures, the pace of relationship building is slower than in others. Don't try to force a close relationship that in the other person's culture would take more time. But also don't be reluctant to form a close relationship faster than your native culture would consider appropriate if people you are living or working with develop close relationships faster. The key is to match the pace of relationship building to the culture you are operating in, regardless of your preferences.

7. If you are a senior leader, try to build relationships with other senior leaders inside your company or in other companies. Senior leaders typically suffer from some isolation because of their position in the hierarchy. They don't have as many peers to talk to or share ideas with. CEO networks or similar groups are useful ways to build history power with other people at your level who are likely to be experiencing some of the same challenges you are.

ATTRACTION POWER

WHAT DIMINISHES THIS POWER SOURCE?

1. Behaving in ways that others consider unattractive; for example, being arrogant, too pushy, too aloof, too cold or distant, unfriendly, harsh, overly cynical, and so on. Attraction is partly about having an attractive, friendly, welcoming personality.

2. Not taking care of your appearance; being slovenly or unkempt. Generally, you should match the appearance norms of the groups you associate with, but a general rule of thumb is to dress slightly better than those norms. When you take care of your appearance, you show pride and self-confidence, and you become a role model for others in the group. Beware, however, of dressing *substantially* better than

others in your group. Then you may appear vain, which can diminish attraction power.

3. Having poor personal hygiene. In most social circles, poor hygiene is a real turnoff. Don't go there.

4. Trying to be funny by being offensive; telling inappropriate jokes; telling jokes at the expense of others who are not present.

5. Demonstrating unacceptable bias (such as racial discrimination). In many social arenas, especially among more educated people, not only is such bias inappropriate but it is usually considered offensive, if not unethical. It also diminishes others' perceptions of your character.

6. Forcing yourself on someone else; violating someone's personal space; imposing your beliefs on someone (like trying to convert someone to your religion or sect after he's indicated he's not interested). Also, don't be loud, aggressive, rude, blunt, harsh, or crude.

7. Behaving unethically; being dishonest; demonstrating a lack of integrity.

8. Showing that you don't care for anyone but yourself. Self-centered people are unattractive.

HOW TO BUILD ATTRACTION POWER:

1. Make yourself attractive to others by avoiding attitudes and behaviors they deem unattractive. Generally, you make yourself attractive by being kind and reasonable, open and friendly, and warm rather than cold—and avoiding every one of the eight bad behaviors listed previously.

2. Seek out people with whom you have some commonality. Show interest in them, engage them, spend time with them, and listen to what they have to say. People who are good listeners are generally more attractive than those who aren't.

3. Boost your self-confidence. Self-confident people are more attractive, just as winners are more attractive than losers.

4. Take pride in your appearance. Whatever physical characteristics you were born with or now have, make the best with what you've got without becoming obsessive about it.

5. Smile more and develop a sense of humor if you don't have one. Research shows that people who smile more often are more attractive to others. And a sense of humor has been cited as the number-one element in attractiveness, even above physical appearance. Smiling and laughing are key elements of a winning personality.

6. Be kind, caring, generous, and giving. Those characteristics are far more attractive than being cruel, uncaring, selfish, and possessive.

7. Be yourself, but try not to be too eccentric. People who are eccentric are often perceived as strange, weird, or odd—which most people do not find attractive.

8. Develop a skill others find satisfying or entertaining. Learn to play the piano or guitar. Learn to be a good storyteller. Learn to tell tastefully amusing jokes. Then share your skill without trying to be the constant center of attention (which is boorish and unattractive).

9. Be authentic. People are wary of those who wear masks or appear to be hiding something.

10. When you are working in or visiting another culture, show awareness of the social norms and protocols in that culture and abide by them to the extent possible. Showing respect for the culture and its people, customs, and traditions is attractive to the people in that culture.

11. Be aware of and, when necessary, conform to the social norms of the people you are with. At the senior levels of management in modern companies, for instance, there are unwritten rules of behavior that leaders are expected to follow. Those unwritten rules obviously vary with the culture of the company. You need to be savvy enough about the social norms in your company to know how to interact properly with others at your level, at higher levels, and at lower levels. In organizational cultures that are more conservative, you need to behave with a certain amount of decorum. In looser, typically younger cultures, you need to know how to be a vital member of your peer group without overdoing it. It may sound like I'm preaching conformity, and to a certain extent I am. Standing out from the crowd may have its appeal, but it can also make you an unattractive outlier. The best leaders are authentically themselves yet also know how to operate within the social norms of their culture and organization.

12. If you are a senior leader, make yourself available to people at lower levels in your company, and be yourself when you do. Show them that

you are a human being. If the occasion arises, be helpful to them in some way—through coaching, mentoring, or simply suggesting a good restaurant you just discovered. Ask what they're reading or seeing, and tell them about a book you just read or a movie you just saw. These kinds of things increase your attraction power with employees.

CHARACTER POWER

WHAT DIMINISHES THIS POWER SOURCE?

(Hint: Many of the behaviors that diminish attraction power also diminish character power.)

1. Making commitments you don't keep; saying you will do something and then not doing it; and, especially, promising to do something for someone and then failing to do it.

2. Being dishonest or deceitful; lying; hiding the truth; allowing someone to believe something that is not true; covering up something that ought to be revealed.

3. Behaving in a cowardly fashion; lacking courage; being unwilling to confront a wrong or stand up for what is right.

4. Being inauthentic; disguising your true feelings or real intentions; wearing a mask.

5. Lacking humanity; being unkind, unfair, or unjust; looking out only for yourself.

6. Being arrogant, unforgiving, imprudent, or immodest; bragging excessively about yourself or your accomplishments; being self-centered.

7. Acting impulsively; being unable to manage yourself.

8. Being sarcastic; criticizing others behind their back; showing bias against others for their race, religion, gender, or national origin.

HOW TO BUILD CHARACTER POWER:

1. Ensure that you manifest impeccable integrity in everything you do.

2. If you have done something that would legitimately call your character into question, then work hard to correct the situation. Admit the error

and accept responsibility for it. Determine what you should have done differently and do those different things in the future.

3. If your character is being called into question for reasons that don't seem fair, try to understand why. Sometimes people have inaccurate perceptions or make false assumptions. If that's true, then try to correct those perceptions or assumptions.

4. Don't commit to more than you can deliver. People sometimes appear to lack integrity because they overcommit and underdeliver.

5. Practice what you preach. If you don't, you will appear to be hypocritical.

6. Review the VIA Classification of Character Strengths (chapter 5). Identify the areas where you could be stronger and then work on developing those areas.

7. Focus mostly on being authentic. Worry less about how you present yourself and more about who you really are. If the authentic you is someone who lacks integrity or does not manifest strong character, then you need to do a fundamental reexamination of yourself. Seek guidance from a counselor, spiritual leader, coach, therapist, or someone else who can help you through a deep transformation of yourself. Accept that character flaws are as difficult to conceal as strong character is to fake.

ROLE POWER

WHAT DIMINISHES THIS POWER SOURCE?

1. Leaving a position or being in a position whose scope of authority and responsibility has been redefined or abridged.

2. Using legitimate role power inappropriately or excessively, which can cause resistance or rebellion; relying on command-and-control methods when delegation and inspirational leadership would be more effective.

3. Relying on punishment and fear to enforce your authority. Negative reinforcement diminishes your moral authority and people's respect for you and will undermine any role power you have. In effect, you lose the consent of the governed.

4. Being a lame duck. Even if you are highly respected, when people know that your tenure in a role or position is ending they are going to be looking beyond you and start positioning themselves for your successor.

5. Failing to use or underutilizing badges of authority. (On the other hand, overusing your authority can cause a loss of respect, so balance and good judgments are key).

6. Being unsuccessful in the role; losing people's confidence in your ability to lead. If you are an ineffective manager or leader, people will vote with their feet and leave your group or the company, or become disengaged and less productive. A high turnover rate will expose your inabilities and ultimately cost you the role. Being successful in leadership and management roles is critically important if you want to maintain or grow role power.

HOW TO BUILD ROLE POWER:

1. Build your qualifications and capabilities for roles of increasing responsibility and authority and then seek those positions. When you have those roles, don't assume that what you've done before will make you successful again. Go through a thoughtful onboarding process and remain open to learning.

2. Perform well in your current role; create demand for yourself by doing whatever you are doing now extremely well. Sustaining and increasing role power depends on success in your current role.

3. If you are in a management or leadership position, pay particular attention to the people side of management. One of the principal causes of derailment is failing to manage people effectively. It is harder than it looks, and many people promoted to management positions are not trained or prepared for it. So don't take people management lightly.

4. Use your role power judiciously. Don't be autocratic or overbearing. Remember that role power depends on the consent of the governed.

5. Strive to be a good role model. If people look up to you, your role power will be increased.

6. Act as a mentor, coach, or teacher. Developing other people reinforces your seniority and experience and reinforces the power of your role.

7. Judiciously use some of the badges of authority discussed in chapter 6. It is unwise to flaunt your role power, but the subtle use of badges of authority will reinforce the role power inherent in your title or position.

8. Increase your role power. If you are a senior leader in your company, then you already have substantial role power—at least in your domain. To increase your role power, you still need to prepare yourself for and seek positions of greater responsibility and leadership breadth.

RESOURCE POWER

WHAT DIMINISHES THIS POWER SOURCE?

1. Losing access to or control of the resources others need.

2. Having the resources you control become irrelevant, unnecessary, or readily available from other sources.

3. Hoarding the resources you control and forcing people to find alternatives, which will force them to find substitutes and eventually make your resources irrelevant to them.

HOW TO BUILD RESOURCE POWER:

1. Acquire important resources yourself or seek organizational roles that include control of resources that others need.

2. Seek positions where you will have budgetary authority. In organizations, this is usually a key resource to control.

3. Try to be born to wealth (I'm joking). If you are like most people, though, then accept that you'll need to work hard to achieve ownership or control of significant resources. Typically, building resource power requires patience, perseverance, and hard work over a long period of time.

INFORMATION POWER

WHAT DIMINISHES THIS POWER SOURCE?

1. Not having or losing access to information that is important, relevant, timely, and scarce.

2. Hoarding information or not disseminating it effectively. Information has power only if others know you have it and when you disseminate it to them in a beneficial manner. Power comes not only from being needed but from being the source that satisfies needs.

3. Failing to organize information effectively, so people can't use it, understand it, or determine what's most useful to them.

4. Giving people information that is inaccurate or incomplete. They will learn not to trust the information you give them, and that obviously diminishes your information power.

5. Being unreliable; not being there when people need you. When they conclude that you are unreliable, they will find more reliable sources if they can.

HOW TO BUILD INFORMATION POWER:

1. Build your capabilities in each part of the RADIO mnemonic—that is, know how to retrieve, access, disseminate, interpret, and organize information. Start by improving your *access* to information. Acquire as much information as you reasonably can in your areas of interest using public sources, including Internet sources. Although this information is publicly available, you can often distinguish yourself and build information power because relatively few people will dig deep enough into all the public sources. To the extent possible, also develop private and deep private sources of information in your areas of interest. This information is much scarcer than deep public information.

2. Develop your skill at *retrieving* information quickly. Simply having access is not enough; you must be able to retrieve it effectively and efficiently.

3. Be an *interpreter* of information. Remember that you can gain tremendous information power from interpreting information that others might already have but have not interpreted as insightfully as you. Reread the section in chapter 7 on interpreting information. Creating powerful and insightful interpretations may not be easy (or else everyone would do it), but it is the most effective and powerful way to gain information power.

4. *Organize* information in ways that make it more useful for other people.

5. Build your skill at *disseminating* information effectively.

NETWORK POWER

WHAT DIMINISHES THIS POWER SOURCE?

1. Being too independent or isolated; not connecting with other people.

2. Having a limited network or a network consisting principally of people with whom you already have strong ties.

3. Networking only with people who have relatively fewer other ties themselves. Build networks with other people who are also well networked.

4. Being uncommunicative, reserved, or withdrawn. If you engage infrequently or have little to offer the people in your networks, your network power will diminish.

5. Failing to maintain your network, especially your weak ties.

6. Failing to reciprocate with people in your network; never adding value to them through your other connections.

HOW TO BUILD NETWORK POWER:

1. Become a more attractive networking partner by developing reliable expertise in an important area. Being a knowledge resource is one key way to attract others to your network.

2. Become an information resource (see chapter 7). It is especially important to master public and deep public sources of information, as well as private sources where that information can be shared without violating a trust. You can strengthen your information power by developing your skill at retrieving, organizing, and disseminating information. If you can provide information in an easily accessible and useful way, you will gain power. However, the greatest way to build information power is to discover a unique way to interpret information that is accurate, insightful, and helpful to others.

3. Be a solid performer; if possible, an exceptional performer. People are drawn to those who have good performance reputations because they want to be associated with success, so if you are an exceptional performer they will see you as a role model. This is a phenomenal attractor of others to your social networks.

4. Be helpful to others. When someone asks for help or advice, be responsive. Follow through and ensure that they got what they needed.

Although these are well-worn tips, the fact is that not everyone is responsive. Some people aren't helpful or don't follow through, and their bonds of trust eventually lose adhesion.

5. Do favors for people. It's a way of being helpful to them, and they will feel obligated to reciprocate. However, don't do favors in a transactional manner. If it's strictly quid pro quo, people will soon learn that you are only out for yourself and will treat you the same way. Greater power comes from being the kind of person who is selflessly collaborative and cooperative.

6. Ask others for help or favors. This is known as the Ben Franklin strategy. He had a fierce opponent in the Continental Congress, and he asked this opponent for help. Afterward, the opponent began supporting Franklin. When others feel like they have helped you, it strengthens their bond to you.

7. Involve people in important events, projects, or activities whenever you have the opportunity to do so. Reaching out to others is one of the best ways to strengthen your bonds with other people.

8. Find ways to connect the various people in your network to people outside their networks, especially when it helps them do their jobs better or discover some opportunities they hadn't known existed.

9. Be highly communicative. People at the hub of social networks invariably communicate more than people who are at the periphery of those networks. Communication increases visibility, and visibility strengthens bonds. However, the communications must add value, not noise.

10. Ensure that your social network in your organization reaches into other levels of the hierarchy. Researchers at Accenture's Institute for High Performance Business studied the networking habits of top talent, and they identified three important characteristics of high-performers' networks: They create ties that bridge (a) hierarchical levels, (b) functional and organizational lines, and (c) physical distance.[1] So, start building connections with managers above your boss's level. If you are several levels up in the hierarchy, build bridges with managers below the level of your direct reports. Your comfort level may be with your boss, peers, and direct reports, but it is essential to build bridges beyond that.

11. Build connections outside of your department or function and outside of your organization. Volunteer or otherwise become involved in multidisciplinary or cross-functional teams or task forces. Get to know people as broadly as you can within your own organization. Also, build connections with customers, partners, suppliers, vendors, and others outside of your company.

12. Try to build bridges with people in other physical locations—in other regions of the company or other parts of the world. Social networking tools like LinkedIn, Plaxo, Facebook, and MySpace may be helpful here.

13. Nourish your connections. Social networks do not spontaneously maintain themselves. To keep the bonds sticky, you have to nourish your contacts the way you nourish plants in a garden. If you don't tend to them, they will die or become infested with weeds. Remember that weak ties are the ones that make your network the most vibrant, but these are the ones that will lose their adhesion if you don't periodically tend to them. How do you tend to them? Pick up the phone. Send a message or a referral. Ask for advice. Add some value. Communicate. Cultivate. Nourish.

REPUTATION POWER

WHAT DIMINISHES THIS POWER SOURCE?

1. Doing anything that diminishes the community's perception of your character or quality.

2. If you are living or working in another culture, failing to abide by or show respect for that culture's social norms.

HOW TO BUILD REPUTATION POWER:

1. Remember that a reputation takes a long time to build. You need to understand the behavioral expectations and social norms in your company, community, or social group and behave accordingly *and* consistently.

2. If you err, accept responsibility, redress the grievance, and then don't do it again. Most people are more forgiving than they are forgetful.

They may forgive an isolated mistake or oversight but not repeated gaffes.

3. Know who the opinion leaders are in your company or community. Know how they shape opinion and what they think of you. You can't build a good name only with them, but it is wise to know what they think and how they communicate their perceptions to others.

4. Think about the consequences of your decisions and actions before you do things that could create the wrong impression or cause the people you work with to reassess their view of you.

5. Think of your reputation as "the brand called You." Take very good care of it. It is one of your most important assets. Avoid impulsive decisions and behaviors that could backfire and destroy your reputation. Young people who take risqué photos of themselves with their cell phones and send those digital photos to friends are flirting with reputational disaster. Information sent electronically has a phenomenally long half-life. When it comes to reputation, it is better to be discreet than sorry.

6. Be kind and thoughtful toward others, take good care of yourself and those you are responsible for, abide by the company's norms, work hard, and perform well. Few things build a good reputation faster than consistent high performance—but don't achieve it at other people's expense.

7. Beware of being too vocal about your own achievements. If you do something extraordinary, it won't hurt if others talk about it, but bear in mind that blatant self-promotion is frowned upon in most cultures.

8. Strive to join institutions whose reputations will enhance yours. Institutions have reputations, too, and your reputation will be based partly on the institutions you belong to. Like it or not, this is how the world works, so go to the finest college you can, earn a prestigious degree, compete for awards that would add to your personal brand, and try to join companies or other institutions with excellent reputations. It would be naïve to assume these things don't matter. They do.

9. If you are a senior leader in your company, be aware that you live and work in a glass bubble. People will be hyperaware of how you look

and behave. They will be overly sensitive to how you speak to them and others. Because you live and work in a glass bubble, you need to ensure that you don't come across as arrogant, aloof, angry, insensitive, petulant, or above it all. If you behave in those ways, people will talk about it, and it will diminish your reputation power.

10. Most of all, work on being a solid performer, a great team member, a fine leader, and if not *the* best, then among the best at whatever you choose to do.

WILL POWER

WHAT DIMINISHES THIS POWER SOURCE?

1. *You do.* This power source depends entirely on your will. You can choose to act or not. You can choose to make a difference or not. You can choose to lead or to follow, to be at the front of the room or at the back, to stay silent or to speak up, to take the initiative or wait for someone else to do it. Nobody can give you will power and no one can take it away. It is entirely up to you.

HOW TO BUILD WILL POWER:

1. You don't need anything other than yourself. Just do it. In that fine film *Dead Poets Society* (1989), John Keating (played by Robin Williams), a teacher at a boys' school, leads his students to a display of photos of students from long ago. As the boys are staring at the images, Keating says that when those photos were taken the boys in them were just like boys today. They felt the same way. They believed they would do great things. And now the boys in those photos are pushing up daisies. Keating wonders if those boys made of their lives what they were capable of making. He imagines their ghosts whispering their legacy to the boys now staring at their faces in the photos. He imagines they would tell the boys to seize the day and live life to the fullest. So it is with will power. All it takes to build it is you.

Carpe diem.

POWER SOURCES SELF-ASSESSMENT

How powerful are you? This self-assessment is designed to help you gauge your sources of personal and organizational power—as well as your strength of will—and then help you identify areas for development. As with any self-assessment, the more honest you are about yourself the more accurate your results will be. As you respond to these forty-four statements, be as realistic about yourself as you can. For the items in the following exercise, indicate on a scale of 1 to 10 how accurately each statement describes you. Circle "1" if the statement is *not at all true of you* and "10" if the statement is *very true of you.*

PERSONAL POWER SOURCES

Knowledge Power

1. I am highly knowledgeable and skilled in areas of importance to the people I work with.

(not at all true of me)   1   2   3   4   5   6   7   8   9   10   (very true of me)

2. My areas of expertise are special enough that they differentiate me from most other people.

(not at all true of me)   1   2   3   4   5   6   7   8   9   10   (very true of me)

3. Many people are aware of my knowledge and skill and value me for it. They consider me an expert and often ask for my opinion or advice.

(not at all true of me)   1   2   3   4   5   6   7   8   9   10   (very true of me)

4. I have many symbols of knowledge power, such as an advanced degree, a special role or title, awards, prizes, certifications, publications, or other honors.

(not at all true of me)   1   2   3   4   5   6   7   8   9   10   (very true of me)

Knowledge power total _____

Expressiveness Power

5. I am a gifted and experienced speaker. I use language well. I speak clearly, concisely, and effectively.

(not at all true of me)   1   2   3   4   5   6   7   8   9   10   (very true of me)

6. In meetings, I participate more than most people and make more comments or suggestions. I usually have more presence in the group than other people.

(not at all true of me)   1   2   3   4   5   6   7   8   9   10   (very true of me)

7. I often communicate to either everyone in my organization or large groups within it. Known as an excellent writer and speaker, I have a great deal of visibility in our company.

(not at all true of me)   1   2   3   4   5   6   7   8   9   10   (very true of me)

8. I frequently communicate my ideas through books, white papers, articles, television or radio appearances, blogs, social networks like Facebook or LinkedIn, and conference presentations.

(not at all true of me)   1   2   3   4   5   6   7   8   9   10   (very true of me)

Expressiveness power total _____

History Power

9. I am very good at building close relationships with other people. I have quite a few customers, colleagues, and others I work with whom I consider friends.

(not at all true of me)   1   2   3   4   5   6   7   8   9   10   (very true of me)

10. I excel at making connections with people I've just met. Outgoing and friendly, I am able to establish rapport and trust with others fairly quickly.

(not at all true of me)   1   2   3   4   5   6   7   8   9   10   (very true of me)

11. I am the type of person who joins groups. I belong to a number of clubs, committees, boards, teams, and other groups where I regularly interact with people based on common interests.

(not at all true of me)   1   2   3   4   5   6   7   8   9   10   (very true of me)

12. I am very active on social networking sites like LinkedIn, Plaxo, Facebook, MySpace, or Twitter.

(not at all true of me)   1   2   3   4   5   6   7   8   9   10   (very true of me)

History power total _____

Attraction Power

13. I have the kind of qualities most people like, and I rarely do anything that would offend anyone else or cause her to think I'm arrogant, pushy, or distant.

(not at all true of me)   1   2   3   4   5   6   7   8   9   10   (very true of me)

14. I take care of my appearance, and most people would consider me to be physically attractive or charming.

(not at all true of me)   1   2   3   4   5   6   7   8   9   10   (very true of me)

15. I am outgoing and very good at engaging people. People enjoy being with me, and many of them think I'm funny or interesting.

(not at all true of me)   1   2   3   4   5   6   7   8   9   10   (very true of me)

16. People have told me that I am charismatic.

(not at all true of me)   1   2   3   4   5   6   7   8   9   10   (very true of me)

Attraction power total _____

Character Power

17. I am totally honest, and people know that about me. They would never question my integrity.

(not at all true of me)   1   2   3   4   5   6   7   8   9   10   (very true of me)

18. I always speak the truth as I know it. It may sometimes be unpleasant to be completely candid with people, but I would never hide the truth just to make someone feel better or to avoid a conflict.

(not at all true of me)   1   2   3   4   5   6   7   8   9   10   (very true of me)

19. People consider me courageous. I stand up for what I believe is right, even in the face of resistance and opposition from powerful people.

(not at all true of me)   1   2   3   4   5   6   7   8   9   10   (very true of me)

20. I don't preach one thing but do something different. I walk the talk, and if I make a promise, I never fail to keep it. People know they can trust me.

(not at all true of me)   1   2   3   4   5   6   7   8   9   10   (very true of me)

Character power total _____

ORGANIZATIONAL POWER SOURCES

Role Power

21. I have a management role in my company that gives me a great deal of formal authority and responsibility for the group and people I manage.

(not at all true of me) 1 2 3 4 5 6 7 8 9 10 (very true of me)

22. I may try to lead through influence rather than authority, but I have the power to make final decisions.

(not at all true of me) 1 2 3 4 5 6 7 8 9 10 (very true of me)

23. I have been very successful in every leadership or management position I have had in my company.

(not at all true of me) 1 2 3 4 5 6 7 8 9 10 (very true of me)

24. I am one of the most senior managers or leaders in my company.

(not at all true of me) 1 2 3 4 5 6 7 8 9 10 (very true of me)

Role power total _____

Resource Power

25. I own or control key resources other people need to do their jobs.

(not at all true of me) 1 2 3 4 5 6 7 8 9 10 (very true of me)

26. My role includes budgetary authority, and other managers or departments need to seek my approval for discretionary spending.

(not at all true of me) 1 2 3 4 5 6 7 8 9 10 (very true of me)

27. In my role, I manage people's schedules or assignments, or I control access to key people.

(not at all true of me) 1 2 3 4 5 6 7 8 9 10 (very true of me)

28. I own or control significant financial resources.

(not at all true of me) 1 2 3 4 5 6 7 8 9 10 (very true of me)

Resource power total _____

Information Power

29. I have access to deep public or private information that many other people do not have access to.

(not at all true of me)   1   2   3   4   5   6   7   8   9   10   (very true of me)

30. I am highly skilled at interpreting information and presenting it in a form other people value and could not get from any other source.

(not at all true of me)   1   2   3   4   5   6   7   8   9   10   (very true of me)

31. In my job, I manage information that helps others do their job, including information they could not readily obtain elsewhere.

(not at all true of me)   1   2   3   4   5   6   7   8   9   10   (very true of me)

32. I conduct research or otherwise generate new information that is valuable to other people and gives them fresh insights.

(not at all true of me)   1   2   3   4   5   6   7   8   9   10   (very true of me)

Information power total _____

Network Power

33. I am well connected inside and outside my company. I know hundreds of customers, colleagues, partners, suppliers, peers, and friends in multiple organizations and locations.

(not at all true of me)   1   2   3   4   5   6   7   8   9   10   (very true of me)

34. My networks include a number of important people who also have many large networks of their own. Through my own and their networks, I have tremendous reach.

(not at all true of me)   1   2   3   4   5   6   7   8   9   10   (very true of me)

35. I am a very active networker. I continually reach out to the people I know and maintain my ties with them.

(not at all true of me)   1   2   3   4   5   6   7   8   9   10   (very true of me)

36. Many people want me to be part of their network because of my role, title, position, expertise, reputation, or some other reason that makes me an attractive network member.

(not at all true of me)   1   2   3   4   5   6   7   8   9   10   (very true of me)

Network power total _____

Reputation Power

37. I have an excellent reputation in my company. People hold me in high regard.

(not at all true of me)   1   2   3   4   5   6   7   8   9   10   (very true of me)

38. People I've just met often tell me that they've heard good things about me.

(not at all true of me)   1   2   3   4   5   6   7   8   9   10   (very true of me)

39. My performance at work has always been outstanding. I am known as a person who gets results.

(not at all true of me)   1   2   3   4   5   6   7   8   9   10   (very true of me)

40. People in my company often ask me for advice, coaching, or mentoring.

(not at all true of me)   1   2   3   4   5   6   7   8   9   10   (very true of me)

Reputation power total _____

WILL POWER

41. I know where I want to go and what I want to do, and I am fiercely determined to get there.

(not at all true of me)   1   2   3   4   5   6   7   8   9   10   (very true of me)

42. I am not easily discouraged. Even unforeseen obstacles and repeated failures could not deter me from my course.

(not at all true of me)   1   2   3   4   5   6   7   8   9   10   (very true of me)

43. I am a dreamer, but I know that dreams are not enough. I have a proven history of acting on my dreams and making them a reality.

(not at all true of me)   1   2   3   4   5   6   7   8   9   10   (very true of me)

44. One of my strengths as a leader is my formidable will power. I never waver. Nothing can get in my way.

(not at all true of me)   1   2   3   4   5   6   7   8   9   10   (very true of me)

Will power total _____

SCORING

In the spaces below, take your power source scores and then multiply each score by the indicated factor and total the result. The factors reflect the relative strength of each of the power sources based on my research. The highest possible score is 1,200.

Personal Power Sources

Knowledge power ($\times 2$) = _____
Expressiveness power ($\times 3$) = _____
History power ($\times 1$) = _____
Attraction power ($\times 1$) = _____
Character power ($\times 3$) = _____
Subtotal personal power sources _____

Organizational Power Sources

Role power ($\times 3$) = _____
Resource power ($\times 1$) = _____
Information power ($\times 1$) = _____
Network power ($\times 2$) = _____
Reputation power ($\times 3$) = _____
Subtotal organizational power sources _____

Will power ($\times 10$) _____

TOTAL _____

Interpreting Your Self-Assessment Score

Obviously, the higher your total score, the more powerful you are in your company or organization. However, if you are interested in building your power, the total score is less important than your scores for each element of power. Note which of your power sources is weakest, and which items had the lowest scores. You may identify some developmental opportunities. Of course, some capabilities may not be easy to build in the short term. Regarding item 28, for instance, most people cannot easily build or gain control of significant financial resources except over a longer period. Nonetheless, as a starting point, identify the power sources you would most like to build, and then return to that section of this chapter and identify the suggestions you could act upon. Make them part of your development plan.

An important caveat about this self-assessment is that the weights assigned to each element of power reflect the relative importance of each power source based on our research. However, in real life, these weights would depend to some degree on the context. If you work as a scientist in a biomedical research firm, then knowledge and reputation power would probably be weighted more heavily. If you are a senior loan officer in a bank or mortgage company, then resource power would have higher weight. If you work for a public relations firm, network power would be considerably more important, and so on. Remember that power is relational and depends on the context in which you are working, so view your results accordingly. The key questions are these:

1. Which sources of power are most important for your role in your company and industry? You might want to rank them and apply your own weighting scheme.

2. Are you weaker than you should be in any of the more important power sources you identified? These are the areas you should focus on in your development plan.

3. If you aspire toward positions of greater responsibility, look ahead. Which power sources would be most important for you to be promoted to those positions? And which of your sources of power would need to be stronger for you to succeed in those positions? Building those sources of power should become part of your longer-term development plan.

At the outset of this book, I noted that you cannot become more influential or have more impact as a leader unless you understand the elements of power and build the power base you need to be effective in whichever domain you are working. Without power, there is no influence or leadership. If you have read this book and reflected thoughtfully upon the challenges outlined at the end of each chapter, you should now have a good understanding of the elements of power and have the tools you need to become a more powerful person.

To learn more about how power and influence work in different cultures around the world, go to www.kornferryinstitute.com, www.theele mentsofpower.com, or www.terryrbacon.com. Good luck. Bonne chance. Buena suerte. Viel glueck. Καλή τύχη. Buona fortuna. 幸運. 행운을 빕니다. Goed geluk. Boa sorte. Удача.

NOTES

INTRODUCTION

1. John R. P. French Jr. and Bertram Raven, "The Bases of Social Power," in *Studies in Social Power,* ed. D. Cartwright (Ann Arbor: University of Michigan Press, 1959).

2. Katharine Graham, *Personal History* (New York: Vintage Books, 1998).

3. Jone Johnson Lewis, About.com: Women's History, "Katharine Graham Quotes," http://womenshistory.about.com/od/quotes/a/kay_graham.htm (accessed May 2009).

4. Ibid.

5. "Religion: Enterprising Evangelism," *Time,* August 3, 1987.

6. William Shakespeare, *Julius Caesar,* act IV, scene 3.

7. The Sonning Prize is awarded biennially by the University of Copenhagen to statesmen, authors, philosophers, film or theater professionals, and others for contributions to European culture. Other recipients have included Winston Churchill, Albert Schweitzer, Bertrand Russell, Niels Bohr, Laurence Olivier, Arthur Koestler, Karl Popper, Hannah Arendt, Simone de Beauvoir, Ingmar Bergman, and former United Nations High Commissioner for Human Rights Mary Robinson.

8. For a full transcript of Václav Havel's acceptance speech, see http://userweb.cs.utexas.edu/users/vl/notes/havel.html.

9. Ibid.

10. Shakespeare, *Julius Caesar,* act II, scene 1.

11. David C. McClelland and David H. Burnham, "Power Is the Great Motivator," *Harvard Business Review,* January 2003, 118. (This article was originally published in 1976.)

CHAPTER 1: THE POWER OF KNOWLEDGE

1. You can find a summary of Baconian evidence for Shakespeare authorship at www.sirbacon.org/links/evidence.htm.

2. Randy Howe, ed., *Here We Stand* (Guilford, CT: Lyons Press, 2009), 173.

3. Howard Gardner, *Frames of Mind: The Theory of Multiple Intelligences* (New York: Basic Books, 1983); *Multiple Intelligences: The Theory in Practice* (New York: Basic Books, 1993); and *Intelligence Reframed: Multiple Intelligences for the Twenty-First Century* (New York: Basic Books, 2000).

4. J. P. Guilford, *The Nature of Human Intelligence* (New York: McGraw-Hill, 1967).

5. Robert J. Sternberg, *Thinking Styles* (Cambridge: Cambridge University Press, 1999).

6. Daniel Goleman, *Emotional Intelligence* (New York: Bantam Books, 1995), 161.

7. Michael M. Lombardo and Robert W. Eichinger, *FYI: For Your Improvement, A Guide for Development and Coaching*, 5th ed. (Minneapolis: Korn/Ferry International, 2009), 389.

8. Academy of Achievement, "Maya Angelou Interview," January 22, 1997, www .achievement.org/autodoc/page/ang0int-2.

9. Much has been written about learning organizations. For example, see Peter Senge, *The Fifth Discipline: The Art and Practice of the Learning Organization* (New York: Doubleday, 1990).

10. For more on the cold fusion debacle and continuing interest in the concept, see Charles Platt, "What If Cold Fusion Is Real?" *Wired* 6, no. 11 (1998), www.wired.-com/wired/archive/6.11/coldfusion.html.

CHAPTER 2: THE POWER OF ELOQUENCE

1. "As a Teenager, Obama Discovered a Talent for Charismatic Speeches," *Arizona Daily Star*, January 16, 2008.

2. Cameron Anderson and Gavin J. Kilduff, "Why Do Dominant Personalities Attain Influence in Face-to-Face Groups? The Competence-Signaling Effects of Trait Dominance," *Journal of Personality and Social Psychology* 96, no. 2 (2009), 491–503.

3. Ruth Golden et al., *The Rhetoric of Western Thought: From the Mediterranean World to the Global Setting*, 9th ed. (Dubuque, IA: Kendall/Hunt Publishing, 2007), 79.

4. George Will, "The Cosmopolitan," *Washington Post*, August 3, 2008, B7.

5. D. K. Simonton, "Presidential Style: Personality, Biography, and Performance," *Journal of Personality and Social Psychology* 55, no. 6 (1988), 928–36.

6. Jeffery Scott Mio et al., "Presidential Leadership and Charisma: The Effects of Metaphor," *Leadership Quarterly* 16, no. 2 (2005), 287–94.

7. Kurt Kister, "A Leader Who Can't Communicate," *The Week* (April 3, 2009), 13. (This article originally appeared in *Suddeutsche Zeitung*.)

8. Ben Roberts, "Underestimating Bush's Intelligence," *CounterPunch*, November 13, 2002, www.counterpunch.com/roberts1113.html.

CHAPTER 3: THE POWER OF RELATIONSHIPS

1. Robert B. Cialdini, *Influence: The Psychology of Persuasion*, rev. ed. (New York: William Morrow, 1993), 167.

2. Leon Festinger, Stanley Schachter, and Kurt Back, *Social Pressures in Informal Groups: A Study of Human Factors in Housing* (Palo Alto, CA: Stanford University Press, 1950).

3. "Chinese Blog Claims Top Spot," *The Age*, July 19, 2007, www.theage.com.au/articles/2007/07/19/1184559939166.html.

4. Sino-angle blog comment, http://sino-angle.blogspot.com (accessed March 26, 2009). Xu Jinglei's blog is written in Chinese. The translator is unknown.

5. Irwin Altman and Dalmas A. Taylor, *Social Penetration: Development of Interpersonal Relationships* (Geneva, IL: Holt McDougal, June 1973).

6. L. A. Baxter, "A Dialectical Perspective on Communication Strategies in Relationship Development," in *Handbook of Personal Relationships: Theory, Research, and Interventions*, ed. Steve Duck (New York: Wiley, 1988), 257–73.

CHAPTER 4: THE POWER OF ATTRACTION

1. John R. P. French Jr. and Bertram Raven, "The Bases of Social Power," in *Studies in Social Power*, ed. D. Cartwright (Ann Arbor: University of Michigan Press, 1959).

2. An early, influential study on attractiveness is "What Is Beautiful Is Good" (1972) by K. Dion, E. Berscheid, and E. Walster. Ellen Berscheid and Elaine Walster summarized their and other research in "Beauty and the Best," *Psychology Today* 5, no. 10 (1972), 42–49. In this list, I am summarizing some of their findings, as well as findings from other researchers. Many of the studies on attraction have used college-age students as subjects, which may bias the results toward greater emphasis on physical appearance.

3. M. P. Zanna and S. J. Pack, "On the Self-Fulfilling Nature of Apparent Sex-Differences in Behavior," *Journal of Experimental Social Psychology* 11 (November 1975), 583–91.

4. Virginia Lashbrooke, interview with the author, March 31, 2009.

5. Aristotle, *On Rhetoric*, trans. George A. Kennedy (Oxford: Oxford University Press, 2006), 25.

6. Robert B. Cialdini, *Influence: The Psychology of Persuasion*, rev. ed. (New York: William Morrow, 1993), 173.

7. Joel A. Gold, Richard M. Ryckman, and Norman R. Mosley, "Romantic Mood Induction and Attraction to a Dissimilar Other," *Personality and Social Psychology Bulletin* 10, no. 3 (1984), 358–68.

8. James Carville, a Democrat, was the lead political strategist for Bill Clinton, the forty-second U.S. president. Mary Matalin is a Republican strategist and former colleague of Karl Rove and Dick Cheney, arch conservatives in the George W. Bush administration. They claim not to talk politics at home.

9. D. S. Hamermesh and J. E. Biddle, "Beauty and the Labor Market," *American Economic Review* 84, no. 5 (1994), 1174–94.

10. Markus M. Mobius and Tanya S. Rosenblat, "Why Beauty Matters," *American Economic Review* 96, no. 1 (2006), 222–35. Their findings were based on a controlled laboratory experiment.

11. Tiziana Casciaro and Miguel Sousa Lobo, "Competent Jerks, Lovable Fools, and the Formation of Social Networks," *Harvard Business Review* 83, no. 6 (2005), 2–3.

12. Ibid., 3.

13. Susan Estrich, *Ann Coulter and the Right-Wing Church of Hate* (New York: HarperCollins Publishers, 2006).

14. Max Weber, *The Theory of Social and Economic Organization* (New York: Free Press, 1997).

CHAPTER 5: THE POWER OF CHARACTER

1. John P. Kotter, *John P. Kotter on What Leaders Really Do* (Boston: Harvard Business School Press, 1999), 106.

2. Aristotle, *Prior Analytics*, trans. A. J. Jenkinson (Whitefish, MT: Kessinger Publishing, 2004), 99.

3. Kevin Cashman, *Leadership from the Inside Out* (San Francisco: Berret-Koehler Publishers, 2008), 45.

4. Christopher Peterson and Martin E. P. Seligman, *Character Strengths and Virtues: A Handbook and Classification* (Oxford: Oxford University Press, 2004). Reprinting of this classification is with permission of the VIA Institute on Character. © 2004 Values in Action Institute.

5. Interested readers can take this survey and receive a free report at the VIA Institute on Character website, www.viastrengths.org/VIASurvey/tabid/55/Default.aspx.

6. An excellent resource is Michael M. Lombardo and Robert W. Eichinger, *FYI: For Your Improvement, A Guide for Development and Coaching* (Minneapolis: Korn/Ferry International, 2009).

7. Joseph P. Lash, *Eleanor and Franklin* (New York: W. W. Norton & Co., 1971), 28.

8. "Eleanor Roosevelt: Shy Young Girl," The Biography Channel website, www.biography.com/video.do?name=politicalfigures&bcpid=1740037438&bclid=1764764685&bctid=1797091569.

9. Rexford Tugwell, "Remarks," *Roosevelt Day Dinner Journal*, Americans for Democratic Action, January 31, 1963.

10. Among the many news stories on John Thain's ouster from Bank of America, see Charlie Gasparino, "John Thain's $87,000 Rug," www.thedailybeast.com/blogs-and-stories/2009-01-22/john-thains-87000-rug/; Bill Saporito, "The Deeper Truth About Thain's Ouster from BofA," www.time.com/time/business/article/0,8599,1873835,00 .html; Julie Creswell and Louise Story, "Thain Resigns Amid Losses at Bank of America," www.nytimes.com/2009/01/23/business/23thain.html; Josh Fineman and David Mildenberg, "Thain Pushed Out at Bank of America After Merrill Loss Widens," www.bloomberg.com/apps/news?pid=20601087&sid=aF.bqMdzXm0Q; and "Was John Thain Right About Merrill Lynch Bonuses?" http://blogs.wsj.com/deals/2009/02/02/the-nitty-gritty-details-on-those-merrill-lynch-december-bonuses/tab/article/.

11. In one of the clearest signs of the financial sector's willingness to forgive and forget, in February 2010, Thain was appointed chairman and chief executive of CIT Group for a total compensation package of up to $7.5 million.

12. Cashman, *Leadership from the Inside Out.*

13. Nick Paumgarten, "The Humbling of Eliot Spitzer," *The New Yorker*, December 10, 2007. Used with permission by Nick Paumgarten.

14. Henry Goldman and Karen Freifeld, "Spitzer Quits as New York Governor; Paterson Elevated (Update 9)," March 12, 2008, www.bloomberg.com/apps/news?pid=news archive&sid=aRNjACiEfCjA&refer=home.

CHAPTER 6: THE POWER OF ROLE AND RESOURCES

1. Michael Useem, "America's Best Leaders: Indra Nooyi, PepsiCo CEO," *U.S. News & World Report*, November 19, 2008.

2. John R. P. French Jr. and Bertram Raven, "The Bases of Social Power," in *Studies in Social Power*, ed. D. Cartwright (Ann Arbor: University of Michigan Press, 1959).

3. John P. Kotter, *John P. Kotter on What Leaders Really Do* (Boston: Harvard Business School Press, 1999), 100.

4. Ibid., 107.

5. Jeffrey Pfeffer, *Managing with Power: Politics and Influence in Organizations* (Boston: Harvard Business School Press, 1994), 89.

CHAPTER 7: THE POWER OF INFORMATION

1. Stewart Brand, "Transcript from the Hackers Conference," *Whole Earth Review*, May 1985, 49.

2. Tom Clancy, *The Hunt for Red October* (Annapolis, MD: Naval Institute Press, 1984) and *The Cardinal of the Kremlin* (New York: G. P. Putnam's Sons, 1988).

3. Atul Gawande, "The Checklist," *The New Yorker*, December 10, 2007, http://www .newyorker.com/reporting/2007/12/10/071210fa_fact_gawande.

4. Ibid.

5. For more information on the Leadership Architect framework, see www.lominger .com or www.kornferry.com.

6. For a thoughtful and factual examination of Ann Coulter's pronouncements, see Joe Maguire, *Brainless: The Lies and Lunacy of Ann Coulter* (New York: William Morrow, 2006).

CHAPTER 8: THE POWER OF NETWORKING

1. Ana D. in discussion with the author, April 2009. Used with permission.

2. Mark Granovetter, "The Strength of Weak Ties: A Network Theory Revisited," *Sociological Theory, Volume 1* (1983), 202. Granovetter's initial study on this subject was published in 1973.

3. Ibid., 209.

4. Malcolm Gladwell, *The Tipping Point: How Little Things Can Make a Big Difference* (New York: Little, Brown, 2000), 48.

5. Ibid., 55.

6. Dean Pagani, "One Pager—White House Chief of Staff," Media Attache blog, comment posted November 11, 2008, http://mediaattache.blogspot.com/2008/11/one-pager-white-house-chief-of-staff.html.

7. Naftali Bendavid, "The House Rahm Built: How Chicago's Profane, Ruthless, Savvy Operative Remade the Democrats in His Image," *Chicago Tribune,* November 12, 2006, 1.

8. CNBC.com, citing "Portfolio's Worst American CEOs of All Time," www.cnbc.com/id/30502091?slide=17.

9. Project for the New American Century, www.newamericancentury.org/.

10. Barton Gellman, *Angler: The Cheney Vice Presidency* (New York: Penguin Press, 2008), 35.

11. Ibid., 384.

12. Ibid., 393.

CHAPTER 9: THE POWER OF REPUTATION

1. Tina Brown, "Elizabeth Edwards Fed Herself to the Vultures," *The Daily Beast,* May 21, 2009, www.thedailybeast.com/blogs-and-stories/2009-05-11/elizabeth-edwards-fed-herself-to-the-vultures/.

2. Jenice Armstrong, "Why Edwards Book Now?" *Philadelphia Daily News,* May 6, 2009, 37. Used with permission of *Philadelphia Daily News.* Copyright© 2010. All rights reserved.

3. Michael Goodwin, "John Edwards Is a Cad, His Wife's a Partner in Grime," *New York Daily News,* May 6, 2009. © New York Daily News, L. P. Used with permission.

4. Ibid.

5. Kyle Smith, "A Wife Less Ordinary: The Motives Behind Elizabeth Edwards' Public Walk of Shame," *New York Post,* May 9, 2009, www.nypost.com/p/news/opinion/opedcolumnists/item_uWV7yGz7o23ObdtabXm7lI.

6. William Shakespeare, *Othello, the Moor of Venice,* act 3, scene 3.

7. For more on this five-to-one ratio, see Terry R. Bacon and David G. Pugh, *Winning Behavior: What the Smartest, Most Successful Companies Do Differently* (New York: AMACOM, 2003), 53.

8. "Warren Buffett Quotes," http://www.theoracleofomaha.com/2009/12/warren-buffett-quotes-on-life.html.

9. Tom Peters, "The Brand Called You," *Fast Company,* December 18, 2007, www.fastcompany.com/magazine/10/brandyou.html.

10. Christopher Peterson and Martin E. P. Seligman, *Character Strengths and Virtues: A Handbook and Classification* (Oxford: Oxford University Press, 2004), 36.

11. Ibid., 52.

12. Brad Stone and Claire Cain Miller, "Jerry Yang, Yahoo Chief, Steps Down," *New York Times,* November 18, 2008; Jessica E. Vascellaro, "Yang to Step Down as Yahoo CEO," *Wall Street Journal,* November 18, 2008; and Associated Press, "Yahoo Co-founder Jerry Yang Steps Down as CEO," November 17, 2008, www.google.com/hostednews/afp/article/ALeqM5hBGB1AVX8xcAcu2jobSbHeY0JWaA.

CHAPTER 10: POWER IN ORGANIZATIONS

1. Reinhold Niebuhr and Robert McAfee Brown, ed., *The Essential Reinhold Niebuhr: Selected Essays and Addresses* (New Haven, CT: Yale University Press, 1987).

2. Aldous Huxley, "Variations on a Philosopher," *Themes and Variations* (1950), quoted in PoemHunter.com, www.poemhunter.com/quotations/famous.asp?people=Aldous%20Huxley&p=15 (accessed March 19, 2010).

3. Ichak Adizes, *Corporate Lifecycles: How and Why Companies Grow and Die and What to Do About It* (Paramus, NJ: Prentice Hall, 1988).

4. "The World's 50 Most Innovative Companies," *Fast Company,* March 2010, 54.

5. Caitlin McDevitt, "What We Learned About Mark Zuckerberg This Week," The Big Money.com, March 5, 2010, www.thebigmoney.com/blogs/facebook-status/2010/03/05/what-we-learned-about-mark-zuckerberg-week (accessed April 4, 2010).

6. John Kenneth Galbraith, "In Pursuit of the Simple Truth," *The Guardian,* July 28, 1989, 23.

7. Kevin Maney, "SAS Workers Won When Greed Lost," *USA Today,* April 21, 2004, www.usatoday.com/money/industries/technology/2004-04-21-sas-culture_x.htm (accessed March 28, 2010).

8. For more information on learning agility, see *FYI for Learning Agility* (Minneapolis: Lominger International, a Korn/Ferry Company, 2010).

9. John Kotter, *Power and Influence: Beyond Formal Authority* (New York: Free Press, 1985), 17.

10. Ibid., 18.

11. Bernard Ryan Jr., *Jeff Bezos: Business Executive and Founder of Amazon.com* (New York: Ferguson, 2005), 48.

12. Academy of Achievement, "Jeff Bezos Biography," June 24, 2009, www.achievement .org/autodoc/printmember/bez0bio-1 (accessed April 5, 2010).

13. Charles Horton Cooley, quoted in Book of Famous Quotes, www.famous-quotes .com/author.php?aid=1676 (accessed March 29, 2010).

14. Bethany McLean and Peter Elkind, *The Smartest Guys in the Room: The Amazing Rise and Scandalous Fall of Enron* (New York: Penguin Books, 2004), 101.

CHAPTER 11: THE POWER OF WILL

1. Ayn Rand, *The Fountainhead* (Indianapolis: Bobbs-Merrill), 1943.

2. Margaret Mead, quoted in *And I Quote: The Definitive Collection of Quotes, Sayings, and Jokes for the Contemporary Speechmaker,* rev. ed. (New York: Thomas Dunne Books, 2003), edited by Ashton Applewhite, Tripp Evans, and Andrew Frothingham.

3. Ron Allen, "More About Sister Mary," *The Daily Nightly,* November 25, 2005, http://dailynightly.msnbc.com/2005/11/more_about_sist.html; and Tom McGrath, "The Good Generation," *Philadelphia Magazine,* June 2, 2009, www.phillymag.com/articles/the_good_generation/.

4. Project H.O.M.E., "'Most Influential Honor' Presents an Opportunity to 'Finish the Job of Ending Homelessness,'" news release, May 1, 2009, www.projecthome.org/pdf/news/122.pdf.

5. Ibid.

6. Peace One Day vision statement, www.peaceoneday.org/objectives.aspx (accessed June 4, 2009).

7. Peace One Day, "The Story So Far," www.peaceoneday.org/en/about/story (accessed July 6, 2010). To learn more about Gilley's journey and the establishment of the annual, international Peace Day, see also *The Day After Peace,* a feature documentary, available at Peace One Day's website.

8. Theodore Roosevelt, "The Man in the Arena," speech at the Sorbonne, Paris, France (April 23, 1910). From the Almanac of Theodore Roosevelt, www.theodore-roosevelt.com.

CHAPTER 12: HOW TO BECOME MORE POWERFUL

1. Rob Cross, Robert J. Thomas, and David A. Light, "How Top Talent Uses Networks and Where Rising Stars Get Trapped," Research Report, Accenture Institute for High Performance Business, April 2006, 8, http://origin.www.accenture.com/NR/rdonlyres/9D263CA5-85A9-41C2-A7BB-904A4E03A2DE/0/HowTopTalentUsesNetworks.pdf.

INDEX

ABOUT THE AUTHOR

Terry R. Bacon is a senior partner and scholar in residence in the Korn/Ferry Institute, the research center of excellence for Korn/Ferry International, the world's leading talent management firm. For more than thirty years he has been a thought leader, innovator, teacher, coach, and consultant to global businesses in leadership, management, business development, and interpersonal skills. In 1989, he founded Lore International Institute, a widely respected executive development firm that was acquired by Korn/Ferry International in 2008.

Terry is a prolific author and speaker. He has written or cowritten more than 100 books, articles, white papers, and research reports, including *Selling to Major Accounts, Winning Behavior, The Behavioral Advantage, Adaptive Coaching, Powerful Proposals, What People Want, Leading in a Boundaryless Organization, Leading for Empowerment, Leadership Through Influence, High-Impact Facilitation, Interpersonal and Interactive Skills, Proposing to Win,* and *Effective Coaching.* He has given presentations on such topics as leading in challenging times, balanced leadership, respect, accountability, the life cycle of companies, behavior-based selling, what people want from their managers, leaders developing leaders, the ideological foundations of adaptive coaching, global account management, developing client relationships, behavioral differentiation and the customer experience, and developing the C-suite.

He received a PhD from the American University in 1977 and a BS in engineering from the United States Military Academy at West Point in 1969. He has studied business and management at The Wharton School (University of Pennsylvania), the University of Chicago, Stanford University, and Harvard Business School. In 2007, 2008, and 2009, he was named by *Leadership Excellence* magazine as one of the "top 100 thinkers on leadership in the world."

For more information about Terry's books, ideas, and research, visit his Facebook page or websites: www.terryrbacon.com and www.theelements ofpower.com. For more information on Korn/Ferry International and its suite of talent management services, see www.kornferryinstitute.com or www.kornferry.com.